T0369067

My Favourite Election Anecdotes and Snippets

Carl W. Dundas

AuthorHouse™
1663 Liberty Drive
Bloomington, IN 47403
www.authorhouse.com
Phone: 1-800-839-8640

Published by AuthorHouse 02/07/2012

ISBN: 978-1-4567-9710-2 (sc)
ISBN: 978-1-4567-9711-9 (e)

This book is printed on acid-free paper.

Contents

Anecdotes and snippets mapped randomly over a period of approximately thirty years and include elections in 89 countries set out in alphabetical order in the Annex hereto.

Note about the Author

Carl W. Dundas, LL.B, LL.M (Lon.), Barrister-at-law (Gray's Inn) is an Election Expert and Maritime Delimitation Consultant. Mr. Dundas is also experienced in governance, democratic development, election organisation and Law of the Sea matters.

Before joining the Commonwealth Secretariat in November 1980, Mr. Dundas was a member of the Attorney-General's Department in Jamaica. In 1973, he was appointed to the post of Legal Counsel and Director of the Legal Division of the Caribbean Community (CARICOM) to oversee the implementation of the Treaty Establishing the Caribbean Community, of which he was a leading negotiator. As Principal Legal Advisor, he drafted legal instruments in respect of, *inter alia,* rules of origin, common external tariff, a harmonised scheme for fiscal incentive to industry, regional laboratory service, a regional shipping service, regional food corporation and regional agriculture research and development institute.

While in the service of Jamaica, Mr. Dundas, as the Technical Adviser to a Joint Select Committee of both Houses of Parliament, which dealt with constitutional and electoral reform, eventually became the first Director of Elections 1979-80. His extensive experience in constitution drafting, particularly the provisions relating to election management bodies and his wide experience in drafting legislative frameworks for petroleum and hard rock mineral exploration, gave rise to service in many countries of the Commonwealth, including Barbados, Botswana, Guyana, Kenya, Malawi, Samoa, Seychelles, Solomon Islands, Vanuatu, and Cook Islands.

He has given technical assistance in electoral matters in many countries, including Aceh, (Indonesia), Antigua & Barbuda, Botswana, Cayman Islands, Guyana, Kenya, Lesotho, Liberia, Malawi, Mozambique, Nigeria, Sierra Leone, South Africa, Tanzania/Zanzibar, and Zambia; and has been assigned to observe elections in many countries, including Bangladesh, Guyana, Kenya, Liberia, Malaysia, Malawi, Pakistan, Mozambique, South Africa, Tanzania/Zanzibar, and Zambia. He has also advised on election organization and management in Jamaica, Kenya, Liberia, Malawi, Mozambique, Nigeria, South Africa, and Sierra Leone.

Mr. Dundas led Commonwealth Secretariat's electoral technical assistance missions to Guyana, Kenya, Malawi, Namibia, Nigeria, Sierra Leone, South Africa, Tanzania/Zanzibar, and Zambia. He carried out assignments in areas such as designing electoral frameworks for a neutral and impartial electoral management body, the establishment of instruments for the transition from a military one-party to a multiparty system, and has organised capacity-building seminars and workshops.

Constitutional reform, particularly relating to the fundamental provisions dealing with election legislative schemes, is a focal area of his specialization. Consequently, he has undertaken assignments in this area in Guyana, Lesotho, Malawi, South Africa, Tanzania (Zanzibar) and has advised on electoral legislation in Antigua & Barbuda, Cayman Islands, Jamaica, Kenya, Lesotho, Liberia, Malawi, Nigeria, and Sierra Leone.

Mr. Dundas has led the Support Team to the Commonwealth Observer Missions to elections in Malaysia (1990), Zambia (1991), Kenya (1992), Guyana (1992 & 97), Malawi (1994), Mozambique (1994), Tanzania (1995), Zanzibar (Tanzania), Trinidad & Tobago (2000). He also served as technical adviser to the Commonwealth pre-election Observation Group to Namibia in 1989 and to the Commonwealth Observer Group to South Africa in 1994.

Mr. Dundas was Chairman of the Electoral Boundary Delimitation Commission of the Cayman Islands in 2003. As an Election Legal Consultant from 2001to 2006, Mr. Dundas advised many election management bodies (EMBs) on reform and modernisation, including Aceh (Indonesia), Antigua & Barbuda, Botswana, Cayman Islands, Guyana, Lesotho, Liberia, Nigeria, and Tanzania.

In 2006, Mr. Dundas took up an appointment as the Chief of Party of the International Foundation for Electoral Systems' (IFES') African Union Support Program (funded by USAID) to advise the African Union on the establishment of a Democracy and Electoral Assistance Unit.

Other Works by the Author

Practical Steps in Negotiating Maritime Boundary Agreements: A Guide to Small States, Commonwealth Secretariat (1991)

Organising Free and Fair Elections at Cost-Effective Levels, Commonwealth Secretariat (1993)

Dimensions of Free and Fair Elections: Frameworks, Integrity, Transparency, Attributes, and Monitoring, Commonwealth Secretariat (1994)

Let's Talk about Elections—The Themes (ed.) Commonwealth Secretariat (1997)

Discussion of Election Issues in Commonwealth Africa (ed.) Commonwealth Secretariat (1998)

Compendium of Election Laws, Practices and Cases of Selected Commonwealth Countries—Volume I, Part I, Commonwealth Secretariat (1996)

Compendium of Election Laws, Practices and Cases of Selected Commonwealth Countries—Volume I, Part 2 Commonwealth Secretariat *(1998)*

Compendium of Election Laws, Practices and Cases of Selected Commonwealth Countries-Volume 2, Part 1, Commonwealth Secretariat (1999)

Compendium of Election Laws, Practices and Cases of Selected Commonwealth Countries—Volume 2, Part 2, Commonwealth Secretariat (1999)

Election Management Bodies: Constitutive Instruments—Commonwealth Secretariat (1999)

Improving the Organization of Elections A 2006 Perspective Ian Randle Publishers (2006)

Observing Elections the Commonwealth's Way: The Early Years, Ian Randle Publishers (2007)

Preface

This work on election anecdotes and snippets is aimed at providing light reading for democratic elections enthusiasts about the funny side of elections in all democracies, mature, as well as in new and emerging ones. This collection of random anecdotes and snippets drawn from elections in almost 90 countries over nearly three decades and touches elections ranging from villages of China, national elections in Taiwan, and presidential elections in France. The full range of elections covered stretches across the globe.

Read about the EMBs that allow candidates to print and distribute their ballot papers; Spain p.163-4, Madagascar p.193; and the EMB that allows polling station electoral officials to be selected by lot from among the electoral list of the station (Spain) p. 164. Read about how Hugo Chavez, the candidate was fined for not obeying campaign rules (p. 95) and the voting method by voting marbles and ballot drums (p208)

See glimpses of electoral environments in emerging democracies in east Europe and central Asia. Read about the performance of electoral structures which are considered a fourth branch of government in Central and South American countries. Read about the electoral environment in local elections in Albania and China, as well as city government challenges in Vancouver, Canada.

Get the occasional chuckles when reading about the inability of the EMBs of Russia, Ukraine, and emerging democracies of east Europe and central Asia, to create a level playing field, particularly relating to media access and the use of publicly owned resources by incumbents.

Read about hints of subtle and not so subtle ways of attempting to rig and steal elections when registering political parties and candidates in east European and central Asian emerging democracies.

This work gives a bird's eye view of the growing successful application of electronic voting and counting of votes in national elections in some Latin American countries, particularly, Brazil, Mexico and Venezuela, as well as in South Asia, particularly Bhutan and India.

Read about the valiant struggle to promote enhanced democratic elections in Egypt by the Judges' Club p. 183-4. Also see arguments in Belize for and against the use of mobile phones in polling stations p.134.

Carl W. Dundas,
Abuja, Nigeria, August 2011.

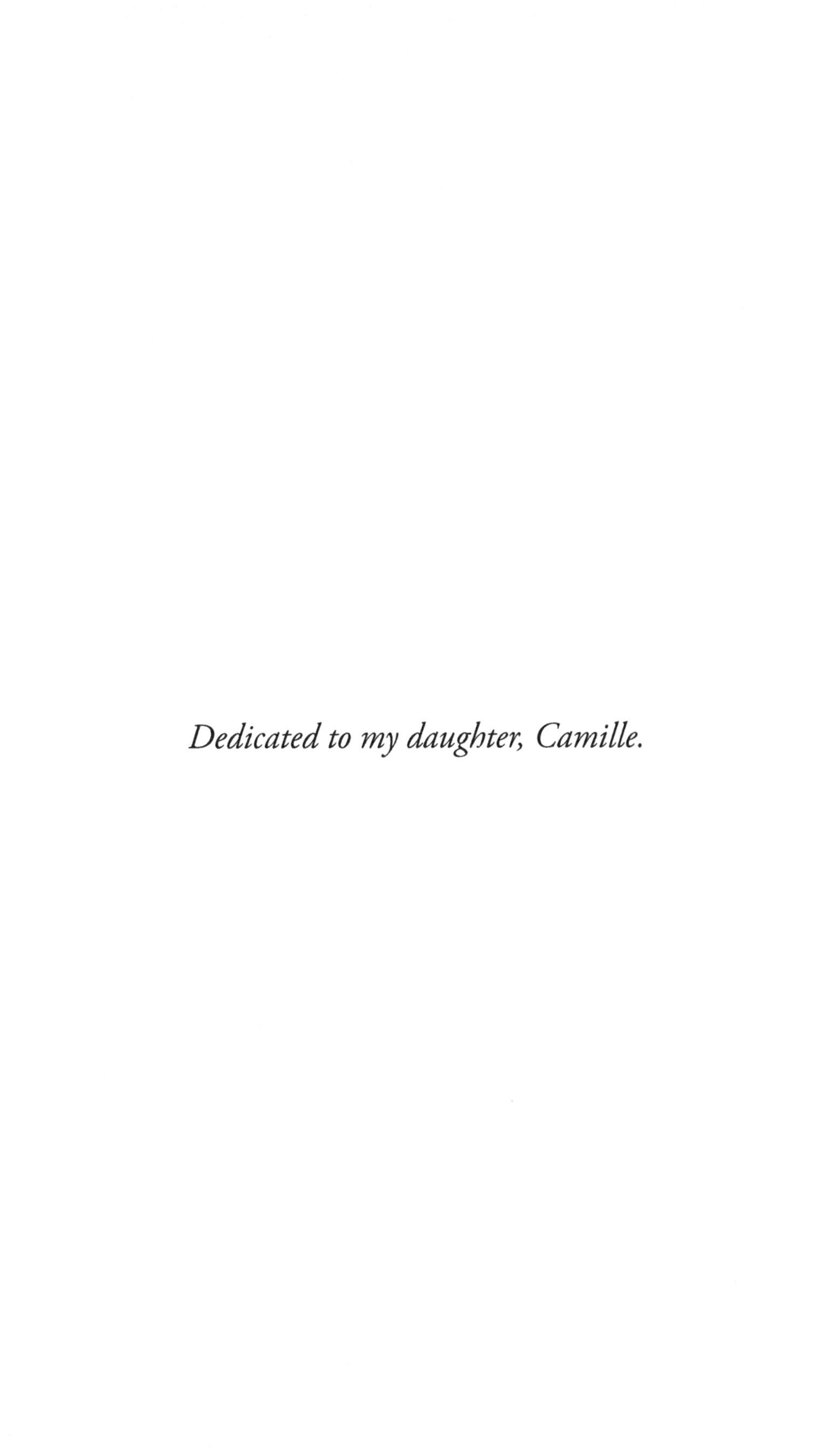

Dedicated to my daughter, Camille.

Introduction

Multiparty democracy is on the rise in Eastern Europe, Central Asia, and the African Union. It is a subject of deep and serious dimensions, but there is enormous fun mapping randomly the funny and lighter side to organizing democratic elections.

In an ideal world many election processes would be quite simple and straightforward activities. These include creating fair constituencies'/ electoral districts' boundaries, registering eligible voters, and preparing for polling. However, in the context of fierce competitive political contests for state power contestants often bend existing rules of the contests, and by so doing a continuous stream of checks and balances has to be put in place.

It is not often that one takes time out from offering consultancy advice on serious election issues to identify funny election anecdotes and snippets from election instruments and reports, but that's what this light work does. It is aimed at bringing hidden funny moments in election organization to a wider audience. It's like going backstage of a theatre after the play has ended. However, it is also aimed at presenting the electoral environment in which elections take place and identify the weaknesses which impact adversely the outcome.

The Narrator: Carl W. Dundas

Polling Preparation

A Mathematician

A certain returning officer with a background of mathematics teaching at secondary and tertiary levels lost the will to perform on the job on the eve of elections. Confusion took over his mind as he started overseeing the packing and distribution of ballot materials to presiding officers. He was unable to properly manage the distribution of election materials and supplies to the polling stations in the constituency for which he was returning officer. He was relieved of his job as a returning officer on the morning of Election Day.

Polling Conduct

The Priest

An Anglican priest in his mid-forties, full of life and with an outgoing personality, was a returning officer for the constituency in which resided. He performed competently over the preparation for polling. However, on Election Day he lost his will to work. He was unable to manage the affairs of his constituency on polling day and had to be replaced by another officer. When asked what had gone wrong with him, the priest answered that he simply froze up. He was overwhelmed by the excitement and busyness of Election Day activities.

Burning Ballot Boxes

Party Activists

Frustrated by the perceived loss by their constituency candidate in a general election, the party activists set fire to the storeroom that housed the ballot boxes that contained the ballots. A preliminary count of the ballots at the polling stations had already taken place before the fire and statements of the count had been issued to representatives of the stakeholders present at the polling station at the time. Much to the surprise of the party activists concerned, a winner was declared notwithstanding that no final count was possible.

Partisan Security Officers

Tampering with Ballot Papers

A candidate, fearing that the ballots would be tampered with before the final count, asked the election managers to allow the ballot boxes to be stored at the headquarters building for security reasons. That was not allowed as it was against the election rules. The election managers strengthened the security of the premises to 19 personnel, but that notwithstanding the security was breached and several ballot boxes were tampered with in such a manner that the count had to be settled in a final count by a Magistrate.

Inflexible Procedural Rules

Misplaced Batch of Enumerated Persons

During the processing of field data in a registration of voters exercise, a batch of data for 109 persons was received at the processing centre and subsequently could not be accounted for. The rules in place at the time regarding corrections to the voters' register did not allow any changes after the cut-off date. The lost batch of data was found the day after the cut-off date kicked in and could not be entered in the register. Although it appeared that the misplacing of the lost batch of data was due wholly to clerical error and was not intentional, a particular political party was upset and did not rule out sabotage.

Multiple Voting

Members of Police Force

In a certain jurisdiction, the police and army voters enjoyed advance polling and due to misplaced confidence, these voters were not subject to the strict identification process as other voters. These voters were required to vote where they were assigned and not where they were registered during the registration exercise. (In previous elections, these voters could either vote where they were registered or where they were assigned at the time of polling.) Many of these voters voted according to the new rules, that is to say, where they were posted, and then went back to where they were registered to vote a second or third time. When they turned up at where they were registered, they discovered that their names were no longer on the register for that polling station and that there were not sufficient ballot papers to accommodate them. The situation caused a certain measure of confusion and the advance polling had to be re-run. In the meanwhile before the re-run took place, the EMB gave permission to analyse the voting pattern of the advance voting that took place and it was discovered that there was a pattern of multiple voting by a number of the voters, several had voted many times. The findings were made public and some individual police personnel were identified and names sent for investigation and prosecution. The re-run of the advance polling lost its appeal and only a few hundred persons who had not voted in the first round turned up to vote at the re-run.

Threats to Polling Staff

The activists of a candidate, who was unlikely to win the election in the constituency, set about intimidating a number of presiding officers in a remote part of the constituency. The upshot was that many polling stations were opened late or not at all on Election Day. Re-polling in the constituency was avoided only because the successful candidate won by a landslide and the unopened stations, even if all the voters on the register for those stations voted for the losing candidate, the latter could not win.[1]

The Priest and His Teenage Nephews

Pre-election Conflict

Observing pre-elections preparations in post-conflict apartheid Namibia threw up many sad stories by ordinary Namibians. But perhaps there was none more revealing than that of a priest who, in audience with Commonwealth international observers, told of his decision to disown his two nephews who had been persuaded to join the apartheid-backed fighters against SWAPO, the freedom fighters of Namibia. The priest told the observers that he had last seen his nephews during that summer of 1989 and they had become killing machines of civilians who they believed had been sympathisers of SWAPO. The priest told of how the boys were trained along with Bushmen in the bush to kill men women and children without regard and that each boy had admitted to so killing tens of people under the apartheid regime during the conflict. Then he expressed the view that it would take many months, if not years, to erase their de-humanised minds and restore their normal teenage behaviour so that they could re-join the community in the village.

Border Incident (1)

While international observers to the preparations for the post-conflict elections in Namibia in 1989 were visiting north central Namibia, some of the observers strayed over the border between Namibia and Angola to take photographs. The attraction was a border post in the vicinity of Oshikango where the Angolan and Cuban troops were said to have inflicted heavy losses on the South African in an air encounter which hastened

---

1 The foregoing incidents took place when the author was Director of Elections in Jamaica in 1979-80.

the South African to sue for peace and agree to UN supervised elections. Momentarily, after straying across the border with Angola, the observers saw Angolan soldiers emerging from the bush and formed a circle around them with guns and bayonets drawn at the ready. The Angola soldiers were muttering something (apparently in Portuguese) and motioning to the observers to stop taking any photos. The observers momentarily froze with fright! The incident was soon settled as the UN security personnel with the observers indicated to the Angolan soldiers that nothing more than a few photos were being taken.[2]

Border Incident (2)

Some international election observers do like to taste of a bit of adventure. At the end of the Pakistan general elections in 1993, a couple of Commonwealth observers sought and obtained permission to visit the Khyber Pass. It was very generous of the Pakistani authorities who arranged a big armed escort of several vehicles in front and behind the vehicle carrying the guests. On reaching the Border Post between Pakistan and Afghanistan (after travelling through the Khyber Pass), the observers had tea with the Governor of the Border Post who showed his visitors the shots that had been directed at the building in which the tea was being served. The Governor however assured the visitors that they were completely safe at his Post. The Governor then invited the visitors to meet the leader of the Mujahadeen faction who controlled the border area of Afghanistan. The visitors agreed and crossed the border into Afghanistan. The visitors took photographs with the Mujahadeen leader and some of his fighters. Just then a mighty shell fire rang out across the valley! The visitors held their breath with fright, but that was it, there was no further shelling. Nevertheless, the Governor and his guests quickly bade farewell to the Mujahadeen leader and his men and went back to the Border Post on the Pakistani side.

---

2 This incident took place during election preparation in Namibia in 1989. The author was technical advisor to the Commonwealth pre-election observation mission.

On the Road to Kahuta

Security Concerns

Not having been informed that foreigners were not allowed to be driven on the road to Kahuta, in Pakistan in 1993, two international observers while on their way to visit pre-election polling sites preparedness in the Kahuta area were detained for more than an hour at a check point. The guards who were both army and police personnel were not helpful and not courteous. They did not explain the reason why the observers were stopped, but merely gave them forms to be filled up as to their particulars. The observers were subsequently released upon the intervention of the Election Commission whose Chairman apologized profusely in not informing the observer group that the area involved was one of national security and was out of bounds to foreigners.[3]

Ceramahs

A *ceramah* in an election context was a meeting held in an enclosed area such as a house, hotel or a meeting hall. This was the only type of political meeting allowed in Malaysia in the early 1990s. The police had to give permission for such a meeting and if it attracted 20 or more people in public areas and if in the opinion of the police the meeting could be detrimental to public order and security. In a particular case, the organiser of a meeting in a park obtained a permit from the police authorities; the permit was withdrawn and later reinstated. Apparently, that procedure was used to prevent certain candidates from giving timely notice of their meetings to the public at the particular venue.

---

3 The area was said to contain research laboratories on atomic energy.

Bulk Registration

The practices of bulk registration by party activists or extended family members use to take place in some jurisdictions. However, it always had the potential to lead to irregularity, as was reported in Malaysia in the early 1990s. Many voters complained that they were registered by unknown persons in constituencies to which they did not belong without their knowledge. The EMB admitted that false particulars and signatures had been used by certain groups to make the changes affecting many thousands of voters without their knowledge. The matter was so serious that it was brought up in the Parliament and new procedures were introduced to govern a voter's change of constituency.

Phantom Voters

The phenomenon of phantom voters occur in many countries, but primarily in continental countries with extensive borders with neighbouring states. These voters are often so called because they are on the voters' register often times legitimately, but they cannot be found at their address during election campaign periods. They may be working or otherwise residing over the border. The matter can become politically sensitive, as when the Chief Minister of Kelantan State in Malaysia in 1990 announced that 21,100 'phantom' voters had been discovered on the roll of his State.[4]

State of Emergency and Elections

During the run up to the elections in 1991 in Zambia, there was a state of emergency in place and upon the dissolution of the Parliament the state of emergency could not be lifted constitutionally, as that could only be done by the Parliament. The Government undertook not to use its powers under the emergency laws during the election campaign period. However

---

4 The author was leader of the Commonwealth Support Team to the Commonwealth Election Observation Mission to Malaysia.

there were widespread allegations of bogus evening curfews in some rural and urban districts where people were illegally picked up and detained overnight.

Insult to International Observers

A few days before the 1991 presidential and parliamentary elections in Zambia, the ruling party placed full page advertisements in one of the leading newspapers saying, among other things, that, 'most of the so-called observer groups are in actual fact not election monitors, their assignment is to facilitate the removal of UNIP Government and replace it with a puppet one like had happened in many parts of the world'. The advertisement further stated that 'the strategy of imperialism is to use so-called election monitors to influence the outcome of the elections in favour of the MMD.' 'In the event that UNIP wins the elections, which is most likely, the observer groups will certify that the elections were not free and fair'. The observer groups that were in the country chided the ruling party for placing such an advertisement, when it had agreed with the EMB to invite the observers. They demanded a retraction of the advertisement and an apology, both of which were forthcoming.

Incumbency

Zambia in 1991 was an example of how difficult it was for the process of de-linking the ruling party machinery from that of government. The one-party machinery lasted for 17 years during which time there was little or no difference between the UNIP, the ruling party and the government. When the election campaign period came, many senior party officials still held government jobs and used public property, including vehicles and offices, to do party campaign work. [5]

---

5 The author was the leader of Commonwealth Secretariat Support Team to the Commonwealth Election Observation Mission to Zambia in 1991.

Elections in Conflict Environment

In February1980 when the elections were held in Southern Rhodesia leading to the creation of the independent State of Zimbabwe, the conflict had not properly ended. There was a state of emergency in force and the environment was still rather unstable politically. The reports suggested that the police broke up political rallies using tear gas, and arrested a large number of party workers, including some candidates. Certified polling agents were arbitrarily detained hours before polling began. Intimidation was widespread, and curfews restricted movement during the election campaign period.

Election Rumours

On the eve of polling in the post-conflict pre-independence elections of 1980 in Southern Rhodesia, observers were bombarded with rumours about the invisible dye to be used to identify those persons who had voted. They had to carry out tests using a variety of cleaners and creams to satisfy themselves that there was no truth in those allegations.

In a similar vein, rumours circulated that it was possible to put additional ballot papers into sealed ballot boxes by removing the wooden handles from their sides. The observers investigated the allegations and found that it was quite impossible to stuff ballot boxes in that manner, as the handles were not set into the sides of the boxes, but were fixed on to the outside by means of two screws. When a handle was removed, and as the screws were placed through from the inside of the box, only two small screw holes through which ballot papers could not pass, could be seen. The observers had no difficulty in pronouncing the construction of the ballot boxes satisfactory.

The Cockerel

Commonwealth observers of the Southern Rhodesian election 1980 confirmed that there were examples of party supporters soliciting the support of persons waiting to vote by walking up and down the queues. A number of those waiting signalled their support for their party by flapping their elbows and making a crowing sound. This was done by supporters of ZANU (PF) whose symbol was the cockerel.

Sir Shridath Ramphal's Admonition

To Observers of the Elections of Southern Rhodesia 1980

You are there neither to whitewash what is unworthy nor to bring an adversary (and, therefore, imperfect) approach to bear on an electoral process that must by any standard be an enormously delicate and arduous undertaking.

I believe, however, that you have a higher, if more indirect task; it lies in your being as much as in your doing. The fact that these elections will be observed by you on behalf of some forty countries—whoever else may be observing all or part of them—must itself be a factor that cannot be discounted by anyone. In a sense, merely by going, you assist the process of making this election free and fair—and become something of a custodian, if only by exercise of a constraining influence.

I do not want to here go into specifics; nothing you see or hear in London, on the radio, on the television, in the press, from the front-line states, from the British Government or, of course, from me, are a substitute for being there and hearing from the people and the parties. In recent months reports covering Rhodesia have been subject to an unusually high degree of press management. You will not be entirely free of it Southern Rhodesia—but you will have been there the best chance of making up your own minds.

The air is replete with allegations and counter-allegations—there are South African forces in Rhodesia where they should not be; there are Rhodesian forces deployed an auxiliaries 'at large' when all parties, save for limited emergency situations, were to be disengaged and confined to base. There are remaining political detainees in Southern Rhodesia and in Mozambique. Inevitably, they all now become your concern, for they concern the environment of the election.

A Chief's Diplomatic Illness

International election observers who were visiting the Caprivi Strip in Namibia made an appointment to pay a courteous call on an important Chief of the area. The Chief however was a supporter of the pro-apartheid political factions of the area and he merely pleaded diplomatic illness and opted out of the appointment. He instead sent his 'Prime Minister' to address the observers. The 'Prime Minister' was some 40 minutes late and that prompted the observers to wonder if he also had fallen ill diplomatically. However he eventually turned up and after going through the customary rituals exchange thoughts with the observers.

The Frostiness of a Political Leader

During the run up to the 1980 elections in Southern Rhodesia, President Bishop Muzorewa became frustrated with the Commonwealth observers and lost his patience when they asked through their Chairman, Ambassador Rajeshwar Dayal, to see him. In his response to Ambassador Dayal's request, the President recalled that the Ambassador was reported as saying that he had raised the question with the Governor of alleged breaches of the Lancaster House Agreement by the Security Force Auxiliaries and that the subject of violations of the ZANLA[6] and ZIPRA[7] elements had not arisen during the discussions. He then wrote that 'I am, therefore, astounded that you chose to ignore these during your discussions with Lord Soames and furthermore that you have not taken the opportunity to refer to these publicly since your unfortunate remarks concerning allegations of breaches by the Security Force Auxiliaries which was a complete misrepresentation of the actual situation. I challenge you to present to me evidence of any such incident as those covered in the communiqués I have mentioned attributable to Security Force Auxiliaries.'

---

6 Armed wing of Mr Mugabe's Zimbabwe African National Union (Patriotic Front).

7 Armed wing of Mr Nkomo's Patriotic Front.

'Under the existing circumstances, I am left with no other conclusion but that you arrived in this country with pre-conceived ideas, that you are no way impartial, a state of mind I consider to be absolutely essential if the forthcoming election is to be judged fairly and that you hold a very distinct bias in favour of particular political parties and their armed wings to the detriment of other parties contesting the election.'

Missils (Processions)

Canvassing for Votes in Bangladesh

Bringing out of missils is a particular kind of canvassing for votes during an election campaign period. While variation of their form and label exists in other south Asian countries, in Bangladesh missils are particularly colourful and exuberant. They take various forms including processions on foot, on bicycles, holding party symbols aloft while chanting or singing party slogans. Missils may also include cavalcades of rickshaws or trucks crowded with party supporters. Occasionally, the exuberance and excitement associated with missils spill over into clashes between the different groups of marchers.

'Mastans' of Bangladesh

Mastans were described as 'violent hoodlums' who operated out of communities in the pay of those who wished to create havoc at election times. Their activities from time to time included mounting attacks on polling stations and causing mayhem in the villages away from polling stations to frighten away persons intending to vote. These disturbing events were described as the combination of 'muscle and money' designed to inflict election irregularities on the election process.

Burka and Impersonation

In Bangladesh the women often wear the traditional burka during voter registration and also polling. Due to the very competitive nature of politics in that country, the supporters of political parties often lodge complaints against their opponents that the burka is used to perpetrate impersonation at the polls. However, international observers have found these fears to be generally unfounded.

Coloured Finger-Nail Polish

Attempt at Multiple Voting

A Bangladeshi young lady, apparently resolved to attempt multiple voting, went to the polling station with the fingernails on her left hand only well done over with coloured nail polish. The indelible voting ink was to be placed on the left thumb-nail. Her case immediately raised the suspicion of the election officers and party agents. As if to verify the young lady's pure intentions, a woman voter in the queue rushed to her aid claiming to be her mother-in-law. She was quickly challenged by a party agent, and there the matter rested.

The 'Iffy' Conclusion

The uneasiness of the Commonwealth observers with their own findings in respect of the Ugandan elections of 1980 can be seen in their following conclusions as follows—

'Some, at least, of these difficulties could have been mitigated, even in Uganda's situation, *if* the Electoral Commission had been more efficient and imaginative body than proved to be the case; *if* the Military Commission had not delayed a final decision and announcement on the venue and the manner of the count till just three days before polling; *if* there had been a mechanism for continuing consultation between the Electoral Commission and all the political parties, sitting together, to consider and resolve difficulties as they arose; and *if* logistical arrangements for the distribution of balloting material had been made with a greater degree of thoroughness.'[8]

Partisan EMB

In the run up to the 1980 Ugandan elections, three candidates of an opposition political party whose nominations had been formally notified many days earlier were peremptorily disqualified by the Electoral Commission on 8 December, 1980, less than two days before Election Day. The reason given for the disqualification was that the nomination papers were filed after 12 noon on nomination day, 25th November. International observers enquired into the matter and established to their satisfaction that the nomination papers had in fact been filed in time. The observers' efforts to have the situation rectified proved unsuccessful.

Multiple Errors

Five candidates were declared unopposed in the 1980 Ugandan elections because their prospective opponents failed to produce the required tax clearance certificates. The Electoral Commission however confirmed to election observers that it had granted verbally a temporary deferment to the prospective candidates. It was not made clear under what legal authority the Commission gave the temporary deferment order. The prospective candidates were disqualified by the returning office whose decision was final, subject only to inquiries by a court during a petition hearing after the election were held.

Spontaneous Moral Coercion

During the Referendum in Gibraltar in 1967, a complaint was lodged by some voters that public interest in the referendum was so widespread

---

8 The emphasis had been added.

and the support for one of the two choices being put to the people so apparently overwhelming, that only the more courageous would publicly criticise the referendum or show a preference for the alternative choice. The situation, it was said, had given rise to spontaneous moral coercion by the vast majority whose enthusiasm for the referendum and its second choice could be seen from the extensive decorations all over Gilbraltar. The Observers investigated the allegation and found no evidence of social pressure amounting to public intimidation.

'Imported' Voters

During the 1992 elections in Kenya, voters and party agents alike coined the phrase 'imported voters' to describe persons who were allegedly brought into marginal constituencies to prop up candidates in danger of election defeat. In the Mombasa district where such allegations were rife, a bus believed to be carrying 'imported voters' was stoned. A group of voters who asked others waiting in line whether this was the polling station they were looking for were hounded away by the crowd, while another group of voters who could not speak Swahili and were identified as refugees from Somalia were chased away.

The Party Strongman

In the Mvita constituency in Mombasa, during the 1992 elections, a polling station was suddenly moved, without notice or consultation under the pretext of securing more spacious premises, on the morning of polling day to a location. The new location however was opposite the district headquarters of the ruling party whose chairman was reputed to be a party strongman. Opposition party agents would have none of it and demanded that the polling station be removed back to the original site. The opposition eventually won, but not before several hours were lost and polling started several hours late!

Ninakula hapa na ninalala huko

'I eat here and sleep there'

This is a Swahili saying which is aimed at playing down the potential influence of money on politics. It conveys the idea that potential voters would happily accept gifts, but would still vote in the manner they wished, reinforced by the expectation of the secrecy of the ballot. Many voters resorted to this saying when asked about the influence of money and other gifts designed to influence their vote.

Nomination Day Irregularities

Many prospective candidates in the parliamentary and civic elections of Kenya in1992 complained of serious irregularities that prevented them from handing in their papers on nomination day. There were some 43 prospective opposition candidates at parliamentary and civic levels who reported that they were hindered from presenting their nomination papers. Some had their papers forcibly taken from them (in some cases by security personnel); others were abducted either from their homes or while on their way to the nomination centre and taken into the forest before being released late into the evening when the nomination proceedings were completed. As a result of these irregularities, 16 parliamentary seats were declared unopposed in favour of the ruling party, KANU.

Mischievous Act

Prior to the elections of 1992, the Kenyan Attorney General and the Electoral Commission attempted to shorten the period required by law for the political parties to nominate their candidates. Opposition parties interpreted the Attorney General's erroneous finding that there was an error on the face of the law, to be an attempt to favour the ruling party. The law required the EMB to allow not less than 21 days to political parties to nominate their candidates to contest an election. The Attorney General changed the phrase 'not less than' to 'not more than' 21 days, and the EMB proceeded to act thereon and purported to allow the parties no more than 9 days. An opposition party took the Attorney General and the EMB to Court and won. The Judge who heard the case said that there was no error in the law to be rectified, and that the Legal Notice published by the Attorney General effected a substantial change which had been sneaked in mischievously. In considering the issue, the Commonwealth observers concluded that the Electoral Commission, in remaining silent about the purported change of a legal provision that would affect adversely the opposition parties, and by setting a period for the party nominations well short of the 21 days normally allowed for that purpose, gave an impression of acting in favour of the ruling party, the Kenya African National Union (KANU). [9]

Admonition of the Chairman of an EMB

The Supreme Court of India in the case of T. N. Seshan, Chief Elections Commissioner (CEC) of India, recalled with disapproval the CEC's behaviour thus: 'the decisions taken by the CEC from time to time postponing elections at the last moment, of which he has made mention in his petition, have evoked mixed reactions. This we say because the CEC uses them to lay the foundation for his contention that the entire exercise was malafide. Some of his other decisions were so unsustainable that he could not support them when tested in Court. His public utterances at times were so abrasive that this Court had to caution him to exercise restraint on more occasions than one. This gave the impression that he was keen to project his own image. That he has very often been in the newspapers and magazines and on television cannot be denied.'

On the Status of an EMB Chairman

The Supreme Court of India ruled on the status of the CEC thus: 'One of the matters to which we must turn is the question of the status of an

---

9 The author led the Commonwealth Secretariat Support Team to the Commonwealth Election Observation Mission to the 1992 elections.

individual whose conditions of service are akin to those of the Judges of the Supreme Court . . . In the instant case, some of the service conditions of the CEC are akin to those of the Supreme Court Judges, namely, (i) the provision that he can be removed from office in like manner and on like grounds as a Judge of the Supreme Court; and (ii) his conditions of service shall not be varied to his disadvantage after his appointment. It appears . . . . that the CEC had suggested that the position of the CEC in the Warrant of Precedence needed consideration. This issue he seems to have raised in his letter to the Prime Minister in December 1991. It becomes clear from Shri Godbole's reply dated July 25th 1992, that the CEC desired that he be placed at No.9 in the Warrant of Precedence at which position the Judges of the Supreme Court figured. It appears from Shri Godbole's reply that the proposal was considered but it was decided to maintain the CEC's position at No. 11 along with the Comptroller and Auditor General of India and the Attorney General of India. However the course of the hearing of these petitions it was stated that the CEC and the Comptroller and Auditor General of India were thereafter placed at No 9A.

Election Expenditure

Keeping Accounts

In dealing with the issue of whether the Elections Commission could instruct candidates contesting elections to keep accounts and in a proper format, Mr Justice Raveendram of the Karnataka at Bangalore, stated that any expenditure incurred by a political party or by any other person, in connection with the election of the candidate, if authorised by the candidate, becomes a part of his election expenditure, the question was whether he should keep account of such expenditure or ignore that expenditure for the purpose of his accounting. The candidate would have to maintain accounts of the expenditure incurred or authorised by him or his election agent. Once any expenditure is treated as the election expenses of the candidate, whatever may be the source, the candidate becomes liable to maintain accounts in respect of such expense, even if it is incurred by a political party or any other person. The requirement that the candidate should account for all expenditure authorised by him, which may include any expenditure incurred by a political party, is thus justified.

Ballot Paper Error

In the preparation for the general election in Guyana in 1992, local opinion and the members of the Elections Commission were split on whether to have locally printed ballot papers. The decision was taken to print the ballot papers abroad in the USA. When the printed ballot papers were received in Guyana, two significant errors were found on the face of the ballot papers. In the first case the name of the major political party alliance was incorrectly reflected on the ballot papers—instead of the title of the 'PPP/Civic' list of candidates was printed only as PPP. Secondly, the title of the list of candidates of the UGI was printed as the United Guyanese International instead of Union of Guyanese International. The error in the first case was considered to be so serious that the elections were almost derailed

An EMB's Inability to Decide

The indelible ink used to indicate persons who had voted came under close scrutiny. Ink used in elections prior to 1992 in Guyana was considered to be below specification and was replaced. However inexplicably the EMB that decided to replace the old ink could not agree on what to do with the old ink and so it was kept in storage much to the displeasure of the EMB's members who were nominated by the opposition parties. The ink was only disposed of when international observers prevailed upon the EMB as a whole to publicly dispose of the ink—the disposal was done openly under the gaze of the observers!

Pitsos

Pitsos or rallies are the principal method of political campaigning in Lesotho. They have a distinct indigenous flavour which places emphasis on the transmission of important statements in group gatherings. They are used to convey a political party's message or manifesto. Pitsos may be held at the national or local level, but the local pitsos are considered to be particularly important.

Containment of Bureaucratic Interference

In August 1993, the Caretaker Government of Pakistan, in an endeavour to contain bureaucratic meddling in the pending elections, launched a massive re-shuffling exercise, transferring thousands of bureaucrats at the provincial and district levels to new postings. The Government also dissolved local bodies and froze their funds, thus depriving thousand of politicians elected to those local bodies that managed municipal, district, town and village councils of crucial source of patronage. Previously, those politicians, during election times, used funds and resources at their disposal to mobilise voters for partisan party interests.

Political Advertising at Polling Stations

A practice used to exist in Pakistan whereby candidates issued chits bearing their picture or political symbol to voters. These chits were intended to facilitate the polling process. They were issued at tents set up by political parties outside the polling station and contained the voter's name, registration number, polling station and booth number. Many chits were promptly discarded in the polling station after the voters voted, introducing political advertising in the polling station and possibly compromising the secrecy of the voter's ballot in the first place.

Pre-election Demise of the 'Independent Homelands'

The 'independent homelands' of Bophuthatswana, Ciskei, Transkei and Venda were in focus just prior to the 1994 elections in South Africa. Though not without initial worry, three of the 'independent homelands', namely, Transkei, Venda and later, Ciskei, incorporated the transitional legislation into their statutes and prepared for the elections. Bophuthatswana however refused to follow that example and sought help from the sympathisers of the dying apartheid regime. Matters came to ahead when, on the 11 March 1994, the far-right Afrikaner Weerstandsbeweging (AWB) with a contingent of about 500 paraded through Mmabatho, the capital of Bophuthatswana, firing shots and killing several black South Africans. Later that day the Defence Force of Bophuthatswana took action against the AWB killing three of their number. Meanwhile, the civil service, army police rose against the leader of Bophuthatswana, Lucas Mangope who was forced from power. The South African Government appointed two co-administrators to run the territory until after the elections.

Selection of Voting Sites—Extraordinary Measures

Widespread violence and intimidation in some parts of South Africa, particularly in KwaZulu Natal and the Pretoria/Witwatersrand/Vereeniging (PWV) areas during the run up to the 1994 elections, led the Independent Electoral Commission (IEC) to adopt extraordinary measures in selecting voting sites. Security precautions were uppermost in the contemplation of the Commission. Thus each station was required, where possible, to have an outer zone of 1,100 metres, called a controlled area, an intermediate zone called he 'inner perimeter' and an inner zone, called the 'election centre'. The stipulated specifications plus the need to accommodate anticipated large numbers of party agents, monitors and observers, required a relatively large space for each station which was seldom attainable.

Spilling Over Effect of the Security

The security needs of the election quickly clashed with IEC's quest to offer good quality election services to voters. Thus when the IEC proposed to set up 9,000 voting stations, the security services promptly indicated that that number had to be reduced as there were not enough security personnel to service so many stations. The IEC wanted to provide one voting station for a maximum of 3,000 voters per station in order to avoid any voter having to walk more than 10 km to a station. The security services proposals would have resulted in drastic reduction of the numbers of voting stations in some areas, for example, from 1800 to 900 in Transkei, from 495 to 320 in Ciskei and from 245 to 70 in Soweto. Eventually, the matter was settled at the eleventh hour between the IEC, the South African Police and the political parties. The agreed number of voting stations stood at 9,739.

Voter Education-

In apartheid South Africa, black and coloured South Africans were for the most part disfranchised and were not familiar with voting procedures. That situation made voter education necessary for the 1994 elections. The IEC was unable to meet all the needs of the prospective voters in respect of voter education and relied on civil society organisations to help out in some parts of the country. Thus more than 100 CSOs were in action in this regard in the erstwhile 'independent homelands'. Complaints were filed in many parts of the country by CSOs and political parties against white farmers who refused entry to voter education trainers on to their farms.

Crash Courses

The late entry into the election campaign by the Inkatha Freedom Party (IFP) made it necessary to resort to crash courses in voter education in KwaZulu Natal and the PWV areas of South Africa immediately before the 1994 elections. In Kwa Zulu Natal the Air Force dropped more than 5 tons of voter education leaflets, particularly in the rural areas, during the last weekend before the polling, although due to the high rate of illiteracy in those areas, the effectiveness of that last-minute approach was doubtful.

Media Monitoring

Media monitoring became strict during the run up to the 1994 South African elections that political correctness suddenly rushed to the fore. Thus a proposed political satire captioned 'One man, one volt' was dropped on the grounds that it was politically incorrect and might infringe the election laws or the spirit there of.

Election Campaigning-Mandela Effect

Mandela castigated some of his supporters for their lack of restraint towards the right of other political parties to put across their campaign platform. In an instance, Mr Mandela reprimanded his supporters for their intolerance towards the National Party in the townships, saying that the injustices inflicted on the people by the NP could not justify counter measures that subverted fundamental freedoms and basic democratic values.

No-Go Areas

During the campaign period leading up to the 1994 elections, there were a number of 'no-go areas'. Complaints were made by the National Party and the Democratic Party that they were unable to campaign in the townships which were dominated by the African National Congress. White-owned farms in Northern and Western Cape and the Orange Free State were 'no-go' areas for the ANC and other black parties. The IEC and the political parties adopted various strategies to overcome the 'no-go obstacles'. For example, in Northern Cape and the Orange Free State, ANC officials seeking to reach farm workers distributed party campaign materials and conducted voter education among school children and instructed them to pass on the knowledge and information to their parents. Activists joined the workforce on the farms and visiting priests were used to conduct voter education. The NP held road shows in some places such as Soweto and ended its rallies by singing liberation movement songs like *Nkosi Sikelel' iAfrika (God Bless Africa.)*

Operation Access

The IEC launched operation access to facilitate free access for political parties to campaign and conduct voter education in 'no-go' areas. Operation access was based on the principle of each political party was allowed to take 10 supporters to meetings in transport provided by the IEC. Each party spokesperson was given 10 minutes to speak, the order of which was determined lot. Generally, operation access was successful, but in some instances it was unsuccessful, as in the East Rand squatter camp of Phola Park, an ANC stronghold, where the operation access vehicle was turned away on the grounds that the IEC was trying to split the community by introducing new political parties into the area.

A Late Contestant

In 1994, the Inkatha Freedom Party (IFP) joined the election race one week before the elections. In order to catch up on campaigning, their supporters converted posters which had urged voters to IFP 'when the time comes' to 'the time has come'. The IFP also sought to make the best use of being at the bottom of the ballot paper by adapting the slogan of the National Party which was previously at the bottom of the ballot paper, that, '*To be top, vote at the bottom*'. The IFP also ran advertisements seeking to capitalise on its position on the ballot paper thus: '*Put your cross in the last block and come first, so the last shall be first*'.

A Voter's Virtue

A reporter visited a tented voting station at 5.30 a.m. in Soweto on polling day in the 1994 elections, he saw an old lady at the front of a queue. When the reporter caught up with her again at 11.00 a.m. still at the front of the queue, the old lady said to him, *Perseverance, my dear, is the mother of success.* A similar theme was echoed by a commentator in one of the newspapers in South Africa thus: *black South Africans learnt what white South Africans already knew: how to vote. White South Africans learnt what black South Africans knew: how to wait.*

Prisoners' ballots

At the largest prison, the Johannesburg Prison, with 6, 500 prisoners at the time of the 1994 elections, voting were predictably chaotic. The election supplies for the stations at the prison did not arrive on time and the polling did not commence until 1.30 p.m. to the clanging and cheers of prisoners in their cells in close proximity to makeshift voting stations in the mess halls. There were seven mobile teams moving from block to block to conduct the polling. The largest block with nearly 2000 prisoners presented difficulties as many prisoners did not have their temporary voter's card (TVCs) which was held by prison officers on behalf of the prisoners. The TVCs were carried around by officials from cell to cell to locate the owners. That procedure went on until 3.00 a.m. in the morning.

Flashes of Chaos

The opening hours of the general voting in the 1994 elections in South Africa presented flashes of chaos in many urban voting stations. Materials were short or unavailable. Stations were unmanned or without materials and the scene was generally one of confusion initially. Slowly, but very slowly as the day wore on, materials began to arrive and polling commenced, late, but the very long queues began to shorten. Some of the reasons advanced for the initial chaos were—last minute changes and additions to voting stations, breakdown in the management of the supplies at many warehouses where there were no final lists of voting stations to facilitate allocation of supplies to the Deputy District Electoral Officers (DDEO), and overzealous DDEOs who collected more boxes of ballot papers than was necessary.

Election Sabotage?

Some of the mistakes in the election logistics management were so elementary that some stakeholders wondered whether there was intentional wrong doing on the part of some election officials. For example, there was non-delivery of materials, or materials sent to wrong addresses. In Transkei, large quantities of ballot papers were found at an airport warehouse and in the PWV area the IEC monitors, after polling was finished, found several hundred thousands of unused ballot papers in two warehouses, which should have been distributed to centres in Thokoza, Katlehong and Soweto. These findings led to the allegation of sabotage. The IEC summonsed four warehouse managers for an explanation.

Strike by Election Officers

The reconciliation of the ballot account prior to counting the votes was beset by problems. Firstly, instructions that the ballot box seal had to be checked to ensure that it contained the appropriate number as recorded by the presiding officer reached some counting officials after the reconciliation exercise was completed. Secondly, reconciliation was hampered by inaccurate or unavailable statements. Thirdly, disputes developed over ballot box seals and even with respect to counting procedures. Fourthly, counting was delayed at centres in some areas where the counting officials went on strike over payment of duty allowances.

Ballot Boxes 'Full of Grass'

Many rumours and alleged mischief surrounded the counting of the ballots. The rather complex procedure of nine steps dealing with the delivery, storage, reconciliation, counting and publication of results confused the counting process and triggered suspicions that they were designed to allay. In some counting centres, such as Nasrec in Johannesburg, rumour reached high points where it was said that ballot boxes were found 'full of grass'.

Party Polling Agents' Error

In the 1993 July presidential and parliamentary elections in Seychelles, party agents were trying out a new procedure whereby they were only taking down the page and line number of voters' names. At the end each hour, the list was delivered to a central area nearby and the names were appropriately crossed out. This new procedure created confusion in one case resulting in a candidate claiming that scores of voters had voted twice, because their page and number had been recorded twice. At the end of polling however the candidate discovered that his agents had made an error in cross checking the names. The two agents at the station divided up their tasks, one recording announcements by one polling clerk and the other from two other polling clerks. Both agents recorded the announcement of the page and line number in their separate sheets of paper and on subsequent cross-checking, it was made to appear as the same voter had voted twice.

Extra Ballot Security

In order to enhance the security of the ballot, the Seychelles EMB in 1993 July elections decide to require the ballot papers to be placed in envelopes. The envelopes rendered the counting procedure somewhat cumbersome as ballots-presidential and parliamentary had to be removed from the envelopes before being sorted. The introduction of the envelopes considerably lengthened the counting process and the reason given for the procedure was that of an extra security measure.

A Pastoral Letter

Sensing that the one-party system in Malawi was rapidly approaching its twilight era, in March 1992, the Roman Catholic Bishops issued a pastoral letter stating that Malawians lived in a climate of mistrust and fear. The Bishops complained that the fear of harassment and mutual suspicion generated a society in which the talent of many lay unused and in which there was little room for initiative. The pastoral letter went on to state some of the concerns thus: academic freedom was seriously restricted; exposing injustices was considered a betrayal; speaking out about some of the evils of society was considered slandering the country; and monopoly of the mass media and censorship prevented the expression of dissenting views. The pastoral letter called for an end to political detentions, and for the introduction of accountable government.

The pastoral letter was declared seditious, making its possession a criminal offence. The Bishops were summoned by the police and an expatriate Bishop was expelled. The education institutions of the Chancellor College in Zomba and the Blantyre Polytechnic mounted demonstrations in support of the Bishops and were promptly shut down.

The Discard Box

At the 1994 post-one-party elections, the voting procedure used required each voter to tear out the ballot paper bearing his/her preferred candidates for the presidential elections and place it in an envelop, and placed the remaining ballot papers in the box marked discarded ballots which was placed in the voting booth, while the ballot box was placed outside the booth in the view of polling officials and political party agents. The discard box had two apertures and some voters simply used one aperture for the disposal of the discarded ballot papers and the other for the envelope with the ballot papers. Some discerning polling officers foresaw the problem and sealed off one of the two apertures of the discard box in order to mitigate the confusion of voters.

Radios With Out Batteries

In 1994, the primary medium of mass communication in Malawi to reach voters throughout the country was radio. The voter/civic education programmes were developed with that knowledge in mind. However it soon became evident that while many persons in the rural districts had radios, they could not afford to buy batteries for the radios to listen regularly to voter education jingles and broadcasts. The realization of this problem first surfaced during the registration exercise and was said to be responsible in part for the slow pace of the voter registration and the eventual rather lower than expected turn out for the registration exercise.

Abuse of Incumbency

In the preparation for the 1994 elections, the opposition parties persistently accused the ruling party of abusing their incumbency status. It was said that while the advantages of incumbency constituted one of the immutable realities of electoral politics everywhere, no line could have been finer than that which had existed in Malawi since independence between a ruling party and government For example, the Executive Committee of the Malawi Congress Party (MCP) ranked higher in government protocol than Cabinet. Party vehicles were often used by senior government officials, or vice versa. Junior local party functionaries of the MCP exercised considerable influence over civil servants.

Nyau Dancing

Nyau dancing was part of a traditional ritual for the initiation of young boys into manhood in some areas of Malawi. It was usually a secret ceremony attended by adult males only. The dancers dressed up in masked so that they could not be easily identified. The ritualistic dancing was said to be explicit erotic dances designed to stimulate masculinity. This dancing was forbidden by tradition from performance at political rallies. However it was alleged that the MCP not only used the dancing with its accompanying music to attract large crowd in the villages, but often used the Nyau dancers to perpetrate intimidation and even murder, as their costume prevented easy identification.

Pranks of Opposition Functionaries

Member of an opposition party in the 1994 elections in Malawi, wishing to prove that registration certificates can be procured, disguised themselves as ruling party functionaries and successfully persuaded a Branch Chairman of the ruling MCP to part with his registration certificate. Having made the point and publicising it, the registration certificate was returned to its lawful owner.

The Malawi Young Pioneers

The Malawi Young Pioneers (MYP) was a paramilitary youth wing of the ruling party (MCP). They soon began to over reach themselves intimidating people and threatening peaceful elections. They even threatened the army and in December 1993 and incident with the MYP left two soldiers dead in Mzuzu. The army then attacked the bases of the MYP all over the country forcing thousands of them to flee the country into Mozambique. The MYP were disbanded when the law which had established it was repealed.

Attempts to Curtail the Franchise

Initially, the members of the security forces of Malawi were not allowed to register as voters for the 1994 elections. After the intervention of the Electoral Commission, the Ministry of Defence withdrew their reservations. However the police authorities maintained their objections until the registration exercise was completed, and only relented then. The registration period was re-opened to accommodate the police force, but only a few hundred registered. However, the reluctance to encourage the members of the security forces to participate in the elections persisted with the government arguing that voting by the uniformed forces on polling day would disrupt security arrangements. It appeared though that the real reason for the government's reluctance to encourage voting by the uniformed forces was the fear that the forces might be exposed to politicization.

Electoral Self Help

Mbayani is a densely populated area in western Blantyre without a building suitable for use as a polling station. Until the day before polling no materials had arrived to build polling stations for 7,000 voters. The Supervisory Presiding Officer and his staff set about building a polling centre with stakes and tarpaulin and on polling morning the seven station centre was up and running. The station opened 43 minutes late and was able to close at 6.00 p.m. on schedule. Candles were the primary light source, but one nearby home offered electric lights, using a long cable to facilitate the counting of the votes.

Acts of God and Elections

The Referendum Act 1995 of Bermuda set the date for the Referendum on the independence of that territory from Britain for 15 August 1995. Meanwhile on or around 12 August 1995, storm clouds from Felix were gathering on the horizon, following a familiar path cut by hurricane Emily which hit the island in 1987. The weather bulletin of 1.30 a.m. Tuesday 15 August 1995 (Referendum Day) located Felix, by then a category 1 hurricane, at 70 nautical miles south west of Bermuda. By 7.30 a.m. that same day, the weather bulletin downgraded the hurricane warning for Bermuda as Felix had changed course and was moving away from the island at 9 knots per hour. Hurricane winds were no longer in the area, but tropical storm winds of force 35 to 64 knots were forecast to prevail for the rest of the day abating only slowly. Meanwhile, somewhat understandably, confusion reigned in the minds of the managers of the referendum organisation. Some election officers turned up at polling stations only to adjourn the polls, while others either turned up late or not at all. Eventually, polling was called off and the provisions of the Referendum Act were frustrated. The opponents of the referendum, sensing that the circumstances of the weather might have militated against the 40% yes vote to carry the referendum, cried foul and political interference in causing the cancelling of the polls. A commission of inquiry was set up to examine the complaint. The commission of inquiry found that there was no evidence of political interference. It also found that the evidence showed that the importance of holding the referendum on the date fixed by law was not given proper priority. The commission found that no contingency plans were prepared to deal with the eventuality that the hurricane may have changed course ever so slightly and merely struck Bermuda a glancing blow. It expressed the view that had a calmer look at the weather advisories would have indicated that the storm may well have passed and although conditions would not have been suitable for the holding of a poll, they might have been such the Returning Officers could have opened the polls and adjourned to the next day.

Prospective Candidates

Opposition prospective candidates for the 1980 Ugandan elections complained that they were disqualified for a variety of reasons, namely, for failure to produce the required educational and language certificates, late arrival, detention, forcible prevention from presenting nomination papers, failure to present income tax clearance certificates, failure to have the stipulated number of 12 registered voters in the constituency, and late filing of nominations particulars. The upshot, as one group of international observers put it, was that the outcome of the political arithmetic yielded17 out of 126 constituencies returned unopposed, all in favour of one party.

Inordinate Delays

During the 1980 Ugandan elections, an international observer group found that the polling arrangements in the capital city of Kampala were marred by inordinate and inexcusable delays. In a number of polling stations, polling did not commence until late in the afternoon, while in some no polling took place even at the scheduled hour of the closure of the poll. The observers added that it would be difficult to believe that the delays were due wholly to mere incompetence.

Walvis Bay

Walvis Bay was a South African deep-water port and an enclave in Namibia at the time of independence. Though claimed by Namibia, it was not incorporated into the Namibian territory at the time of Namibia's independence in 1990. Instead, it was being used as a bargaining chip by apartheid South Africa against the newly independent Namibia. Walvis Bay was not only the largest deep-water port on the Namibian coast, but it was an important fish-processing centre. The formal integration of Walvis Bay into Namibia took place on I March 1994 after protracted negotiations.

Post-independence Electoral Adjustments

The pre-independence elections for Namibia were held under Apartheid South Africa, and United Nations' supervision in 1989 in a distinctly post-conflict environment. The 1994 general elections were the first post-independence ones and were being organised by Namibians. The Electoral Commission, established under the independence Constitution, was responsible for organising the first post-independence general elections. The electoral system was proportional representation, list system. The Electoral Commission, through its Directorate introduced administrative mechanisms to enable the election processes to work smoothly. In particular, a supervisor of registration and a registration officer were appointed for each constituency and local authority, as the case may be. Similarly, for the organisation of the elections, the Directorate appointed a coordinator in each of the 13 administrative regions. Election materials were delivered to constituencies and polling districts throughout the country through the coordinators.

No Voters' List at Polling Stations

The Namibian Electoral Commission decided not to make available copies of the voters' register at polling stations in accordance with a change in the law in 1994 because it was felt that substantial number of eligible voters might not be able to vote at their places of registration. The Electoral Directorate felt that if there were not such changes as much as 20% of the electorate might be disfranchised because of the high proportion of migratory voters or the full national register of voters would have to be made available at every polling station.[10] The votes of those persons who voted outside of the constituencies in which they were registered were treated as 'tendered' votes and were counted separately at a central point in the capital, Windhoek.

---

[10] This was due to the nature of the proportional representation electoral system used in Namibia.

Restricted Election Reporting

The public broadcasting system, the Namibian Broadcasting Corporation, (NBC) developed a set of guidelines, in consultation with the Directorate of Elections and the political parties, for fair political coverage before and during the 1994 elections. Paid political broadcasts were not allowed, but each party and the two presidential candidates were allocated free airtime, with television and radio broadcasts of approximately the same duration, whatever the size and strength of the party concerned. Polling day reporting was intentionally restricted to information about the elections, such as turnout, location of polling stations and voting procedures. News reporters were however allowed to report problems that were encountered and step taken to resolve them. References to election issues were not allowed. Only results certified by the Electoral Commission were announced.

Shortage of Affidavit Forms

For some inexplicable reason, during polling in the 1994 elections in Namibia, a large number of persons claiming the right to vote turned up at polling stations without the required means of identification. In such cases, each prospective voter had to be identified by means of an affidavit by one or two voters who could vouch for the identity of the prospective voter. Many polling stations however were in short supply of affidavit forms. At some stations, up to 30% of the prospective voters required affidavits to verify identity. The more enterprising presiding officers set about constructing the affidavit forms by hand. The shortages were caused by underestimation of the demand for affidavit forms. The Directorate of Elections had estimated that each polling station would be supplied with materials to serve about 1500 voters, but had not apparently indicated the amount of affidavit forms that would be needed at each station.

Confusion at Polling Stations

While in general the Namibia polling officials perform well during polling in the 1994 elections, there was a measure of inconsistencies in performance at some stations. At one station, for example, the validity of hundred of votes was put at risk, because the presiding officer applied the rule governing the marking of the ballot papers with the security stamp incorrectly. The stamp was used for all National Assembly ballot papers, but not for the ballot papers used in the presidential elections. At another polling station all the ballot papers were marked on the wrong side!

Resourcefulness in Tackling Polling Problems

At the commencement of polling on Election Day in1994 in the Karas Region of Namibia, it was discovered that the security stamp to mark the ballot papers was not included in the election supplies. The presiding officer promptly made that fact known to the party agents and then to the Directorate of Elections. The presiding officer then secured the agreement of the party agents that voting could start without the official stamp, and placed the unstamped ballot papers into a specially identified ballot box, on the understanding that the ballot papers would be properly stamped when the specially identified ballot box was opened. Although the voting procedural rules were not followed, the preferred option in the circumstances of practical improvisation in a transparent manner was taken over delaying polling and keeping voters in long queues for a prolonged period in hot sunshine.

Errant Party Agents

Some political party agents are always pro-active and seeking to carve a little advantage here and there at polling. Namibia was no exception, and during the 1994 elections, some party agents attempted to use seals bearing party initials and insignia to seal ballot boxes before polling began at the time of closing the boxes after the demonstration of the empty box at the opening of the poll. Some party agents exhibited a persistent practice of trying to speak to voters and seeking to offer help to voters. Some party agents intervened directly whenever they perceived that an irregularity was taking place rather than calling the attention of the presiding officer as provided in the election rules and the code of conduct for party agents.

Soldier-Politicians Embrace of Elections

1996 saw the great embrace in Africa of a form of democratic elections espoused by at least eight soldier-politicians[11] who had previously seized power in *coups d'etats.* Although it was not entirely clear how far one could go in declaring that those elections were free and fair from the viewpoint of the respective stakeholders, there was no doubt that each contestant appreciated the advantages of triggering the motions of elections to test the strength of the prevailing winds of foreign investments in their respective countries. The apparent democratic package was dressed up with the invitation to international election observers to enhance the legitimacy and respectability of the election processes concerned.

Ruling Parties & Reports of International Observers

The ruling party of Malaysia was not flattering about the Commonwealth Observer Groups' report on the General Elections in Malaysia of October1990. Indeed, the Government was unhappy even with the act of issuing an interim report on the finding of the Group. To compound the displeasure of the Government and others, the report did not expressly pronounce upon the freeness and fairness of the conduct of the election, a fact which even many Malaysian journalists remained unaware of for many months.

The Kenyan Government leaned heavily on an infelicitous phrase in the report of the Commonwealth Observer Group to the Presidential, Parliamentary and Civic Elections 1992 that the elections 'constitute a giant step on the road to multiparty democracy' to ward off criticisms that the elections were riddled with irregularities.

In a similar vein, the Zambian Government in 1996 relied on the findings of the Christian Council of Zambia International, Regional and Local

---

11 The 8 countries were Benin, Chad, Equatorial Guinea, Gambia, Ghana, Madagascar, Niger and Sudan.

Ecumenical Partners' Team which had observed the elections in Lusaka Province alone, that the election in that Province was conducted in a free, fair and transparent manner. However, other observer groups, like the local Committee for a Clean Campaign, which observed the election throughout the country, found that the election could not be said to have been free and fair.

Local Elections and Voter Education

The Community Elections Evaluation Group (CEEG) which evaluated the 1995 Local Government elections in South Africa found that there was continuing need for voter education in support of local government elections. It recommended that a distinction should be made between 'voter information' and 'education for democracy'. The report contended that the former covered issues such as where persons register to vote, and how and where to vote, while the latter embraced political accountability and the different tiers of government, among other things. Continuing, the evaluation report, at recommendation 12, proposed that voter information activity should be the responsibility of the Electoral Commission to promote and coordinate. At recommendation 13, the report advocated that an education for democracy programme should be established after consultation with national educational organisations, non-governmental organisations (NGOs) and other elements of civil society, and with political parties.[12]

Judicial Intervention in Local Elections

The CEEG report cited above made a finding and recommendation with respect to judicial intervention in local elections. Indeed it frowned upon it. The report found that the possibility of judicial intervention during

---

12 See evaluation report of the November 1995 Local Government Elections of South Africa by the CEEG, recommendations 12 & 13 in Vol. 1 *The End of the Beginning.*

an election was a controversial issue. It stated that judicial intervention halted the preparations for the 1995 local elections on several occasions, and concluded that judicial intervention can be used negatively to prevent the exercise of legitimate political rights. It recommended that judicial intervention should only be permitted in respect of issues which would fatally flaw an election.[13]

Impact of Voter Education

In measuring the impact of voter education programmes on voters, the findings of the CEEG's report differed sharply from an earlier survey carried out on behalf of the South African Broadcasting Corporation (SABC). The CEEG's report found that only four out of ten respondents to the survey received voter education, while the SABC's survey found that 71% of the respondents received voter education. The discrepancy in the survey may lie in the timing and wording of the questions put. The SABC's survey was immediately after the elections and the CEEG's was done some five months later. Also, the question put by the SABC survey was rather vague, namely, 'have you heard anything on the radio to do with the local community elections?' The question by the CEEG's survey was more specific-along the lines if the respondents had attended, participated or received any voter education.

Change of Political System

A change of the one-party political system to multi-party democracy in Tanzania was ushered in as a result of the positive report of the Nyalali Commission in early 1992. The Commission was set up in February 1991 by President Ali Hassan Mwinyi under the Chairmanship of the Chief Justice Francis Nyalali and mandated to report within one year. 28, 018 or 77.2% of the 36,299 people who expressed their views on the issue supported a continuation of the one-party system. The majority of

[13] Ibid., Recommendation 20.

those favouring the change to multi-party system were in the age group of 18-35. In spite of a clear majority support for the continuation of the one-party system, the Commission recommended the adoption of a multiparty system and the amendment of the Constitution of the Union and the Constitution of Zanzibar to remove the provisions that made Tanzania a one-party state.

Tending the Emergence of Multiparty Democracy

The birth of multiparty democracy in Tanzania was blighted by the denial of the right of independent candidates to contest elections and by stringent application of the rules governing the registration of political parties. In the perceived cause of the defence of national unity and security, a number of applications to register political parties were refused by the Registrar of Political Parties. One such case was that of the Reverend Christopher Mtikila and his Democratic Party (DP). The Registrar of Political Parties refused to register the DP because it opposed the Union between Tanzania and Zanzibar. The High Court upheld the Registrar's decision, but the Court of Appeal overturned the decision of the High Court and ordered the Registrar to deal with the registration of DP in accordance with the principle of law and natural justice. The Court of Appeal's ruling came on 20 October 1995, just over a week before the Election Day. Reverend Mtikila's attempt to seek a court injunction to prevent the election go ahead on the set date of 29 October 1995, in order to give the DP time to participate in the polls, was unsuccessful.

Unique Electoral Position of Zanzibar

Politically and constitutionally, Zanzibar is an integral part of the Union of Tanzania. However, the electoral structure of the Union is shared between the mainland and Zanzibar. There is a National Electoral Commission (NEC) of Tanzania which primarily deals with the organisation of elections on mainland Tanzania. With respect to Zanzibar, a separate electoral commission, the Zanzibar Electoral Commission (ZEC).The two Electoral Commissions are required to consult on various matters, but the ZEC retains autonomy over the elections for the Zanzibar Presidency,

House of Representatives and local councils. The NEC is responsible for the registration, supervision and conduct of the elections for the Union Presidency and Parliament on the mainland and in Zanzibar. It utilises the personnel of the ZEC, the constituency boundaries and the electoral registers compiled by the ZEC in the administration of the Union polls in Zanzibar.

Valliant Attempt to Offer Good Election Services

The National Electoral Commission (NEC) of mainland Tanzania sought to offer good election services to voters on polling day in October 1995. Each of the 40,000 polling stations catered for 300-350 voters. That meant that polling sites not only included public and community buildings such as schools and health centres, but private premises such as small businesses, carpenters' workshops, cafés, and even butchers' shops, notwithstanding the disagreeable smell. In selecting the private premises care was taken to ensure that the owners or occupiers of the premises were non-partisans so far as the political parties were concerned. Some previously used locations were objected to by local party activists. In some stations, when polling began, no furniture had arrived and so the stations operated from the ground, dusty as some were, polling went on until some tables and chairs were delivered. While polling took place without furniture, makeshift voting screens were made from Kangas (brightly coloured cloth), to protect the secrecy of the ballot.

Faulty Ballot Paper Layout

In the 1995 Tanzanian transitional one-party to multiparty elections, political parties were unhappy with the ballot paper layout. Regarding the presidential election ballot papers they complained that the presentation of the photographs of the vice presidential candidates on the presidential ballot paper was confusing to the voters, unnecessarily crowded the ballot paper, and could increase the number of spoilt ballot papers. With respect to the ballot papers for the parliamentary elections, the parties complained that in each constituency the candidates appeared in alphabetical order according to their surnames and therefore parties did not have a fixed place on the ballot papers across the country. The parties also felt that the absence of party symbols on either set of ballot papers would present difficulties in educating their supporters in the voting procedures.

Multi-Party Election Campaign

The euphoria brought on by the multiparty election campaign in Tanzania in 1995 released the energies of many civil society groups, including the church. The reports suggested that churches, prayer houses, and other civil society groups were engulfed in the dynamic momentum of the campaign. Complaints were made against the National Council for Women that some of its leaders were involved in partisan politics and those complaints drew a caution from President Mwinyi. Complaints by some political parties and candidates told of religious leaders who were campaigning for candidates although the NEC had drawn the attention of the public that the Elections Act of 1985 proscribed the use of prayer houses as campaign venues and the use of religion in political campaigns. The Council of Catholic Bishops issued a statement warning religious leaders against direct involvement in campaigning for candidates or parties and urging instead that they take a lead in voter education.

Nyumba Kumi Kumi (Ten-Cell System)

The Nyumba Kumi Kumi or ten cell system was developed by the Chama Cha Mapinduzi (CCH) Party which was the sole and dominant party in the one-party system of Tanzania. The ten cell system denoted that the party was one that was based on very small units of organisation where official party leaders with considerable influence over the population in the community lived among the voters. That party structure was being copies by many opposition parties.

Annulment of Elections in 7 Constituencies

The transitional elections in 1995 on mainland Tanzania experienced some setbacks. Among the most serious was the complete breakdown in the election logistics management in each of the seven constituencies of Dar es Salaam. Polling stations were opened late, very late, or not at all. Election materials reached polling stations very late or not at all, and the late opening and shortages of materials triggered confusion at polling stations. At the end of the polling day, the National Electoral Commission reviewed the reports and annulled the election in all seven constituencies in Dar es Salaam and set a new date for the elections in those constituencies.

Safeguarding the Secrecy of the Ballot

The United Nations team that was coordinating the election observers in Tanzania in 1995 was unhappy about the procedure of placing the voters' registration number on the counterfoils of ballot papers. Other observers also expressed their dissatisfaction with the procedure as it was felt that it was possible to trace how a person voted, if the counterfoils got into the wrong hands. The National Electoral Commission took action by issuing guidelines to presiding officers to secure the counterfoils at the close of the polls and, before the count, place the counterfoils in an envelope and sealed it, and allows any polling agents wishing to do so, to add their seals to the envelope. The envelopes with the counterfoils could only be opened by court order. This procedure met the concerns of all observers and other stakeholders.

Verdict of Commonwealth Observers

The Commonwealth Observer Group which was sympathetic to the efforts of the Tanzanian National Electoral Commission's genuine efforts to deliver free and fair elections at its first multiparty elections stated that the Commission was aware of the logistical challenge posed by the administration of the 1995 elections, it did not have the necessary structure and experience in managing multiparty elections to ensure that all voters wishing to do so were able to express their will on polling. The Group noted that notwithstanding that the voting period was extended until 8.00p.m., the poll had to be continued in some constituencies on 30 and 31 October. They pointed out that the situation was so confused in Dar es Salaam that voting in seven constituencies was annulled and had to be re-scheduled. They concluded that it was evident that one of the contributing factors to the confusion in Dar es Salaam was the inadequate control of the distribution of materials, particularly ballot papers, which had resulted in the shortage of those vital election supplies in a number of different areas.

Inadequate Formula for Delimitation of Electoral Districts

During the preparation for the July 1995 general election in St Kitts and Nevis, there were strong calls from civil society organisations for review of the boundaries of constituencies. The two main political parties, the People's Action Movement (PAM), the ruling party, and the St Kitts and Nevis Labour Party (SKNLP), were silent on the issue. The Constituencies Boundaries Commission was mandated to review constituencies' boundaries at intervals of not less than two years and no more than five years. The Commission carried out a review in 1990, but did not recommend any changes. In the intervening years changes in demography in St Kitts in particular made a review necessary before the pending elections in the view of many stakeholders. They pointed out that a particular constituency in urban St Kitts had twice as many voters as each of five constituencies in St Kitts and three constituencies in Nevis. The two largest parties showed little interest in that issue because voting patterns in the country suggested that they would not be significantly disadvantaged if the boundaries were not redrawn.

Flawed Voting Procedure

For the July 1995 general elections in St Kitts and Nevis, the voting procedure that was stipulated required that the voter handed the ballot paper to the presiding officer after the ballot was marked. The completed ballot paper was then placed into the ballot box by the presiding officer and not by the voter. On the eve of the election, complaints were made about this procedure to the Electoral Commission on the ground that it ran the risk of compromising the secrecy of the ballot. The Commission consulted on the matter, but felt that there was not enough time to introduce the changes proposed, since the consent of the political parties had to be obtained prior to making the changes, and to re-educate the voters in the change of procedures.

An Important CSO Initiative

The civil society organisations (CSOs) of the St Kitts Christian Council, the Nevis Christian Council, the Evangelical Association of St Kitts, the Evangelical Association of Nevis, and the Chamber of Industry and Commerce brokered an agreement among four of the five political parties to establish a code of conduct for the political process. A Committee to Promote Compliance with the Code of Conduct was established to monitor compliance of the parties there with. The Compliance Committee met daily to receive submissions regarding violations of the Code and make recommendations for corrective measures. The initiative of the CSOs was considered a positive contribution to easing tension in the polarised political environment of St Kitts and Nevis at that time.

Returning Voters

A recurring electoral feature known to St Kitts and Nevis (and also to Antigua and Barbuda) is that of voters returning from abroad[14] to vote in the constituency in which they were registered. This feature has it roots in the regime governing registration of voters (how long must some one reside in a constituency to be qualified to vote therein). At the time of the 1995 elections, any person who was qualified to be registered as a voter in a constituency and was so registered was entitled to return from overseas to vote, even if residing abroad at the time of the election. It can make a difference to the outcome of a constituency election, because the constituencies are small (in terms of electorate). While the concept of 'returning voter' was sometimes frowned upon, the traditional view is that

---

14 Mainly from the British and American Virgin Islands, but also from North America and other neighbouring islands like St Maartin.

most political parties benefit from overseas voters and would not want to see it stopped. The practice has also given rise to complaint of financial inducements being offered by political parties to attract overseas voters to exercise their franchise. It was estimated that there were as many as 2000 overseas voters in 1995, a relatively significant figure in the election mathematics of St Kitts and Nevis, particularly in respect of marginal constituencies.

Safeguarding the Distribution of Polling Materials

The procedure for ensuring that election materials and supplies were distributed without tampering was elaborate. It entailed that each presiding officer was provided with a ballot box with a lock and key and with the voters' list for his/her polling station, and the envelopes containing the ballot books. Each ballot book had100 ballot papers and each envelope contained several ballot books according to the number of voters registered at the particular polling station. Each envelope given to the presiding officer was sealed at both ends and the Chairman and members of the Electoral Commission put their signatures across the folds at two ends, so that if anyone opened the envelope at either end, the signatures would be interfered with and it would be obvious that the tampering had taken place. On polling morning the presiding officer was required to show the envelope to the party agents in order to assure them that there was no tampering with the envelope and that it was the same envelope that was received from the Supervisor of Elections in that the seals at the two ends of the envelope were in tact and so were the signature of the Chairman and the members of the Commission.

Electoral Innovations

The Electoral Commission of Ghana was credited with the introduction of a number of innovations for the presidential and parliamentary elections in December1996. Such innovations included the use of transparent ballot boxes which could be sealed; the requirement that voter identity cards should be perforated before the ballot paper was issued to each voter, and the establishment of regular contact with all political parties through an Inter Party Advisory Committee (IPAC). Matters of common interest were discussed at the IPAC meetings and as improved trust amongst the parties, and between the parties and the Commission, grew, political tension began to ease, resulting in reduced political intimidation and violence. The IPAC was replicated in a modified form at the regional and district level where election task forces comprising local administrative officers, security personnel, and political parties dealt with local electoral and political difficulties as they arose.

Getting Polling Stations to Voters

In order to get polling stations within easy reach of voters, the Electoral Commission of Ghana in 1996 designated polling stations as 'temporary structures' and many stations were constructed on open ground sites conveniently placed to serve voters. Some stations were sited near to schools, community centres, churches, mosques and other public buildings. That flexible approach allowed the Commission to set up polling stations in areas where few registered voters resided. In its endeavour to ensure that a polling station was within easy reach of every voter, some stations had too little space available for the smooth operation of the polling process. At some stations, polling screens were poorly positioned and compromised the secrecy of the ballot, as candidates' agents were located too close to the booths, while at other stations the agents were too far away.

The Sandline Affair and Elections

The months before the June 1997 general elections in Papua New Guinea (PNG) witnessed the emergence of a political crisis triggered by what became known as the Sandline Affair. The Government of PNG, in line with its policy to step up efforts to resolve the attempted secession of the island of Bourgainville, the main island in the North Solomons Province of PNG, hired a United Kingdom-based company, Sandline International, to train members of the PNG Defence Force (PNGDF). Opponents of the scheme, which was said to cost some US$35 million, quickly labelled it one of foreign mercenaries to be used in Bourgainville and attracted domestic and international protest. The Commander of the PNGDF, Brigadier-General, Jerry Singirok opposed the scheme and joined the call for the Prime Minister and senior Ministers to resign. The members of the PNGDF and of the public protested in the streets of the capital, Port Moresby, and the 'mercenaries' were expelled from the country. The Prime Minister, Sir Julius Chan, stepped aside in favour of an Acting Prime Minister, Mr John Giheno and a Commission of Inquiry was set up to investigate the Sandline affair. The Commission's report was submitted to the Acting Prime Minister at the end of May during the general election campaign. The Sandline affair formed an issue which was widely debated during the election campaign in the media and at political rallies by Brigadier-General Jerry Singirok and anti-corruption candidates through the country.

Gender Tally

During polling in the PNG 1997 general election, polling officers kept gender tally records to enable the Electoral Commission to find out whether women were participating in the polling process as fully as men. The result was positive and showed that as many women as men voted in the election.

Creation of New Constituencies

During the period leading up to the May 1997 parliamentary elections in Cameroon, a number of new constituencies were created by the President by decree[15] on the same day on which the election date was announced. Administratively, Cameroon is divided into ten provinces which are further divided into Divisions. The Divisions serve as constituencies for the purposes of parliamentary elections. The President had the power to construct the boundaries of Divisions in his sole discretion and so for the 1997 parliamentary elections, the President not only increased the number of Divisions, but re-drew a number of electoral boundaries. Additional

---

15 See President Decree No.97-062, 2nd April 1997.

constituencies could also be created by the President under powers derived by an amendment to the Electoral Law which allowed the creation of 'special constituencies', a phrase which was not defined in the decree. Each constituency was allocated one or more parliamentary seats, depending on several criteria including population density and geographical size. Not unexpectedly, the action of the President provoked strong complaints from opposition political parties.

Multi-tiered Local Commissions

The electoral structure for the 1997 Cameroon parliamentary elections consisted of the Ministry of Territorial Administration (MINAT) and a series of commissions mandated to deal with various specific aspects of the electoral process. Thus there were the commissions for the revision of the register for electors; the commissions responsible for the establishment and distribution of registration cards; commissions responsible for local polling; commissions for the supervision of elections in each Division; the national commission for the final counting of votes; and the constitutional council, which dealt with complaints and which announced the election results.

Dispute Concerning Size and Quality of Register

The voters' register prepared for the parliamentary elections of Cameroon in 1997 was strongly criticized on the grounds of its size and quality. The register contained 3, 719, 774 voters out of an estimated more than 14 million people. According to stakeholders, a reasonable estimate suggested that substantially more persons should have been on the register, since the municipal elections of 1996 had 300.000 more voters on that register. Regarding the quality of the register, stakeholders complained, among other things, that:

- Inadequately publicised schedules of times and places for registration;
- Failure to place the names of registered persons on the register;

- Names of voters appearing in places other than where they were registered;
- Procedure for correcting the register not observed;
- Voter's particulars in the register some times differed from those on their voter's card or national identity card;
- Voters' names appear on the register in locality in which they did not reside;
- Multiple registration;
- People were hindered from registering rather than helped to do so; and
- The receipt for application to register was not accepted as proof of registration.

Faulty Distribution of Voters' Cards

In order to vote at the parliamentary elections of Cameroon in 1997, a voter had to produce a voter's card and prove his/her identity. The local polling commission, however, had discretion to allow a voter to vote without a voter's card, if their name was on the register and they could prove identity. Many stakeholders complained that a large number of persons who had registered did not receive their voter's card before polling day. This was believed to be intentional on the part of district officials who, it was reported, caused voters' cards of many individuals to be handed over to traditional chiefs and other unauthorised persons for distribution.

Campaign Wrappa

'Wrappa' was printed cloth used by political parties in Cameroon during their parliamentary election campaign in 1997. The wrappa was printed in party colours and was used for posters and banners, and clothes for party supporters.

'Reporters not Supporters'

The Union of Journalists initiated a programme called Media for Democracy in the period leading up to the Cameroon election of 1997. About 400 journalists were trained at a workshop on election reporting. At the end of the workshop the journalists adopted a slogan that they should be 'reporters not supporters', aimed at reducing the incidence of biased reporting. Many stakeholders acknowledged however that the ruling party, the Cameroon People's Democratic Movement (CPDM) received unfair advantage above other parties from the electronic media.

Chefferies of L'amidos

Stakeholders in the Cameroon parliamentary election of 1997 complained that many polling stations were set up in houses or compounds (chefferies) of local chiefs (l'amidos) who were known to be supporters of a particular political party. In a particular division, all the polling stations were sited in or near to chefferies.

Selective Disenfranchisement

The poor quality of the register of voters for the 1997 Cameroon parliamentary elections showed up at the polling stations. Many persons who turned up to vote were not known to the polling officials or members of the public, while many who turned up and were known in the area did not find their name on the register. In a particular polling station, all persons, who went to the station up to 4.00 p.m. on polling day, found that their names were not on the register. Many voters were prevent from voting because of discrepancies in the details found on their national ID card and those on their voter's card with those on the register. The problems were widespread and earned the allegation of selective disenfranchisement by some stakeholders.

Insufficient Copies of Counting Reports

Although many assurances had been given about adequate copies of the counting reports at polling stations, including two statements on the matter by the Cameroon Vice-Prime Minister, there were many complaints that a number of stations without the relevant forms, while others were unable to issue more than two copies of the report.

Burning of Ballots Immediately After Count

Rather unusually, the electoral law of Cameroon allowed ballots which have been counted and not subject to challenge to be burned immediately. At least one report of international observers expressed concern at the practice.

Incomplete Voters' Register

The 1997 general election in Pakistan was organised under the auspices of a caretaker government, like the previous election of 1993. The Bhutto Administration was dismissed on 5 November 1996 and election was fixed for February 1997. Before its dismissal from power, the Bhutto Government had initiated a nationwide re-registration exercise in 1995. However, before the completion of the re-registration exercise, it was challenged in the Supreme Court on the grounds that the law permitted a revision of the register only and not re-registration. The Court granted a stay of the re-registration exercise and that Order was in place when the election was held in February 1997. The electoral register which was used for the 1997 election was based on the register used for the 1993 elections, but the register was revised in November and December 1996. The voters' register increased from 52, 326, 021 in 1993 to 56, 573, 956, in 1996. The updating of the voters' lists was done by means of supplementary lists which were sent to returning officers who distributed them to presiding officers. The upshot was that there was no consolidated electoral roll at the national or constituency level. It was not possible to check for multiple registration and that triggered complaints by political parties.

Caretaker Governments and Elections

Caretaker governments are a familiar constitutional phenomenon in Pakistan and Bangladesh. In Pakistan the ability of the President of the day to dismiss the government of the day has led to the administration of the affairs of the State to pass into the hands of unelected bureaucrats. This happened in 1993 and again in 1996. Thus both the general elections of 1993 and 1997 in Pakistan were organised by Caretaker Governments. In Bangladesh, the unique feature of the elected government stepping aside at the end of its electoral mandate and handing over to an unelected Caretaker Government is enshrined in the Constitution. Unsurprisingly, the procedure faltered when in 2006 the term of the incumbent Government ended and the opposition parties challenged the impartiality of the Electoral Commission and of the composition of the Caretaker Government. Riots broke out throughout the country. A state of emergency was declared and the election was postponed for some 18 months. The obviously flawed approach to solving the lack of confidence in the political and electoral system of Bangladesh has been very costly to that country.

Well-Intentioned, but Wrong Approach

During polling in the 1997 general election in Pakistan a number of party agents turned up late on polling day. Notwithstanding the clear rules which required the polls to open at the hour set by law whether or not party agents are present, many presiding officers delayed the opening of the polls at their stations until the arrival of the party agents. That generous approach by presiding officers was contrary to the election rules and unfair to the voters who were waiting in queues.

Gender Hurdles

During the run up to the 1997 general election in Pakistan, tribal leaders and men generally in the North-Frontier Province left international observers in no doubt that they did not favour voting by women. In the Kyber Agency region some men indicated that there would be consequences for women who tried to vote, they would be fined and their houses burnt down. That attitude persisted until polling day and few women appeared to have voted in that area of the Federal Administered Tribal region.

Need for Effective Governance

Against the background of successive democratic elections (1993 & 1997) having to be organised by Caretaker Governments because of an apparent breakdown of democratic governance, the Commonwealth Observer Group was mandated to make recommendations concerning effective democratic governance in Pakistan.

The main thrust of the recommendations was:

Improvement in the Attitude of Opposition Parties

The Group noted that successive opposition political parties did not always conduct themselves in the spirit of democracy. It cited the fact that opposition parties had often urged the President to use his power to dismiss the government. That approach, it noted, appeared to strengthen the power of the Presidency at the expense of Parliament. The Observer Group further referred to the incidence of crossing the floor in the Assembly and thereby changing allegiance through inducements which would not stand public scrutiny.

The Rule of Law

The Group was of the view that a caretaker government should be made to operate within specific limits under the law, and particularly to foster an environment in which credible elections would be held.

Independence of the Judiciary[16]

The Observers suggested that the formula for appointments to the superior courts should be flexible to include the Prime Minister, Chief Justice, and the Leader of the Opposition.

New Political Culture

The Group noted that the lack of the appropriate political culture led to a drift of power from Parliament to President in a manner which distorts the proper functioning of a democratic system. They suggested that in order for Pakistan to achieve an effective and enduring democratic government, participants in the process must change their approach. The Group also suggested that the parliamentarians had to build a new culture based on respect for Pakistan's institutions, each other and for the process of law and of government. They noted that the undue use of the decree-making power of the President which enabled the President to bypass Parliament was one of the causes of the woes of the Parliament. The flaws of Pakistan's parliamentary democracy was compounded, in the view of the Observer Group, by the Opposition encouraging the President to use the powers of dismissal, rather than trying to defeat the Government in Parliament.

Equality for Women

The Group of Observers felt that a fool-proof identity card system, taking account of religious and cultural considerations, could be developed for use by both men and women. They expressed the view that special efforts should be made to assist the women of the tribal areas to move freely to

---

[16] During March of 2007, the President, General Pervez Musharraf who came to power in a coup in 1999, purportedly dismissed the Chief Justice, Mr. Justice Chaudhry, on grounds of misbehaviour, amidst accusations of breaching the independence of the Judiciary and prolonged protestations by the country's lawyers and civil society groups.

vote. They suggested that special directly elected seats for women should be restored and women should continue to have the rights to vote in their own constituencies.

Honest Governance

The Observer Group expressed the wish that the in-coming Parliament would create an Ethics Committee which would provide an additional safeguard for the integrity of Parliament. They also suggested that the new Parliament should preserve the powers of the Accountability Commission.

Error in Polling Officers' Manual

The preparation for the general and regional elections in Guyana in 1997 marked significant improvement on the election of 1992. However, simple errors still turned up in unexpected places. One such error was the failure of the *Manual for Presiding Officers and Polling Place Staff (Manual)* to reflect the then current provisions of the elections law relating to the procedure for counting of votes by the Disciplined Forces. The Manual reflected the rule prior to the change in the law, namely, that the ballots cast by the Disciplined Forces must be intermixed with and counted on Election Day at a designated polling place in each electoral district together with the ballots cast at that polling place. The amending provisions of the elections law[17] had removed the requirement of intermixing of ballots of the Disciplined Forces with other ballots at any designated polling place. The upshot of the confusion was that when the Disciplined Forces on the 10 December 1997 (early voting ahead of general voting on 15 December 1997), voted, international observers were surprised to see the results of the Disciplined Forces votes published in one of the daily papers on 17 December 1997, showing separately how the Forces voted, contrary to

---

17 See Section 7 of the Representation of the People Act (Amendment) Act No. 30 of 1990.

the rules set out in the Manual. The Chairman of the Guyana Elections Commission took responsibility for the apparent misleading information in the Manual and pointed to the relevant amendment to the election law.

Defective Voters' Lists at Stations

As so often happens in emerging democracies, the discrepancies in the voters' register show up in a variety of forms at the polling stations on polling day. Guyana was true to form on polling day on 15 December 1997. Many voters turned up at their respective designated polling stations with their voter's identification card, but found out that their names were not on the voters' register. In some cases there had been an Addendum list of voters for the polling station in question, but amazingly the presiding officer did not refer to it. Party agents were also not alerted to the need to remind presiding officers about the Addendum list in the station; it was left to observers in many instances to remind presiding officers of that fact.

Flawed Votes Tallying

The tallying process of the votes at the general and regional elections in Guyana in 1997 faced a complete break down. In order to speed up the tallying of the votes from the stations, where to counting of the votes took place, the counting officer of each polling station was required to send the origin copy of the Statement of the Poll in an envelope provided for that purpose, along with the ballot box to the stipulated tallying centre. For inexplicable reasons a number of counting officers locked away the Statement of the Count in the ballot box. That development slowed the tallying process and made the release of results patchy and incoherent. In such circumstances, it was not long before total confusion reigned in the counting centre with anxious supporters of political parties shouting suspicious rumours. The confusion was compounded by discrepancies or perhaps lack of synchronization between results agreed between the Elections Commission and party agents and the results announced by the Chairman of the Commission. The situation at the Commission got progressively worse as days passed and the outgoing minority party leader announced on Friday 19 December 1997 that his party would not accept the election results and instead would be challenging them in court.

Premature Announcement of Winner

In the midst of the confusion about the tallying of the votes in the general and regional elections in Guyana in 1997 and before the tallying process was completed, the Chairman of the Elections Commission announced that the ruling party, the PPP/C had secured the largest number of votes. He indicated that he came to that conclusion because on the basis of the Commission's projection, taking account the number of votes counted, the number of votes received by the PNC (the main opposition party) and the number received by the PPP/C, even if all the remaining votes went to the PNC it could not achieve a majority. The Chairman of the Commission then declared that in accordance with the Constitution, he declared the PPP/C the winning party and its leader as President of Guyana, although all the votes had not yet been tallied. Opposition political parties objected to the procedure followed by the Chairman of the Commission and indicated that they would take the matter to court.

Joint Observer Mission

The presidential and national assembly elections in Seychelles in 1998 were observed by a joint mission sent by the Commonwealth and La Francophonie. A team of nine observers from the Commonwealth and La Francophonie was preceded by a joint mission to ascertain whether there was support among stakeholders for a joint observer team and the findings were positive. The Government of Seychelles invited both organisations of which that country is a member to observe the elections. The Commonwealth and La Francophonie first collaborated in a joint election observation mission in Cameroon at the parliamentary elections in 1997.

Funding of Political Parties in Seychelles.

An enactment in 1996[18] allowed for the funding of political parties in Seychelles. The funding formula was based on the percentage of valid votes received by nominated candidates by the respective political parties in the last elections to the National Assembly. The funds were appropriated by the National Assembly and were paid out on or before 30 January each year.[19]

Mixed Electoral System

The register of voters for the 1998 elections in Seychelles stood at 56, 399, a small electorate, that notwithstanding its size supported a mixed electoral system. Twenty-five seats were allocated to a first past the post system and 10 seats on proportional representation system.

Objection to Local Printing of Ballot Papers

The printing of the ballot papers for the presidential and national assembly elections in 1998 in Seychelles assumed nation-wide interest when opposition parties objected to their printing by a local firm which was owned by an alleged supporter of the ruling Seychelles People's Progressive Front (SPPF). The ballot papers were ultimately printed in Singapore.

Emergency Payments

Long queues at payment out points at the Seychelles Ministry of Finance and elsewhere in Victoria shortly before the elections caught the attention of international observers to the 1998 elections and others. Many

---

18 See the Political Parties (Registration and Regulation) (Amendment) Act.

19 An amount of SR7.5 million was appropriated for assistance to political parties in 1997, the first year of the operation of the Fund.

stakeholders complained to the Electoral Commission who wrote to the Ministry of Employment and Social Affairs for an explanation of the distribution of emergency funds at that time. The Principal Secretary in the Ministry replied promptly explaining that emergency payments were made to individuals and families in distress, and indicated the procedure. The Ministry's explanation was not wholly satisfactory to the Joint Observer Mission from the Commonwealth and La Francophonie whose Chairman pointed out that the payment out of large amounts of social security benefits immediately before the elections was likely to lead to misinterpretation. After his re-election, the President, Mr René, said that it was unfortunate that the timing of payments could have given rise to suspicion and indicated that the Government would look into the system of payment.

Mozambique—Public Funding of Political Parties

In preparing for the parliamentary and presidential elections in Mozambique in 1999, the National Electoral Commission, pursuant to the electoral law, distributed public funds in accordance with stipulated criteria to political parties to be used for election campaign purposes. The formula for the funding was based on existing representation of the parties in the National Assembly and the proportion of the candidates presented for the elections in relation to the number of seats in the Assembly.

Phased Voter Education Programme

The Technical Secretariat for the Administration of Elections, STAE, developed a two-phased programme for voter education for the 1999 elections in Mozambique. The programme, which was approved by the Electoral Commission, consisted of phase 1 which focussed on voter registration and lasting from June to September 1999. Phase 2 dealt with the polling process and lasted from November until Election Day in early December 1999. Although the programme was carried on radio and television, and in the print media, it was only in the Portuguese Language, as the election authorities did have the resources to translate it into local dialects. The lack of translation facilities was perhaps cushioned by visuals such as the use of posters, T-shirts and shopping bags.

Polling Extension

Polling was extended into a third day during the Parliamentary and Presidential elections in Mozambique in 1999 because of inclement weather on the second day of polling when some stations opened so late that, in the view of the Commission, the time available to voters was unacceptably limited. That decision was criticized by some stakeholders and by some international observers. The critics felt that the cost of keeping the entire voting machinery open for a relatively small number of voters was not worth it. They felt that, if the law was inflexible then it should be amended to allow voting to continue only in those stations where it was necessary.

South Africa—Post Post-Apartheid Electoral Structures

(1) *Independent Electoral Commission*

The Electoral Act of 1996 vested an independent electoral commission, established by the Electoral Commission Act 1996, with the responsibility for the conduct of elections in South Africa. The Commission was intended to be an independent body subject to the Constitution and the law. Its primary role includes promotion of conditions conducive to holding free and fair elections; compiling and maintaining the voters' register; registering political parties; establishing cooperation with parties; reviewing and making recommendations about election legislation; promoting voter education; demarcating electoral constituencies; adjudicating disputes of an administrative nature arising out of the organisation of elections; and administering monies allocated by Parliament for party funding.

(2) *Electoral Court*

An Electoral Court was established by the Electoral Commission Act of 1996 with a similar status as that of the Supreme Court. The Court has final jurisdiction over breaches of the Electoral Act and Codes of Conduct established under the Act. Its decisions and orders are not subject to appeal or review.

(3) *Party Liaison Committees*

Section 5 of the Electoral Act allows the Electoral Commission to set up Party Liaison Committees at national, provincial and municipal levels. The committees were chaired by representatives of the Commission. The work of these committees was facilitated by conflict analysts within the Commission's structures at the national and provincial levels, and mediators were identified at the provincial level.

Challenge to Use of Bar-Coded ID Documents

The system of bar-coded identification documents required under the Electoral Act 1996 of South Africa was challenged by two of the political parties, the New National Party and the Democratic Party, on the grounds that up to four million people who held other forms of identification papers and had not applied for the new documents, would be disenfranchised. The parties lost the case in the Cape Town High Court and they appealed to the Constitutional Court, asking that Court to declare the requirement of bar-coded ID documents unconstitutional and unfair. That Court also dismissed the action holding that voters had sufficient time to acquire the prescribed ID book and that the documents used previously belonged to the apartheid era and were no longer appropriate.

Public Funding of Political Parties

The funding of South African political parties is done under the Public Funding of Represented Political Parties Act, which confers the responsibility of administering such funds on the Chief Executive Officer of the Commission. Allocation of 90% of the funds to parties should be based on the share of each in the seats in the National Assembly and the provincial legislatures. The remaining 10% is distributed on the basis of a fixed threshold to each party. The party funds received under this formula may be used for a variety of purposes, including promoting the party's influence on public opinion; political education; and strengthening the party's links to the organs of state. This allocation formula has been criticised as being unfriendly towards new political parties.

Flexibility Respecting Special Voting

The Independent Electoral Commission (IEC) of South Africa is clothed with considerable flexibility to designate special voting circumstances, for example, on application the IEC may allow special voting facilities to the disabled, pregnant voters, or those absent form their voting district for good reasons.

Observing Special Voting Abroad

During the June 1999 National and Provincial elections in South Africa, the South African High Commissioner to the United Kingdom, with the concurrence of the Independent Electoral Commission, invited three members of the Commonwealth Secretariat to observe the polling at the High Commission as accredited observers. The special voting at the High Commission was held on 26 May 1999, a few days ahead of the general polling day of 2 June 1999, for all South African voters in the United Kingdom. The accredited observers from the Commonwealth Secretariat submitted a positive report on the conduct of the special voting at the High Commission in the UK.

Prisoners' Franchise

Like the transitional elections in 1994 in South Africa, prisoners were able to exercise the franchise at the elections of 1999. For the purposes of the elections, the prisoners were deemed to be ordinarily resident at the place of incarceration. A total of 213 temporary polling places were set up to allow prisoners to vote, and also those who had registered there before their release from the respective prisons.

Scrapping a Unique Voting System

The Gambia has a unique voting system, which uses, instead of the normal ballot papers and ballot boxes commonly used in Africa, ballot tokens (marbles) and metal ballot drums. Voting materials consist of ballot drums, the bells of ballot drums, ballot tokens and seals for the drums. Ballot drums in polling stations are marked with the pictures and party symbols of the candidates. Polling procedures include showing the empty drums to those present in the station at the opening of the poll. The AU Observers to the Parliamentary Elections of 2007, in their report expressed the view that the unique system was not in keeping with the trend elsewhere in the Union and should be replaced with a single ballot paper on which the candidates' name would be placed.

Incumbency-The Ugandan Treatment

Incumbency gained prominence in the Ugandan presidential and parliamentary elections of 2006. The conditions governing the use of Government resources were set out in Section 27 of the Presidential Elections Act 2005. In January 2006, in compliance with the Act, the Deputy Prime Minister and Minister of the Public Service laid before Parliament the entitlements of the President as follows: "The usual transport facilities provided to the President, the usual security detail facilities provided to the President, the usual personal staff and their facilities attached to the President, the usual information and communication facilities attached to the President". Some stakeholders expressed concern about the presentation, as not many people knew what the "usual facilities" attached to the President were.

Mass Removal of Names from the Voters' Register

In the 2006 Ugandan general election, a number of polling stations reported that large numbers of names of voters were removed from the register without any apparent explanation. The persons concerned had registered and had their voter's card or certificate from voter registration showing that they were eligible to vote at the particular polling station.

They were not informed that that was not longer the case. It turned out that the removal of the names from the register might have been as a result of a change in the law which took place in 2000 requiring only those persons who live in or originate from a particular area may register there, whereas previously persons working in the area could register in that area. It was feared however that the amending law might not have been the only factor at work in those cases, as some names were removed with the help of local tribunals which were believed to have acted on a partisanship basis. It was estimated that some 200,000 voters were affected.

Inconsistent Application of Polling Procedures

In some elections, the evidence of lack of thorough training of election officers is evidenced by shortcomings in many aspects of the conduct of the polling. This was seen to have been the case in Uganda in 2006. Election observers saw insufficient sealing of ballot boxes, and even no sealing at all; the indelible ink was sometimes administered to the wrong finger and in some cases the stamp pad was used rather than pen-like instrument provided for the purpose; some party or candidate's agents were seated too far away from the activity taking place, while other agents were too near to the polling activity as to get in the way of the process. It also appeared that many polling officers were not equipped to deal with contingency circumstances such as shortages of election materials or changes in the weather on Election Day.

Excessive Security or Intimidation

The Uganda People's Defence Force and the riot Police Force were highly visible in some places on polling day and in some towns they conducted tours in their armoured vehicles. That display of military force was interpreted by some stakeholders and some member of the public as a form of intimidation.

Marking Ballot Papers in Plastic Basins

Plastic basins were used for marking the ballot papers in the 2006 Ugandan elections, but were considered to be inadequate. One observer group recommended that use of plastic basins should be dropped and the international practice of using a separate cubicle or a form of screened voting area be used.

Snap Elections

The election stakeholders of Lesotho were expecting the general elections to be held between May and July 2007, but political events led to the dissolution of Parliament on 24 November 2006 and the elections had to be held within 90 days of that date. In the meantime, the registration of voters which began in early October 2006 had to be curtailed, but was extended for 7 days and 25 December 2006 was set for the publication date for the Preliminary register. When that date came, the register revealed lots of errors—some 120,000 records were in raw form and were yet to be processed. The IEC had to engage 3-shift workers to process the data. The situation was rectified and by 15 January 2007, the register was certified with 916,000 voters, though 10,000 photographs were missing.

Row over Printing of Ballot Papers

During the 'provincial elections' in Zanzibar in 2005, a controversy developed between the Government of Zanzibar and the Zanzibar Electoral Commission over who should print the ballot papers for the pending elections. There was an understanding that the printers who printed the ballot papers for the National Electoral Commission (which managed elections on mainland Tanzania) would also print the Zanzibar ballot papers, but the Government of Zanzibar did not favour that arrangement and ordered the Zanzibar Electoral Commission to make a different arrangement on the grounds that there had been procedural irregularities and financial constraints.

Lack of transparency in Changing Constituencies' Boundaries—Zanzibar 2005 Elections

Not unlike many Commonwealth countries, changes to the boundaries of electoral districts or constituencies in Zanzibar may be made on the basis of population density, population trends, means of communication, and geographical features. The census in Zanzibar in 2002 was relevant for this purpose. There was no requirement in the law for the Electoral Commission to consult political parties or to give notice of a review of constituencies. In the review carried out before the election in 2005, the number of constituencies in Pemba, an opposition stronghold, was reduced from 21 to 18 and those in Unguja (a stronghold of the ruling party) was increased from 29 to 32. There were no maps available to show the details of the changes. The main opposition party cried foul and accused the Commission of attempting to gerrymander the registration process.

The Shehas

In the registration exercise of 29 November 2004 through to 26 April 2005, the role of the shehas was prescribed by section 11(2) & (3) of the Election Act as an ex-officio registration agent of the Electoral Commission which cooperated with the registration officials to secure the smooth compliance of the law and procedures relating to the conduct of the registration of voters at the registration office. However, there was widespread perception that the shehas usurped the authority of registration officers and influenced the determination of people's eligibility in a highly partisan manner. Even the presidential candidate of the main opposition party was reportedly refused registration as a voter initially, but that apparent omission was subsequently rectified.

Late Publication of the Permanent Register (PVR)

There were delays in producing and verifying the PVR which resulted in extracts there from being publicly displayed the day before, or on polling day. This confused voters as they did not know whether or not they were on the final verified register, and at which polling station they were supposed to cast their vote.

'Guard the Vote'

The opposition party, the Civic United Front (CUF) took the position during the Zanzibari election campaign that its supporters should guard the vote by keeping watch just behind the 200 metres line from the polling stations. The Government regarded that position as a provocation and a threat to law and order. CUF later called off the 'guard the vote' policy a few days before the election, and thereby reduced the tension which the policy had caused.

Impediment to Free Campaigning?

Contrary to agreements and understandings, without due notice the police stopped an opposition campaign rally which was to be held in Skuli Ya Donge in Unguja by CUF on 9 October 05. The day before the rally was to be held the police informed the Electoral Commission that the venue could not be used for the CUF rally because churches and mosques and schools premises should not be used for rallies. But the police had agreed to the holding of the rally at that venue a month before. Moreover the ruling party, the Chama cha Mapinduzi, CCM, had used schools for rallies. The apparent breach of the understandings on the conduct of the campaign caused considerable tension which resulted in violence during which the police opened fire on CUF's supporters, injuring some 19 people.

Unclear Procedures

The elections in Zanzibar in 2005 revealed some of the pitfalls when election procedures are unclear and or non-existent. After the counting of the votes, the collation process began with the transportation of the election materials and transmission of the results from the polling stations to the collation centres. However, the procedural steps were not uniform. Some observers stated that there appeared to be no plan—as some times agents were present, other times they were not. Some items were guarded by the police, others were not. Some staff remained, others went home. Some boxes were sealed, others were not. Furthermore, the process that was to take place at the collation centre appeared to be unclear, even to the officers in charge of the transfer from the count.

Lack of Transparency— 'No Scoreboards'

In the 2005 Zanzibar elections, many collation centres were likened to hives of confusion, at times tinged with outright disorder, unsurprisingly. The tallying officers were often unwilling or unable to explain how the results were transmitted and added to the totals for the constituencies and presidential results. There were no 'scoreboards' or similar step-by-step indicator available or on display of the results information. There was an absence of any sheets or other posted information at the collation centres. Party agents were often not present at the collation centres, although they were entitled to be there. Some observers complained that it was not possible to establish how the final results figures for each constituency and the presidential election were compiled.

Tampering of Tally Sheets

The Liberian elections of 2005 witnessed a brazen, but unsophisticated attempt to win a senate seat by tampering with tally sheets. Following up on findings of irregularities after complaints by stakeholders about a senatorial election in Gbarpolu, the National Elections Commission recounted the polling places concerned and found that several polling places' result forms were tampered with at the tally centre, advancing one candidate to the junior senatorial position from third place. Consequently, no result was declared for that Gbarpolu senatorial election and the case was submitted to the police for criminal investigation.

Poorly-Managed Tallying Process

The first round election tallying process was not well managed in the Liberian election in 2005. The hand over of sensitive election materials and the tallying process itself was poorly organised and marked by delays and confusion about the procedures to be applied. Some presiding officers did not properly understand how to reconcile the figures for the three elections or the filling out of the result forms. In a similar vein, many party and candidate representatives were poorly prepared, and did not understand either the tallying process or their role in observing that aspect of the election.

Financial Reports

The majority of the candidates of political parties and alliances who contested the 2005 Liberian elections failed to comply with the requirements of the Campaign Finance Regulations to submit the Annual Financial Reports of the parties and alliances and the two campaign financial reports by the extended deadline of 25 October 2005. Only 136 of the 762 candidates submitted their reports within the time limit. One of the two candidates in the presidential run off election, Ellen Johnson-Sirleaf, was among those who failed to submit a first return by 25 October, claiming that the regulations and procedures were too advanced for Liberia. She did later file a first return.

In the Heat of Elections

In the run up to the run off presidential elections in Liberia 2005, the Congress for Democratic Change (CDC) whose candidate was Ambassador George Weah, on the day of the run off election, 8 November 2005, issued the following statement: 'We, the officers and members of the Congress for Democratic Change (CDC), heard with shock and dismay on the local and international media statements from the Chairperson of NEC, Cllr. Frances Johnson-Morris, without justification, referring to the CDC Standard Bearer, Ambassador George Manneh Weah, as being a person who has made reckless and irresponsible statements on the morning of the election day. We consider this statement with others she made indicated infra, as prejudicial of her role as the senior administrator of the electoral process, particularly on the day of the election, as further impinging on the right of the voters to make a free choice. This has created the substantive and constructive effect of campaigning against Ambassador Weah.

Unintended Confusion

During the run off election in Liberia in 2005, voters were persistently told during the election campaign that they were faced with the choice between one female and one male candidate, but on the ballot paper, there were four pictures (one female and three males). The two Vice Presidential candidates who also appeared on the ballot paper were seldom mentioned during the campaign. Some illiterate voters were confused by this.

Mauritius Poll 2005—Positive Findings

Election observes found that polling operations were conducted in an atmosphere of calm and serenity in which voters cast their votes freely. Police personnel were present within sight of polling stations and there was no visible sign of intimidation or harassment or open violence. The police personnel provided adequate security for sealed ballot boxes and voting materials that were transported to counting centres at the end of polling. Candidates' agents were also allowed to accompany the ballot boxes to the counting centres.

Influence of Incumbency?

Opposition parties and domestic observers complained about the large numbers of ballot papers printed, and the Electoral Commission's award of the tender or printing of the ballot papers to Namprint, a company in which SWAPO, the ruling party, was a shareholder. The Commission argued that Namprint bid was commercially attractive and had printed the regional election ballot papers in 1998 and the presidential and national assembly elections ballot papers in 1999. The Commission explained that the extra ballot papers were necessary to ensure that any station did not run short, especially having regard to tendered ballot papers.

Flawed Counting Process

The counting process in the 2004 Namibian elections was flawed. The whole process was reportedly unnecessarily prolonged leading some opposition parties to question the integrity of the outcome of the elections. Election officials kept on postponing the deadline for announcing the first results and apparently had no cogent explanation to justify the undue delay, thus, in the view of one observer group, casting a shadow over the election process as a whole. The view was expressed that the procedures for the administration and counting of tendered votes should be reviewed.

Stringent Measures Governing Qualification to Register as a Voter

The qualification for registration as a voter in Zimbabwe for the 2005 parliamentary elections was considered to unduly harsh. An example of this was the requirement of the physical production of a landlord's identification particulars before a tenant could be registered. New migrants to urban areas were particularly affected and were likely to be disenfranchised under the new rules.

The Zimbabwean Media in 2005

During the period leading up to the 2005 parliamentary elections, the Zimbabwe Union of Journalists (ZUJ) was concerned about the systematic closure of newspapers. The journalists were particularly concerned that the media laws in the country, particularly the Information and Protection of Privacy Act. That Act was thought to be repressive. It also believed to be suppressive of plurality of views, one of the main tenets of democracy.

Observers' Accreditation Fees

Many election observers were surprised to find that the Zimbabwean Electoral Supervisory Commission was charging accreditation fees of US$100.00 per observer at the 2005 parliamentary elections. When applied to the African Union Observation team, the charges were in violation of clear guidelines in the AU Declaration on the Principles Governing Democratic Elections in Africa—in particular the stipulation that Member States should refrain from imposing any fees and or charges on AU Observers, for example, registration or accreditation fees. The AU Observer Team to the Zimbabwe elections recommended that the practice of imposing accreditation fees on observers be discontinued and that the AU guideline be strictly observed.

Advance Special Voting

Observers of the South African 2004 national and provincial elections were impressed by the advance special voting arrangements for persons with disability, the elderly, and security and election officers a day or two before normal polling day. It was felt that it was a good practice that should be emulated by other countries.

Night Voting

Polling at many stations in South Africa during the 2004 elections continued late into the night. That was due in part to the absence of an appropriate minimum threshold number of voters per voting station. That approach, it is believed, would have significantly reduced the voting hours and avoided voting late into the night. The 2004 late night voting was compounded by poor security lighting outside and insufficient lighting inside many stations. In the rural areas, some stations relied on candles and or paraffin lamps, and that adversely affected the voting and counting processes.

Swift Treatment of Complaints

A notable feature of the 2004 South Africa elections was the rapid treatment of election complaints by the Electoral Commission and its staff. For example, when a mayor entered a polling station wearing a party T-shirt, the presiding officer promptly asked him to leave the station.

Compromising the Secrecy of the Vote

A defective procedure in the South Africa 2004 polling procedure revealed that the ballot boxes attendants often were called upon to assist voters to fold their ballot papers and in so doing they were able to see how the voters voted. Undoubtedly, that practice affected the secrecy of the vote.

Prisoners Separated from their IDs

The vote of persons in prison during an election was provided for in section 24B of the Electoral Act of 1998 of South Africa. It so happened that on voting day in 2004, a number of prisoners turned up at polling stations leaving their identity documents at their homes or places of permanent residents far away from the prisons.

Funding Political Parties—The Mozambique Way

The Mozambique Government earmarked US$2 million for funding political parties in 2004 in line with the electoral law. The distribution was as follows: one third for presidential candidates, one third for parties then currently holding seats in Parliament and one third for parties contesting parliamentary elections. The funds were distributed in three instalments, namely, 50%, 25% and 25%. The ruling party, FRELIMO, and the main opposition party, RENAMO, were entitled to $550,000.00 each. The other parties with presidential candidates and contesting all the seats in the parliamentary elections were entitled to US$125,000.00. Those parties which fielded candidates for all the parliamentary seats were entitled to approximately US$33,000.00.

Vote Counting At Its Onerous Best

The 2004 elections in Mozambique revealed, in the view of some observers, an extremely laborious and exhausting exercise, which took several hours and left many polling officials drooping with sleep and fatigue. The process involved numerous checks and balances, which were intended to enhance transparency and reduce the risk of counting errors. But, complained observers, nonetheless it remained quite onerous.

Election of Youth and Handicapped Deputies

In the Rwandan legislative elections on September 29 2003, two Deputies representing youths and one Deputy representing the Handicapped were elected by a special procedure designed for the purpose. The representatives of the youths were elected by 164 members of the National Council of Youths through indirect and secret ballot, and the representative of the handicapped was elected 99 members of the Federation of Associations of the Handicapped through indirect and secret suffrage. The voting process can only commence when the two-thirds quorum of the members had been attained. The voting process was supervised by the officials of the National Electoral Commission of Rwanda.

Election of Women Deputies

The election of women Deputies to the Rwandan Parliament in 2003 took place on 2nd October. A quorum of two-thirds of the Women's Executive Committees of the Provinces had to be attained before the voting could start. Certain other sectors such as senators, which required three-fourths quorum of their electoral college to be attained before voting could commence also fell under this arrangement. The teaching staff of Public Universities and Higher Institutions fell into the schedule of arrangements and failed to attain the stipulated quorum that would trigger voting and so voting was postponed. The system did not find favour with some election observers who recommended that it should be scrapped.

Multiple Procedural Deficiencies

The 2003 Rwandan Parliamentary elections drew criticisms from stakeholders and election observers regarding multiple procedural deficiencies, namely: the simplicity of the ballot boxes impressed, but would generate more confidence if they had seals or lockable devices; the post-counting arrangements for each candidate's ballot papers were unsatisfactory; the absence of serial numbers generated suspicion and did not facilitate; the use of indelible ink would discourage vote cheating and multiple voting; the method of disqualifying candidates of political parties was unsatisfactory; and there was need for the harmonization of training instructions for election officers.

Candidate Registration—Ethiopian Style (at the 2005 legislative elections)

The Ethiopian electoral law provided that prospective candidates should be Ethiopians of 21 years old who speak the language of the region where the registration was recorded with two years residence in the constituencies. With respect to independent candidates, the law required them to be supported by 1000 signatures, but candidates sponsored by political parties needed no such endorsement.

Voting Complaints

At the time of the 2005 legislative elections, the overall complaints procedures were divided up according to categories such as those relating to voters' registration, candidates' registration, and election campaign. There were those procedures that dealt with voting which entailed the setting up of a committee called the Polling Station Disputes Committee. The time frame given such a Disputes Committee was five hours to receive, examine and resolve the complaint. Thereafter, an appeal lay to the Woreda Electoral Office Disputes Committee within twenty-four hours and a decision should be rendered within forty-eight hours. A further appeal may lie to the Woreda Court for adjudication.

Lukewarm Embrace of Local Observers

Some foreign (international) observers were surprised to learn that the National Electoral Board of Ethiopia had initially refused to accredit local observers.

Voter Registration in Ethiopia

The registration of voters for the 2005 legislative elections revealed anxiety regarding the final figures contained in the register. The number of voters was stated to be 25.6 million which the NEBE stated represented 80% of the eligible persons. The confusion for stakeholders stemmed in part from the fact that the popular assumption that 50% of Ethiopia's 71 million inhabitants were 18 years or over. The actual registration results threw up some strange results, as some areas recorded a larger number of eligible voters than were registered voters. On polling day, flaws in the register were quickly revealed. The registers were prepared in longhand and each registered voter signed the register against his or her name after registering. When the voter went to vote, he/she had to sign against his or her name in the register again. On inspection of the registers, many Election Day signatures had no resemblance to the corresponding signatures during registration.

Over-Sized Ballot Papers

The ballot papers for the legislative elections of 2005 in Ethiopia were designed and printed in-house, which was a cost-effective measure and a positive development with respect to sustainability. However, the ballot papers were observed to be too large and rendered with packaging that did not facilitate smooth or speedy counting of the votes. To compound the problem in the view of some observers, the ballot papers were not printed with serial numbers on their counterfoil which made it difficult to track their movement, and did nothing to enhance accountability.

Ethiopian Legislative Elections 2005

A View of Losing Stakeholders

In showing distaste for the preliminary report of the Carter Center which was viewed as too favourable to the National Electoral Board of Ethiopia (NEBE) and the ruling party, the Ethiopian Peoples Revolutionary Democratic Front (EPRDF), the aggrieved wrote that impartiality had been the last thing to expect from the NEBE, and it was a miracle that Carter Center had seen it when it did not exist. NEBE and the Head of the Secretariat, they said, had been appointed by the ruling party, and the Chairman was appointed in violation of Article102 of the Constitution, and what was also unfortunate was that the Chairman of NEBE was also the President of the Supreme Court, and hence Head of the Judiciary, and also Chairman of the National Council of Constitutional Inquiry. Hence, if any opposition party wants to lodge a legal complaint against NEBE and Chairman Kemal Bedri, one does so to Kemal Bedri in his capacity as President of the Supreme Court or to Kemal Bedri as the Chairman of the Council of the Constitutional Inquiry.

Observer Team's Report Silent on Irregularities

The aggrieved stakeholders complained that the Carter Center made no mention of displaced or disappearing ballot boxes, stolen ballot boxes, opened ballot boxes, party agents and domestic observers who were thrown out of vote counting operations, or threats, beatings and harassment of opposition leaders and supporters, and the total failure of the dispute resolution processes of the Complaints Review Boards (CRBs) and Complaint Investigations Panel (CIPs), primarily due to NEBE'S partisanship. It is regrettable that the Carter Center's team still concluded, after seeing such a hostile climate and coverage of less than 15% of the constituencies, that the majority of the constituency results based on the May 15 polling and tabulation were credible and reflected competitive conditions. In spite of all the several problems enumerated in the report, Carter Center was still saying that Ethiopia had free and fair elections, and that was clearly not true.

Stakeholders—Winners' Response to Criticism

The Prime Minister, Meles Zenawi, in a letter to the press rebutted many assertions in the report published by the European Union Election Observation Mission. In a picturesque passage in the rebuttal letter, the Prime Minister wrote that the problem with the Arithmetic of the EU-EOM was that the fact told a different story. You see, he said, the winner in Ada 1 and 2 was the Coalition for Unity and Democracy (CUD) (opposition party). The complainant was the United Ethiopian Democratic Force (UEDF) (opposition party). The complaint was made against EPRDF (ruling party) despite the fact that it had lost both constituencies. As soon as the investigations started, the UEDF recognized that it had targeted the wrong party and recognized that if the investigations proceeded the EPRDF might be the ultimate beneficiary. It quickly pulled the rug from under the EPRDF's feet and declared it had withdrawn its complaints as it had a right to do. Where there is no complaint, there is no investigation. Ada 1 and 2 were passed without investigation and the CUD allowed to retain both seats. The only investigation carried out by the Complaint Investigations Panel (CIP) before the EU-EOM arrived was that of Adama 2. The time it took to carry out one real investigation was identical both before and after the EU-EOM arrived.[20] But the EU-EOM was not interested in the facts, because if they were they could have been saved the embarrassment of being caught lying by simply asking the CIP what had happened. They needed to trash the CIP and blame it on the EPRDF so they did not check their facts. They simply assumed that the natives would go back to their bad undemocratic ways if the prying eyes of the EU-EOM were temporarily absent.

---

20 The EU-EOM had stated that three complaints were dealt with within just 4 days before their arrival, while afterwards each complaint took at least three days to debrief all witnesses- supporting the view that the procedures were followed only as long as international observers were present.

Guns and Polling Stations in Ethiopia

It is not unlawful for an Ethiopian to go about his/her normal business with a gun at hand. There are some places where this is not allowed. One of these is a polling station. People must leave their guns 500 meters away from a polling station. The reason behind the law that prohibits the carrying of guns within 500 meters of polling stations is not because the sight of guns would intimidate the voters. Why should the sight of some one carrying a gun 499 meters away from a polling station intimidate voters, while the sight of some one carrying a gun 501 meters away from the does not? The reason for the regulation is to prevent some one from killing voters in the heat of contested election. It is known that the effective range of the guns that are held by civilians is less than 500 meters. If we can keep guns away from their effective, the risk of killings in voting stations would be removed.

The Infamous Meragna 'Assassination'

In his article criticizing the EU-EOM Report on the 2005 elections, Prime Minister Meles Zenawi said of this incident: 'Was the deceased a witness of the opposition? The answer is no. Parties submit the list of their witnesses to the National Electoral Board of Ethiopia (NEBE) before the hearings start and as the NEBE has said, Ato Wudu was not on the list of witnesses that CUD submitted for the hearings in Meragna. Did Ato Wudu die on 16th July? The answer is yes. Did he testify for CUD in Meragna? The answer is an emphatic no, for two reasons. First, the hearings were supposed to start on 18th July, two days after he died. Unfortunately, on the 18th July CUD walked out of the hearings in Meragna, as a result of which Ato Wudu who was in any case already dead could not testify. None of the CUD witnesses testified in Meragna, even those that were already dead. So how could the EU-EOM come with the allegation that he was assassinated five days after he testified? The logical answer is that in this case not only did they not try to check the facts, facts that were a matter of public record, but they did not even listen well to the opposition. The opposition accusations were that he was killed to prevent him testifying. Normally, the EU-EOM would report the accusation of the opposition accurately and conclude that the EPRDF is guilty. This time they forgot to report the accusation of the opposition accurately before they pronounced the EPRDF guilty.

Observation Mission Becoming Part of the Problem

In his letter to the press, Prime Minister Meles Zenawi alleged that the EU-EOM in Ethiopia had become part of the problem rather than the solution, beginning with the highly speculative report they leaked, a report, he said he believed, significantly contributed to the June events. He said Ethiopia had to learn from its experience, and therefore had to ask why such shoddy piece of work was issued in the name of the EU-EOM. He attributed it to the author of the report who, he said, was peddling a series of ideas on reforms which she (the author) said was necessary for Ethiopia. The Prime Minister alleged that the ideas of the author of the EU-EOM report were in substance the same ideas, which the opposition had been peddling, including a government of national unity, which the ruling party had rejected.

A Stakeholder Gone Caustic

In his three-part article to a local newspaper, the Herald, (August27, 30 and 31 2005), the Ethiopian Prime Minister criticized the writer of the EU-EOM election report in the following manner:

'All of the bad ideas were discussed with her in the spirit of partnership enshrined in the Coutonou Agreement that exists between Ethiopia and the European Union. She was told that these are bad ideas unacceptable to the EPRDF (the ruling party). The good lady can apparently not take no for an answer from the natives. She had a card in her hands, the report of the election observation, that in unscrupulous hands could be used as hostage to blackmail the EPRDF into accepting those really bad ideas, and she appears to have gone for it. The good lady apparently does not know her Ethiopian history, or her EPRDF's. She apparently does not understand that as soon as these merely bad ideas become tainted by association with an election observer turned self-appointed colonial viceroy hell-bent on twisting the arms of the government to force it to accept her dictates, merely discussing the ideas, let alone accepting them, becomes unthinkable. The good lady does not appear to understand that what her action succeeded in doing is put the last nail in the coffin of her 'recommendations'.

Stealing Elections Brazenly—Panama 1989

Popular expression was confirmed by the parallel vote counting exercise conducted by the Catholic Church laity and the opposition, and the vote was so clearly in favour of the opposition presidential slate and contrary to the Noreiga government, the Panama Defence Force (PDF) manipulated the vote count and, when that ploy failed, annulled the election.

Acts of a Partisan EMB

In 1989, the Electoral Tribunal of Panama was accused of partisan behaviour for allegedly designating pro-government splinter factions as recognized parties. It was slow in dealing with complaints and did not treat them fairly. It nullified the elections of May 10, 1989 on basis of Election Day difficulties caused by the opposition and foreign interference.

Flawed Second Tier Counting

Major problems developed in the second tier of counting of votes at the regional counting boards at the 1989 Panama elections. Difficulties arose from attacks by the PDF and paramilitary forces. The difficulties were perpetrated by the National Counting Board, which was responsible for tabulating the results in the presidential election, apparently collaborated in the irregularity by accepting forms transmitted from the regional boards that were obviously forged.

A Reluctant Host

In the 1989 elections, the Panama authorities, in an apparent attempt to deter US nationals from visiting Panama for the elections, the Ministry of Tourism announced that US citizens would have to obtain a visa from a government-recognized consulate. The consulate in Tampa, Florida, was the only one so recognized. Previously, US nationals were required only to obtain a tourist card from an airline. Further, the Ministry of Commerce informed the hotel where the Institutes planned to accommodate the delegation that, during the election period, the hotel must obtain permission from the Ministry before any guests could be registered, and that no private meeting would be permitted in the hotel The Government also required all private leasing agencies to obtain government authorization before renting vehicles to foreign groups.

Elements of a Stolen Election

The opposition in the 1989 Panama election complained that government used unfair campaign practices, fraudulent vote counting, tampered with voters' cards, bought votes, upheld frivolous challenges to opposition votes and stole tally sheets.

Human Rights

The Inter-American Commission on Human Rights visited Panama from February 25 to March 3 1989 and received numerous complaints of alleged human rights violation such as torture, mistreatment of prisoners, police brutality, illegal arrests, and undue delay in processing of criminal cases, ineffectiveness of writs of habeas corpus, prolonged period of in communicado detention and arbitrary seizure of private priority.

Election Irregularities—Panama Style

Insufficient number of ballots or the ballot papers of the opposition were not in voting booths, opposition party agents were not located in a manner that allowed them to properly observe and verify voters' cards. They also complained that they were not allowed to sign the tape on the ballot box, as required by law. Voters were omitted from the register of voters. The secrecy of the ballot was compromised at some voting stations, because of the lack of proper screens. The opposition reported that the government distributed false credentials to their supports. There were reports of multiple voting by the PDF members and by government supporters.

'Relay Voting'

A voter was given an envelope with ballots for the government alliance before entering the station. He then received an empty envelope in the station and proceeds to the ballot booth. He would then return into the station and deposit the pre-filled envelope in the ballot box, and return the empty envelope to those who had organize the bogus scheme in exchange for money.

The Bishops Spoke Out

The Bishops spoke out for the nullification of the 1989 election—they said veiled or expressed threats, then restrictions on assembly and free expression, the assaults and thefts of ballot boxes and tally sheets, the mobs of military and para-military personnel attacking property and people were some of the flagrant acts with which they have tried to resist the popular will.

What moral justification, they asked, could there be to disperse with beatings and bullets men and women who commit no other crime than that of demanding peacefully their rights? What moral justification could there be to terrify the population with hordes fed with hate and a false nationalism that does not recognize nor respect the individual and rights of other Panamanians.

The US President's Comments on the Panama Election 1989

'All nations in the democratic community have a responsibility to make it clear through our actions and our words that efforts to overturn constitutional regimes or steal elections are unacceptable.'

Restrictions on National Election Observers

The 1993 electoral law of Mexico allowed national observers to be accredited as individual and not as organisations. The election observer must not have been a member of a political party in the three years prior to the elections. The law did not guarantee that national observers would have access to the voter registration list prior to the election. Subsequent reform of the electoral law in 1994 removed most of the restrictions of the earlier restrictions.

Removable Indelible Ink

During the voting process of the 1990 Nicaragua elections, it was discovered that the indelible ink used to indicate that persons who had voted was readily removable with the use of chlorox. Tests confirmed the allegation. That discovery strengthened the fear of multiple voting. The party campaign managers were informed and they and observers reached an understanding that if no widespread cases of multiple voting were discovered during the counting of the votes, the parties would respect the results of the poll.

Observers and Quick Counts

In the Nicaragua elections of 1990, the international observers of the Organization of American States (OAS) and the United Nations (UN) carried out independent comprehensive tabulations and 'quick counts' or projections of the presidential elections. The quick counts were based on samples of 8-10 percent of the vote. Observers from the OAS mission were assigned polling sites at which they were to observe the entire count and collect their designated copy of the tally sheet along with a copy for UN. The UN assigned its observers to specific polling sites to observe the presidential count, record the figures on a specific form, and then do the same at a second site. In that way, the UN was able to obtain more rapid results for their quick counts. The methodology of the two organizations complemented each other and provided for a comprehensive monitoring and verification of the entire process. The projections produced by the quick count proved to be accurate as measured against the subsequent results reported by the election management body.

An Aborted Election

The Haitian elections set for November 29 1987 were cancelled due to violence. A non-military Provisional Electoral Council (CEP) was established in May 1987. It was composed of nine members drawn from different sectors of Haitian society. The Council of National Government (CNG) was frequently at odds with the CEP. The election environment soon became charged with violence, triggered in part by the perception that the CNG was condoning violence. On November 3 the CEP's offices were burnt down, after the CEP had rejected the candidacies of many individuals who were believed to be sympathisers of Duvalier. On the morning of Election Day, November 29, shooting broke out and 34 people were killed in and around Port-au-Prince. In an attempt to avoid further violence, after three hours voting, the CEP cancelled the polls.

Contribution to Elections—Haitian Style

The contribution to the Haitian 1990 elections was a multinational affair. Assistance was coordinated in part by the UN General Assembly. The US came forward with 2 million dollars, Canada contributed election materials, Germany picked up printing costs, France supplied the ballot papers and assisted with civic education, and Venezuela took care of the fuel. Important contributions came from Italy and Taiwan.

Election Violence—The Haitian Way

During the lead up to the 1990 elections, violence, not unlike that which caused the 1987 elections to be aborted, returned and many people were killed. Perhaps one of the more violent incidents occurred in Pétionville, a wealthy suburban north of Port-au-Prince. Just as presidential candidate Aristide was finished addressing a rally, the electric lights were cut and two men jumped out of a jeep, one hurled a grenade at a group of pedestrians and the other opened fire with a machine gun. Seven people were killed and 50 badly hurt.

Another Example of 'Quick Count'

The Organization of American States (OAS) and the United Nations (UN) agreed to carry out limited parallel vote tabulation (quick count) for the 1990 Haitian elections. The UN and OAS quick count relied on presidential results from a random sample of approximately 130 polling stations. The quick count was designed with two goals in mind-to determine if any presidential candidate had obtained over 50 percent of the votes, the total necessary to avoid a run-off, and if no candidate got a majority, to determine which two candidates had the largest number of votes. The mechanism worked to satisfaction and results began to flow in from observers in the field as soon as the counting of the presidential ballots by the Departmental Election Office (BED) was completed. Although the quick count sample was small, it took longer than planned, but projected nearly 70% of the votes cast for candidate Aristide. The final results which were released on 24 December 1990 (8 days after Election Day) showed Aristide winning 67.5% of the votes.

An Archbishop Outburst

During a homily on January 1 1991, a pro-Duvalier cleric, Archbishop Wolff Ligondé labelled President-elect Aristide a 'socio-Bolshevik' whose intent was to build a dictatorship. The Archbishop's utterance triggered an avalanche of violence against the prelate; his residence was burnt down by Aristide's supporters. They destroyed the Vatican nuncio's residence, the

Catholic Bishops' Conference headquarters and a 387-year-old cathedral. Archbishop Ligondé, the nuncio and their church officials went into hiding. The rampage by roving mobs continued against the supporters of Duvalier regimé for a week.

A Post-Election Coup

Fast on the heels of the unrest triggered by the Archbishop's verbal attack on Aristide, a rejected prospective candidate who had served the Duvalier regime, on January 6 1991, with the assistance of armed supporters, abducted the Acting President, Ms Trouillot at her private residence and took her to the National Palace. There she was forced to broadcast her resignation. On the 7 of January 1991, Lafontant who carried out the abduction announced that he had assumed provisional presidency of Haiti. The coup failed and Lafontant was arrested. Meanwhile, supporters of president-elect Aristide set about destroying Lafontant's party headquarters and offices, and also the personal property of other political party leaders throughout the country. Fifty people were killed in aftermath of the attempted coup.

Election Day Drawbacks

At 1990 elections in the Dominican Republic, the quality of the electoral materials was of inferior quality. The ink used to stamp the election forms was unusable in some cases or too pale to read.[21] Some electoral officials did not turn up at their designated mesa. Some electoral officials were not familiar with the electoral law. It was not clear to some electoral officers operating the mesas whether or not persons who received their registration cards after January 16 the last day of registration for the 1990 elections should be allowed to vote. There was no common interpretation of the rule of relating to persons waiting in lines to vote at the close of the poll

---

[21] There were 6, 663 mesas, or voting precincts, for 3, 275, 570 voters, an average of 492 voters per mesa.

at 6 p.m. on Election Day. Some officers interpreted the rule to mean that people should be in the mesa at 6 p.m. in order to vote.

'Colossal Fraud' or Clerical Error

The losing principal opposition candidate (Juan Bosch) described the unfolding results of the 1990 election in the Dominican Republic as a 'colossal fraud'. That the result was very close only served to heighten the political tension during the counting of the votes. The tally sheets (form 6) were not all returned to the headquarters of the Central Electoral Board (JCE) in a timely manner and so it was not possible to determine who had won the elections. Furthermore, form 6 was incorrectly distributed in the capital and as a result some of the forms carried numbers that did not correspond to the mesa where the voting took place. The election officials had to rewrite the mesa number on each form so affected. Again, in some cases the number on the JCE seal that stamped at the mesa did not match the number on form 6. The Electoral Board judged that as many as 80 percent of the forms might carry the wrong number.

Election Fraud—what is It? (22)

Two opposition parties which contested the 1990 Dominican Republic elections alleged that those elections were fraudulent. To support their allegation they cited the following:

- The late arrival of ballot papers which caused voting to be delayed;
- Tally sheets (form 6) did not arrive at some mesas and as a consequence blank sheets had to be substituted;
- Some tally sheets were not signed by the mesa officials and or party poll watchers;
- That the mistake in numbering of the tally sheets (form 6) created problems for the Electoral Board, as the computer processed the forms according to the mesa where the form was supposed to be used and not where they were actually used.

- In some cases there was more than one form 6 with different results for the same mesas;
- In some cases, the total number of votes recorded on the form was incorrect;
- Thousands of military personnel, who were prohibited from voting, voted; and
- The names of deceased persons appeared on the register of voters and facilitated multiple voting.

The Electoral Commission of Zambia 1991

The Electoral Commission of Zambia in 1991 consisted of three members, one of which was chairman, Mr Mathew Ngulube, Deputy Chief Justice. One member became attracted to the main opposition party and resigned from the Commission. He was never replaced.

Secrecy of the Ballot under Scrutiny

In the lead up to the1991 election in Zambia, stakeholders, particularly international observers, expressed concern about the secrecy of the ballot. The reason was that each ballot was numbered along with the stub, or counterfoil. When the ballot was issued to a voter, the polling official wrote the registration number of the voter on the counterfoil. Thus it was possible, at least in theory, to trace a given ballot to a particular voter even after the ballot was cast. The justification for the practice was that it facilitated detection of unofficial or improperly cast ballots. As the Electoral Commission stated, voters had no reason to fear the politicians or government officials would trace how ballots had been cast as only the High Court, in response to a formal petition challenging the validity of an election, could examine the ballots and ballot stubs.

Counting at District Centres versus Polling Sites

The venue for the counting of votes in the Zambian elections of 1991 was at the centre of a controversy. The Electoral Commission preferred to hold the count at the traditional district counting centres, but the stakeholders—opposition political parties, international and domestic observer groups, wanted the count to be carried out at the polling sites. They argued that it was a common practice in democratic countries and that it would trigger suspicions about ballot box tampering during transport to the counting centres. The Commission did not agree with the stakeholders' arguments, and advanced several reasons to support its case, namely:

- At the close of the poll at 6 p.m. is already dark and that would affect the counting process adversely as many sites had no electricity or suitable lighting;
- Counting at polling sites would require increased security to prevent possible disruption or manipulation of the count and to prevent any violence after the result was announced;
- Political parties might not have sufficient personnel to field agents at every polling station during the count;
- Training election officials to service 3,489 polling stations would pose problems;
- Counting at polling stations might enable candidates to determine which localities supported specific candidates.

De-linkage of Ruling Party and the State

Zambia in 1991 provided an example of a one-party system of government giving way to a multiparty democracy. The de-linking of the ruling political party from the government posed considerable difficulties. The United National Independence Party (UNIP), the ruling party, initiated the 'de-linking' of party and state institutions, and the Cabinet directives gave UNIP employees and officials notice to vacate government houses, demanded the return of all government property on loan to the UNIP—from vehicles to stationery—and ordered the resignation of government employees who desired to work for the party. The de-coupling of the party and government proved to be only of partial success, for the government was alleged to have allocated funds to the UNIP from the national budget while the other political parties did not receive any allocation. Also, at the local level, the ruling party and the state organs were merged—by the Local Administration Act 1980.

State of Emergency

At the time of the 1991 elections in Zambia, there was a state of emergency in place which required a police permit to hold a rally or any meeting with more than 5 persons. The stakeholders in the pending elections wanted the state of emergency to be lifted before the beginning of the election campaign on the ground that the state of emergency was incompatible with a free campaign. It was alleged that that the police often denied rally permit to the opposition, while they seldom required such permits of the ruling party. At one point President Kaunda agreed to lift the state of emergency and authorized former President Carter to announce that the state of emergency would be lifted by September 30 if peaceful conditions continued to prevail. However, the Attorney General of Zambia advised the President that he had no legal authority to lift the state of emergency without the concurrence of the National Assembly, which had been dissolved several weeks earlier. The President claimed that he was unaware of his lack of competence to lift the state of emergency and undertook not to implement restrictive measures under the state of emergency.

Objection to Parallel Vote Tabulation

Observers connected to the Carter Center set up a Z-Vote project, which was aimed at undertaking parallel vote tabulation (PVT) exercise on polling day during the 1991 elections. The leaders of the ruling party strongly objected to the proposal on the grounds that there was no good cause for the PVT exercise, as the election results would be out within 48 hours. Furthermore, the party officials felt that the PVT could cause unnecessary disorder, especially when the projections erroneously pick a losing candidate or party as winner. Television broadcasts called the PVT proposal a 'foreign scheme' to undermine Zambian sovereignty, and fears were expressed that the exercise would leave the country on a precipice for social order. Notwithstanding the apprehension of the senior members of the ruling party, UNIP, the leader, President Kaunda, appeared to sanction the PVT in his election-eve broadcast when he urged Zambians to continue to assist the observer groups in every way possible to enable them to carry out their tasks.

Inconclusive Parallel Vote Tabulation

The Z-Vote team organized their independent vote count (or parallel vote tabulation (PVT)). They recruited a network of Zambian to assist with the PVT. The methodology involved the use of polling sites representing ten percent of eligible voters within each of the nine provinces of the country. The PVT, as designed, allowed the observers to verify the officially announced results and to check the integrity of the ballot box conveyance to the counting centres. The PVT in Zambia was not designated to provide a 'quick count' to be announced to the public. The PVT relied on ballot boxes which had to be brought from a given constituency to the counting centre before the tally could begin, thus its findings could not be announced on election night. When twelve percent of the PVT sample was received at its headquarters, it showed that victory was going the Movement for Multiparty Democracy (MMD) way. The official counting process was too slow to facilitate the PVT effectively, but two days after the Election Day the available PVT results showed the MMD's presidential candidate was winning with 74 percent of the votes. Perhaps the landslide results, followed by early concession of victory by the ruling party, put the importance and indeed effectiveness of the PVT in Zambia in 1991 in some doubt.

Unstamped Ballots-Zambia

Many hundreds of ballots from across the country were not stamped with the official as required by the election regulations and thus could not be counted as valid ballots. In one case, the entire contents of ballot boxes from the station were as null and void because the ballot papers were not stamped. In another case a batch of 190 ballots were not stamped and had to be treated as invalid. At yet another station 250 out of 320 ballots were not stamped and met a similar fate.

Multiple Voters' Register

The voters' register used for the November 1992 presidential elections in Ghana was dated, and indeed was originally prepared for the 1987 district assembly elections and partially updated in1991. In the presidential elections, there were also voters' lists which were used for the April 1992 referendum and modified for the presidential elections. Not unexpectedly confusion set in at some polling stations where prospective voters could not identify the names and addresses used in 1987. Others, who had changed addresses and could not identify the address on the then current register, were not allowed to vote.

Hi-jacking an Election Framework

During the Forbes Burnham's years in power in Guyana, the Elections Commission was stripped of its ability to deliver free and fair elections by the transfer of its powers to prepare the voters' register to the Commissioner of National Registration who was under the authority of the Ministry of Home Affairs. By and large, that Ministry gained control over the production of the voters' register and appointments of electoral officials.

A Divided Elections Commission

In 1991, the Guyana Elections Commission erroneously published a flawed Preliminary List of voters. The Chairman of the Commission felt that, with the help of the political parties and the public, the list could be purged of its flaws during the 28-day period for claims and Objections. Two of the opposition members of the Commission promptly went public in disassociating themselves from the Chairman on that issue.

Siege of Elections Commission Headquarters

During the October 5th 1992 elections in Guyana, the Elections Commission headquarters in Georgetown were seized by a violent crowd claiming to be disenfranchised. There was protracted stone throwing at the building and attempts to storm it. The election officials evacuated the building. The violence spread to other parts of Georgetown, resulting in two deaths and extensive damage. In order to defuse the tense situation, the Chairman of the Commission allowed the crowd to vote, although those votes were not counted. As it turned out only 21 percent of those persons who voted were registered voters. The assault on the Commission premises halted after almost nine hours only upon the intervention of the police.

An Unworthy Election to Observe

In 1993, The Carter Center and the National Democratic Institute (NDI) walked away from observing the August 25 presidential elections in Togo. They cited as the reasons for not observing the elections the lack of significant opposition participation and the state of un-preparedness of the electoral machinery. Among the factors that undermined the electoral preparatory process were:

- All major opposition candidates halted their participation in the election process, because of concern over the accuracy of the voters' register and the poor distribution of electoral cards;
- The President of the National Electoral Commission (NEC) had expressed doubts about the readiness of the electoral machinery and requested a postponement of the election. The Government did not agree with the recommendation;
- The voters' register appeared to contain significantly more names than the demographic indicators suggested;
- There was inadequate voter education about the use of electoral cards;
- The indelible ink to be used to stain persons who voted was not reliable; and
- There was widespread abuse of incumbency regarding the use of public resources and the partisan behaviour of some election officials.

Interference with an Independent Quick Count

During the national elections in Paraguay, May 9th 1993, SAKA, a consortium of non-governmental organizations carried out an independent quick count. While the quick count was on the way, the authorities attempted to disrupt the exercise by causing the telephone company, which was facilitating the process, to block many of its lines, thus slowing down the tabulation process.

Irregularities Not Significant Enough

The Paraguayan elections of 1993 threw up considerable irregularities, which included the following:

- Fraud and sabotage marred the voting in some areas;
- Military interference was lurking in the background while the electoral process was on the way;
- There was the authority-inspired disruption to the non-governmental group, SAKA's, quick count exercise; and
- Volunteers trained to observe the vote counts were excluded from some voting tables.

Notwithstanding, the foregoing irregularities, international observers felt that such irregularities did not rise to the level of seriousness that would invalidate the election results.

Closing out Voters

The losing Liberal Party candidate, Mr. Laino, complained that he lost the election of 1993, because the soldiers closed land bridges to prevent Paraguayans from coming home from Brazil and Argentina to vote.

'Dirty Democracy'

Writing in its editorial, the New York Times of Friday 14 May 1993 styled the Paraguayan election as a 'dirty democracy'. It said that enough chicanery took place to mar Paraguay's first-ever democratic presidential election. The editorial pointed out days before the election a key army commander swore that the military would maintain the long-ruling Colorado Party in power whatever the voters decided. It also stated that earlier the Colorado Party's president had promised to win the election by 'assault' and 'special tricks'.

Conditions for Free and Fair Elections—Mexico 1994

In a determined effort to upgrade the conditions in Mexico for the delivery of free and fair elections, the authorities and election stakeholders set about identifying the issues to be tackled. First among such issues were the voters' lists. That task was undertaken by the Federal Electoral Registry (RFE), which carried out an expensive exercise aimed at purifying the voters' lists. The resultant product was considered satisfactory, only two small avenues left to accommodate fraud—namely, the inclusion of non-existent persons in the list, and the omission of qualified persons from the list. The new approach in the compilation of a credible voters' register was accompanied by improvements in the voting and counting procedures, and the use of more satisfactory ballot boxes, polling booths and ballot papers. The regulation of domestic observers was brought in line with international practice, and foreign (international) observers were allowed to observe elections. Moreover, important new steps were introduced to create a level playing field between political parties and candidates contesting elections. Nevertheless, the ruling party, the Institutional Revolutionary Party (PRI) was so strong and its influence so widely felt that the perception lingered that the media was biased in their coverage in favour of the ruling party, and the independence of the Federal Electoral Institute of the ruling party doubted.

An Unusual, though not Unique, Practice

In Panama, after the ballots are counted, the results are written up on an acta (tally sheet), which is signed by the election officials and by poll watchers who wish to do so. After the actas are completed and transmitted, both the marked and unused ballot papers are burnt at each polling station. The purpose of the burning is to prevent the stuffing of ballot boxes, or stealing or swapping of ballot boxes during transportation to the central counting centres.

Curious Election Irregularities

Observers and other stakeholders noticed a curious development during the May 16th 1994 elections in the Dominican Republic. They observed that many prospective voters with valid identification cards were being turned away from polling stations because the official voters' lists did not contain their names. The names of these voters had appeared on the voters' lists that the Central Electoral Board (JCE) had previously issued to political parties. A disproportionate number of the disfranchised voters identified themselves as supporters of the opposition parties. The JCE responded to the situation by extending the voting hours from 6.00 p.m. to 9.00 p.m. and allowed persons whose valid identification cards but whose names were not on the official voters' lists to cast tendered ballots. The extension was not announced on the television and radio until 10 minutes after the closing time of the polls when some stations had already started the counting of the votes and could not respond positively to the JCE's announcement. Notwithstanding that, some 17,000 tendered ballots were cast after 6.00 p. m. by the disenfranchised voters. Some election observers felt that the pattern of disenfranchisement suggested that there was the possibility of a deliberate attempt to tamper with the electoral process. The irregularities resulted in an agreement or 'Pact for Democracy', which stipulated that new elections would be held within two years.

Upgrading an Electoral Framework

Consequent on the widespread election irregularities in the 1994 presidential elections in the Dominican Republic, a Pact for Democracy was entered into by the main political parties calling for electoral reform. The resultant reforms required steps to be taken to:

- Reconstitute the Central Electoral Board (JCE) to enable all board members to be approved by each of the major political parties;
- Enable an improved and reliable computerised system to be put in place which would offer a more accurate voters' list;
- Improve transparency enabling access at all stages of the electoral process to stakeholders and observers, domestic and foreign;

- Allow voters' lists used by officials to be posted publicly well in advance of polling day and remain for a reasonable time; and
- Use a new close college voting system instituted to protect against multiple voting.

Voting Procedure- 'Close College System'

The 'close college voting system' was introduced to the Dominican Republic for the 1996 presidential elections to guard against multiple voting. Under this voting procedure voters were required to turn out during a stipulated period (for this election, women were to come out in the morning and men in the afternoon), sign in, and remain in line at the voting table (station) during the entire sign-in period. The voting process was closed to any voter who was not in line within the prescribed timeframe. Since voters were kept at the station in this manner, there was little opportunity for anyone to indulge in multiple voting, a practice which was well known in earlier elections in the Dominican Republic. As soon as the sign-in period ended, voting commenced in the order in which the voters signed in.[22]

Restrictions on Media Reporting During Elections

In the Dominican Republic, there were extensive restrictions on media reporting during the period of 24 hours before and after an election under the election law. However, for the 1996 presidential elections, there was a lessening of those restrictions, as the Central Electoral Board (JCE) allowed

---

[22] A similar voting procedure (accreditation of voters) has been used in Nigeria where voters turn out to have their particulars checked during an accreditation period on Election Day and once accredited, the voter remains in a queue until he/she votes in the order in which the accreditation took place. However, the procedure does not serve democracy well as intended, because in part due to the ceaseless sun and heat many voters leave the queue before voting and do not return.

privately owned television and radio channels to broadcast their regular programming as long as they did not discuss the electoral process. They were allowed to broadcast the news on the election only when transmitted by the JCE.

Nullification of Vote Through Lack of Official Signature

In the first round of the presidential vote in the 1996 Dominican Republic elections, there were 46,281 (1.54 percent) null votes mainly because the table (polling station) president did not sign the ballot paper. The voting procedure required the table president to sign the ballot only after the voter marked and folded the ballot papers. It was generally believed that many voters forgot to take the ballot to the table for the president of the table to sign it before depositing it in the ballot box. However, some stakeholders charged that partisan table presidents deliberately omitted to sign when they know the preference of the voter was different from theirs. In response to the allegation of partisanship the JCE allowed the ballot paper to be signed by the table president either before or after the voter voted.

The 'Deceased-Living' Voters

In the 1996 Dominican Republic presidential elections, the official registry erroneously excluded some eligible voters who were listed as deceased. When the deceased-living voters turned to vote during the first round of the voting, they were barred from voting. In the run up to the second round (run-off) election, the status of the deceased-living persons again surfaced. One political party wrote to the Central Electoral Board (JCE) contending that the deceased-living persons should not be allowed to vote-not even by tendered ballot. The JCE ruled in favour of the complaining party that those persons listed as deceased on the voters' registry would not be able to vote in the run-off election.

Partisan Entities

In the lead up to the Palestinian elections of 1996, there was not enough time to reach a consensus on a political party law and so provisions were included in the electoral law for partisan entities to register with the Palestinian Authority Ministry of Interior. In order to register as a partisan entity, pursuant to Article 49 of the Palestinian Election Law, an organization had to submit its name, symbol, motto, director's name, leadership structure, a summary of its political and social programme, and a signed document stating that it did not advocate violence. Partisan entities were required to make financial disclosures and were forbidden from receiving financial contributions from abroad.

Election Campaign under Occupation

During the election campaign in the first national Palestinian elections of 1996, candidates campaigning in Jerusalem did not know which sites had been designated for displaying campaign posters or holding rallies. On many occasions Israeli police interrupted rallies and inform the organisers and supporters that the venue was not on the approved list of campaign sites. There were frequent confrontations between Israeli soldiers and Palestinians, during the campaign period, at checkpoints around Jerusalem, due to cars carrying campaign stickers, which the soldiers contended were not allowed.

Illiterate Voters

Although Palestine enjoyed a relatively high literacy rate, the procedure for dealing with illiterate voters was not clearly worked out and as a consequence the secrecy of the vote was compromised at some stations. It was not clear whether or not polling station commission members could assist illiterate voters. Illiterate voters were allowed to bring someone they trusted to help them vote, however, many of them did not do so. The upshot was that such illiterate voters merely asked anyone who was available at the station to assist them. It mattered not whether those persons were election security personnel or candidates' agents. It transpired that polling station commission members were not prepared to properly monitor the assistance given to illiterate voters, particularly where there was a habit of large families entering the polling stations and remaining inside until all family members had voted. There were reported cases of faked illiteracy in order for the voter to satisfy the family, tribe or community members that they voted for a particular candidate.

Voting without Registration Cards

During the Palestine election of 1996, the Central Election Commission (CEC) issued instructions to polling station commission members to allow voters to cast ballots when they could present voter registration cards bearing the number of the polling station, even if their names did not appear on the voter registry list. In such cases, the polling station commission members would add their names and identification numbers to the registration list and give the voter a ballot paper. That announcement solved the problem of allowing voters who had registered but whose names were not on the final list. But this ruling opened up the possibility of multiple voting, as the registration cards were not carefully controlled during the registration process and extra cards could have been filled out unlawfully. Indeed, multiple voting was detected in the districts of Khan Younis (54) where 779 voters were registered, but 1053 voted; and Khan Younis (63) where 560 voters were registered but 890 voted. However, the number of people registered and the number of people voted equalled the number of names added to the voter registration lists.

Comedy of Sleepiness and Errors

The morning after election night during the Palestinian election 1996, several district election officers (DEOs) offices were in a state of disarray. There were bags of ballot papers, empty ballot boxes, voters' lists and other documents strewn over the floor. The DEOs, many of whom were short of two nights sleep, searched through the scattered materials for their forms to compile the provisional results. The pattern was the same from Jerusalem to Hebron, here the mayor, at one stage, announced that 50 ballot boxes were missing to a crowd of candidates, journalists and voters, only to later find that relevant forms with the results were in the storeroom of the municipality. (The polling station commission officials had given instructions that ballot boxes, once emptied of the ballots should be left behind to be collected later. But when the empty ballot boxes were seen abandoned, as it were, stakeholders became suspicious and the belief that manipulation of the election results was taking place, and even more so, when coupled with the news from the mayor that 50 ballot boxes were missing.)

The Imprudence of Releasing Partial Election Results

In the Palestinian election of 1996, for inexplicable reasons the Central Election Commission released partial election results before all the stations had reported all their results. Some of the partial results represented only a small percentage of the votes. When the provisional results were published the following day there was considerable difference in the list of winners from that published in the partial results. The changes in the list winners triggered rumours that the changes were ordered by the Fateh leadership.

Disqualification of the Relatives of a Sitting President

Under the Nicaraguan constitutional reform of 1995, no relative of the sitting president could run for president in the subsequent term. Under that stipulation, for example, Antonio Lacayo, son-in-law of President Chamorro, was disqualified for contesting the 1996 presidential elections.

Election Results by 'Telegram'

In the Nicaraguan elections of 1996, ballots were counted at the voting sites, where tally sheets were completed and copies filled out for each poll worker. The tally sheet information was then summarised on a form called a 'telegram'-so called because of historic reasons; and the election officials took the telegram to the nearest office of the telephone company where the results were dictated over the telephone to the National Counting

Center in Managua. The information so received was used to make up the preliminary count total of the votes.

Village Elections in China

Incremental and Experimental Elections

In 1997, The Carter Center sent a delegation to China to observe village elections in Fujian and Hebei. Village elections were administered by an Election Leadership Committee selected by the Village Committees and Representative Assemblies. In general, villages ranged in size from 1000 to 2500 people. The delegation formed the view that China's approach to elections was incremental and experimental, and that officials were constantly seeking ways to improve the process. It felt that in a decade the village election programme had made real progress.

Essentials of Electoral Legislative Framework

In 1987, China's legislature, the Standing Committee of the National People's Congress (NPC), adopted the Organic Law on the Village Committee of the People's Republic of China (provisional). Article 9 of the law provides: "The village committee chair, vice-chair(s) and members shall be elected directly by the villagers. The village committee shall have a term of three years and its members may be re-elected for consecutive terms." Since then, experiments on directly electing village committees began in the rural areas across the country and were gradually extended to cover all village committees. In order to further standardize village committee elections, the NPC amended the provisional law in 1988 and formally promulgated the Organic Law on the Village Committee. The new law contains detailed provisions on the procedures and operating steps for village committee elections, such as voter eligibility, election organizing institutions, voter registration, secret balloting, confirmation of election results, and removal of village committee members. As a result, a system structure for village committee elections was largely in place, and village committee elections in China's rural areas began entering a new stage of holding standard elections for new terms.

'Villager' versus 'Native Villager'

"Villager" is a legal concept, which refers to a peasant who has Chinese nationality and has lived and worked in a specific rural area for a long time. "Native villager" refers to the natural person who lives in a specific village, has a household registration in the village and has a land ownership relation with the village. Determining whether a person is a native villager depends on two conditions: residence and land ownership. Only a native villager can participate in the village's village committee elections.[23]

Nature of Villagers' Right to Vote

The enjoyment of the villagers' right to vote refers to the legal confirmation and obtaining of the villagers' right to vote. The Organic Law on the Village Committee defines the subject and scope for the enjoyment of the villagers' right to vote and also specifies the conditions and qualifications for exercising the right to vote. In this sense, the enjoyment and exercise of the villagers' right to vote is limited and requires legal definition and protection. The restriction on the villagers' right to vote is mainly designed to ensure the orderliness of the electoral system and to restrain or restrict the enjoyment and exercise of the voting right of special legal subjects according to law. The deprivation of the villagers' right to vote refers to the fact that those who have been deprived of their political rights according to law cannot enjoy the right to vote or the right to be elected under the Constitution.

Encroachments upon Villager's Right to Vote

Failure to elect village committees according to law:

---

23 For the legislative definition of a villager by various regions, please see: Wang Yu: A Study on Legal Issues on Villager Election, Peking University Press, 2002, pp. 2-4.

- The township organizations designate members to village committees.
- The village Party organizations directly or indirectly select members to village committees.
- The former village committees designate members or appoint their own members to village committees.
- A few villagers organize selection of members for village committees without the approval of the villagers' conferences.
- Too few people are involved in selecting members for village committees.
- Reduced the members of village electoral committees without the approval of villagers.

Failure to conduct voter registration according to law:

- Wrong registration done deliberately.
- Incomplete registration done deliberately.
- Repeated registration done deliberately.
- Refuse to register, include those who have switched from agricultural to non-agricultural occupations and those who are peasants but married to non-agricultural workers.

Failure to nominate and select candidates according to law:

- The township authorities designate candidates.
- The village organizations fail to nominate and select candidates according to law.
- Disregard the wish of those nominated and fail to select candidates according to the number of votes.
- Restrict villagers' right to nominate candidates in various ways.

Open confrontation

Open confrontation is a form of villager participation in village committee elections and village affairs. The aim is to seek relief to the encroached voting right. In recent years, it has been quite frequent that the villagers have shifted from political indifference and seeking support to open confrontation in village committee elections and post-election management of village affairs. The main forms of open confrontation include staging open boycott against elections, disturbing the electoral order, organizing elections and recalls, and blocking government institutions.

Lack of constitutional review mechanisms

As China has no review mechanisms for constitutional violations, the villagers find themselves helpless in dealing with the abstract encroachments arising from regulatory documents in their practice of elections

Lack of Motivation

The self-government institutions lack the motivation to offer relief. One is that there are no explicit legal provisions on what electoral disputes can be solved by the village electoral committees. The other is that the self-governing units lack the ability to execute the rules on the protection of the voting right and their authority is still doubtful to villagers.

Basic principles Aimed at Avoiding Encroachment on Villagers' Rights24

The relief for the villagers' right to democratic elections would be enhanced by the following principles that:

- Rights and obligations are inseparable. The villagers' right to vote in village elections must be protected from encroachment by clear procedures.

---

[24] The author of this work participated in an international seminar in China in November 2004 as an expert on the international good practices in resolving election disputes with reference to the Chinese village elections programme.

- Relief is offered in a timely manner according to law. That means that the encroachments upon the democratic rights of villagers should be handled in a timely manner, on the spot and according to law. The institutions and individuals who have been found to have truly violated laws and disciplines as complained should be dealt with promptly.
- Internal relief comes first. The subject of internal relief is the village committee or the village electoral committee, whose relief only covers some minor cases within the self-government unit, such as voter eligibility and minor encroachment upon the voting by villagers. Internal relief is more operable, simple, efficient and cost-effective.

External relief, such as relief by Party and government and power relief, comes second. Of all forms of external relief, relief by Party and government should be a preference, followed by the relief by power organs and then by social relief.

- The principle that judicial relief is the final resort. Judicial relief is the last shield for other forms of relief and only preferred when all other forms of relief do not work or go wrong.

Insufficient Education about Village Committee Elections

To the Chinese peasants who still have no democratic tradition and democratic training, village committee election still represents a new thing. Many villagers do not know what statutory rights they have or how village committee elections should be held. This state of affairs makes it easy for the administrative powers to encroach upon the villagers' right to vote. Therefore, it is imperative to intensify publicity so that the electoral workers can grasp the specific basic knowledge about elections, know the procedures and rules for elections, respect the villagers' substantial and procedural rights to vote, and truly act according to laws and procedures.

What Goes on in Village Elections Machinery?

In March 1998, the Carter Center sent a delegation to observe nine village elections in Jilin and Liaoning provinces. Among the interesting practices they observed were:

- The use of 'roving ballot boxes' which were intended to only accommodate elderly and infirm voters. However, in some villages, the roving ballot box was used for the convenience of most of the electorate. Villages with industry and fishing use the roving ballot box to enable their villagers to vote early in the morning before going to work. In a few cases up to 90 percent of the votes were cast at roving ballot boxes which visited the homes of voters. Although the roving ballot boxes were sealed with a lock that was opened in public view when the box was brought to the main voting station, it was not possible to determine the integrity of the voting procedure used with voting ballot boxes.
- The counting procedure sometimes lacked transparency; for although the ballots were counted in the full view of the assembled voters at the main station, it was not easy to workout what was happening with the counting of the votes. The procedure involved the election officers gathering the ballot papers into batches and then each batch was counted by a group of the election officers.
- Invalid ballots often amounted to between 10 and 15 percent, a bit on the high side. That was probably due to insufficient voter education programmes, or confusion over the method of voting, which requires an "O" to be placed beneath the name of the preferred candidate and "X" beneath the name of the candidate who was being rejected. Some voters placed "O" beneath the names of all candidates.

Indirect Election—Township People's Congress Deputies

Proxy Voting

Proxy voting procedure has always attracted problems, and that was the case with proxy voting at township elections in China. In its report on election observation of two township elections in China, the Carter Center noted certain shortcomings with proxy voting—notably:

- Absence of written authorization from the absent voters, as required by law;
- Some voters dealt with more than the three proxy ballots allowed by the law;
- The possibility of a family or clan member insisting on voting for other family or clan members; or not voting as instructed.

Jamaican General Elections 1997—'Garrison Communities'25

'Garrison communities' were perhaps unique to Jamaica. They originated in government housing schemes where houses were allocated along partisan lines, resulting in entire neighbourhoods owing political obedience to one or other of the two main political parties, the People's National Party (PNP) or the Jamaica Labour Party (JLP). Both the PNP and the JLP sustained garrison communities where the respective party's supporters often used violence to maintain dominance in the community. In each case, election results overwhelmingly came out in favour of the dominant party, due largely to fraud or intimidation. Some garrison communities became large and so influential as to determine the result in a particular constituency.

Late Production of ID Cards

During the lead up to the 1997 Jamaican general election, voter identification cards fell behind in production so badly that the political parties became concerned that voters would not be able to adequately identify themselves at the polling stations. With the election date set for 18 December 1997, by 1st December only 50,000 of the 1.5 million ID cards were produced for distribution. There was widespread belief among the electorate that without ID cards there would large scale election fraud. This feeling was confirmed by a poll which showed two-thirds of the Jamaican electorate feared fraud on Election Day, if ID cards were not distributed. In desperation, the electoral authorities engaged the British firm of De La Rue to help with the production of ID cards. (The primary contract to produce the ID cards was awarded to Cleveland based firm of TRW). Although De La Rue speeded up the production of the ID

---

25 The author was Director of Elections in Jamaica during the 1980 elections, when there were 6 major and 7 minor pockets of garrison-like communities spread across some 8 constituencies in the Corporate Area of Kingston and St. Andrew, and St. Catherine.

cards so that 9 December 200,000 cards were produced; nevertheless, by Election Day only 322,000 had been produced, well short of the required 1.5 million needed.

Consequences of Ballot Papers Security Breach

The main opposition party reported, just over a week before the Jamaican general election in 1997 that it had discovered 250 ballot papers inside a box with registration lists that the Electoral Office had delivered to the JLP headquarters. The ballot papers at the JLP headquarters were checked and found to be genuine. Thereupon, the parties and the Electoral Office agreed to re-certify the remaining ballot papers—1.5 million of them. The accounting firm of Coopers and Lybrand was employed to audit the remaining ballot papers. As a further consequence of the ballot papers security breach, the advance voting by the military and the police was delayed from the 12 to the 15 December 1997.

Special Elections-Liberia 1997

The Special Elections of Liberia was held in a period of relative lull in a civil war that had gone on for nearly 7 years. Given such an unstable atmosphere, it was not surprising to find frequent violent incidents during the election campaign period which began on June 16th.1997. Candidates for the election often complained that the playing field was not level, as the National Patriotic Party (NPP) was better resourced than the others, and it controlled the only radio station that could reach all of Liberia. The complaint about the NPP's short-wave radio capacity earned the sympathy of the European Union and the USAID which promised to enhance the capacity of two local radio stations-assuring alternative FM and short-wave access through out the country—only materialized shortly before the election when two transmitters arrived in Liberia. It was virtually too late to influence the course of the campaign.

No Provision for Refugees to Vote in the July 19 Elections

There was no arrangement for refugees to vote in neighbouring countries. Thus an estimated 600,000 Liberian refugees were deprived of the franchise. The majority of these people were believed to be from Lofa and Nimba counties. It was also reported that large numbers of refugees crossed over the Guinea border to register, but because the demand for registration was not anticipated, it could not be met.

Statement of Hope That Faded Fast

After the Special Election of July 19 1997, which Charles Taylor of the NPP won with over 75 percent of the votes, the Carter Center put out a statement in which they concluded that: 'This election could provide a turning point for Liberia—between a bitter civil war and a hopeful future of prosperity and democracy. The positive future, however, will only come if all parties in Liberia demonstrate their commitment to the peaceful process of democracy-building, allay the fears that some have of others, and rejuvenate a feeling of nationhood and civic pride that will help their country advance. We hope that the spirit of Election Day will guide Liberians in the days ahead. Well, that hope, so eloquently expressed herein, soon turn to decay, as before too long a bloody civil war resumed!

Caciquismo 'Village Strongman'

Despite extensive electoral reform in the 1990s, the phenomenon of the local strongman continued to impact adversely on elections in rural areas of states in Mexico. The caciques or local strongmen influenced elections through illicit means, particularly voting buying, which along with the use of state funds to influence voters continued to be a problem in Mexican elections. Coacción or use of state funds to influence voters may be described broadly as predicating the vote on the delivery of public programmes for a particular party or using public programmes to influence the vote of the electorate. Vote buying can be defined as offering money or goods in exchange for voting for a party or candidate.

Growing Electoral Professionalism and Competence

In transforming itself from a government agency into an independent electoral management body (EMB), the Federal Electoral Institute (IFE) had to devise ways to also transform its almost 8,000 employees into election professionals. At first the IFE, instead of purging the staff, set about minimising the discretion, which the employees possessed by refining the election regulations, improving the register of voters, and engaging outside election observation. The view had also been expressed that the establishment of clearer career track for IFE employers might be appropriate to cement their loyalties to the organization and undermine any ties they might have had to the state and local influences that might compromise their performance.

Nigerian Transitional Elections 1998-99 Local Elections December 5 1998[26]

The Local Elections marked the first of four rounds of transitional elections in Nigerian transformation from a military regime to multiparty democracy. The training of election officers was the key to successful organisation of these elections and so the Commonwealth organised a group of specialist trainers of trainers for two weeks just prior to the elections. However, Nigeria being such a large and diverse country, the training in such a short time, as was available before the elections was never going to turn out well-trained election officers and the insufficient training of some election officers showed up at the polling stations on polling day. Many polling stations opened late and with insufficient election materials. Some polling officers operated in such a manner as to reveal their inadequate training and their imperfect knowledge of the voting procedures. Some polling stations were without indelible ink which would have prevented multiple voting. The accreditation of voters should have taken place on the morning

---

[26] The author was advising the Independent National Electoral Commission on various aspects of the election organisation, as well as overseeing Commonwealth technical support to the INEC for the elections.

of polling, but before voting began; however, in many instances both the accreditation and polling took place simultaneously. There was evidence that the secrecy of the vote was compromised at some polling stations. The regulations governing the local elections were promulgated only days before poling.

State and Gubernatorial Elections January 9 1999

The second round of the transitional elections, that is, for states and governors was held in January 9 1999. The INEC had taken on board weakness observed during the first round at the local elections[27] and organised, somewhat hastily, crash training sessions (again with the help of the Commonwealth, which provided experienced trainers of trainers) with the aim of remedying the weakness identified during the local government elections. The crash training sessions produced some positive improvements, but there were still weaknesses which surfaced on polling day, such as late opening of polling stations, again shortages of vital election materials, breach of the secrecy of the ballot was still in evidence, and indelible ink was absent from some stations.

The Third Round-Federal Legislature (National Assembly) Elections February 20 1999.

No Informal Party Alliance

Shortly before the National Assembly elections, the INEC ruled out any informal political party alliances, as it felt that the electoral law did not allow it. The parties of Alliance for Democracy (AD) and the All People's Party (APP) wanted to form such an alliance but were not allowed to

---

27 The author participated in observation of the local government elections, along with some senior staff, on behalf of the Commission to identify weaknesses in the election organisation with a view to enable the Commission to take remedial action before the third and fourth rounds of polling.

do so. However the INEC held that the two political parties could field candidates on the same platform of one party.

Increased Irregularities

The third round of elections marked a slippage in general management of polling stations and in the election management generally. The inadequacies of the performance of many election officers were exposed to all stakeholders somewhat embarrassingly. There was ballot stuffing on a serious scale in some areas, intimidation witnessed in many constituencies, and bloated results reported in many areas. Considerable damage was done to the credibility of the electoral process during the third round of the elections.

Fourth Round-Presidential February 27 1999[28]

The fourth round witnessed a further deterioration in the quality of election services and organisation. There was open fraudulent conduct in the elections in many states. There was increased ballot stuffing, tampering with ballot papers, and partisanship of election officers who allowed fraudulent activities to take place during and after the polling. There was strong evidence of inflated election results in some constituencies where the turn out was estimated by some stakeholders to be as low as 12 percent, but the announced results suggested a turn out above 80 percent. A good many polling stations experienced general breakdown, due to lack of party agents from the less dominant parties in particular regions and the dominant party agents did as they wished with ballot tampering and ballot stuffing, notwithstanding the presence of election officials.

---

[28] The author observed the fourth round of the election as a member of the Support Team to the Commonwealth Observer Group.

Venezuela—Electoral Reform on a Grand Scale

The lead up to the 1998 legislative and presidential elections in Venezuela was characterised by extensive electoral reform. Venezuela was attempting to do what no other country had done then, that was to integrate an automated ballot counting system with a single national integrated network to transmit the voting results within minutes to a headquarters. The National Electoral Council (CNE) acquired some 7,000 voting machines to achieve its goal. Further, in order to achieve greater transparency and prevent election fraud, party poll workers who had previously managed polling centres were replaced by poll workers recruited from among registered voters by a kind of lottery system. Party agents were allowed to observe the voting process, but not to participate as poll workers, except if there was an absent recruited poll worker. The new approach to recruitment of poll workers put a stop to the Venezuelan election parlance of 'acta mata voto', which was translated as 'tally sheet trumps the ballot'. The phrase summed up the practice whereby party poll workers present at a polling station conspired to tamper with the tally sheets by redistributing the votes of those parties that did not have poll workers present.

The Limits of the Electoral Reforms 1998

The National Electoral Council (CNE) expressed the view a few days before the Venezuelan legislative elections in November 1998, that the new automated voting system would increase transparency, accuracy, and would speed up the delivery of election results. It acknowledged, however, that only 80 percent of the voters would use a fully automated voting system that included both the automatic tabulation of ballots and electronic transmission of results. Another 12 percent would have their votes tallied automatically, but the results would be hand carried to the respective regional electoral council (JER) due to lack of telephone lines. The remaining 8 percent would vote by the traditional method, and the results would be tallied by poll workers at their voting centres. Generally, the reformed system worked well and it enabled more than 70 percent of the results to be reported within a few hours after the polls closed. However, the unfamiliarity of the poll workers with the new system engendered delays in the voting. The number of spoilt ballot was on the high side, although it varied 5-8 percent at the gubernatorial elections, to 10-15 for the senators and deputies, to 16-22 percent in the state assembly elections.

Challenge to the New Automated Voting System

Subsequent to the November legislative elections in Venezuela, the La Causa R political party filed a national challenge to the election on the ground that it was impossible to adequately audit electronically tabulated and transmitted voting results. The Venezuelan electoral law required any voting process to be auditable for it to be valid. However the Supreme Court was unimpressed with the legal action and dismissed the challenge as being without merit.

Changing Candidates Prior to an Election Can Create Problems

The Comité de Organización Politica Electoral Independente (COPEI) and the Acción Democràtica, (Democratic Action Party) (AD) political parties withdrew their support for their own party nominees as candidates for the December presidential election in Venezuela in favour of one candidate Römer. This change created serious problems for the voting machines, as they were not programmed to associate candidate Römer with those two parties. When the substitution was made some of the ballot papers for the elections had already been delivered to the Electoral Council and so it was too late to change the ballot for the presidential elections. Further, the voting procedure enabled a voter to cast ballot for more than one party in the presidential elections if the parties concerned had the same candidate. The voting tabulation software in the voting machine was programmed with information on the alliances and the machine would read ballots with multiple selections for the same candidate as valid. However, the machines would read ballots as null if voters selected multiple parties that were not in an electoral alliance. Thus when AD and COPEI substituted Römer for their original candidates, the pattern of electoral alliances programmed into the tabulating software ceased to be valid. The confusion that came about by the actions of these two parties caused the CNE to change the rules on the day before the elections by announcing that each voter should select only one party on the presidential ballot.

Automation Voting Technology Worked

In the view of many election stakeholders in and observers of the Venezuelan presidential elections of December 1998 was that the automation voting process worked. They were impressed with the smoothness of the operation and the speed with which the CNE was able to announce the results of the elections. At 6.30 p.m. on Election Day the CNE announced the results—that candidate Hugo Chàvez Frias had been elected president with 57 percent of the vote. The turnout was 65 percent.

Mozambique Electoral Law Did Not Allow for PVT

In the lead up to the1999 national elections in Mozambique, the Carter Center sought permission to carryout parallel vote tabulation (PVT) exercise. The main purpose of PVT exercise is to verify the accuracy of the official results and thus to enhance confidence in the process and at the same time facilitating the acceptance of the election results by all sides. The issue was somewhat prematurely publicised and some of the newspaper articles appeared to obfuscate the issue and discredit the plans to hold a PVT. The National Elections Commission (CNE) of Mozambique informed the Carter Center during discussions that the Mozambican law did not provide for PVT and therefore it would be against the law for the CNE to permit it. The Carter Center dropped the plans to carryout the PVT during the 1999 elections.

Positive Indicators from Polls

The 1999 general elections of Mozambique threw up a number of positive indicators, namely:

- The polling was orderly, quiet, and efficient, with few problems;
- The election preparation and conduct generally was good;

- Polling officers were well trained and diligent in responding to voters' needs;
- High levels of women participation-both as polling officials and voters;
- High percentage of participation by party agents from all sides and they worked in harmony;
- The security was well administered and the presence of the police was not intrusive.

Some Negative Factors Encountered

Despite the overall favourable impression formed by stakeholders of the 1999 national elections in Mozambique, some significant negative factors did surface, such as, for example:

- Some voters were unable to find their names on the register;
- Some voter's card contained errors which prevented the holders thereof from voting;
- There was intimidation against the main opposition party in some districts;
- There were some improper campaigning at some polling stations;
- Evidence of insufficient voter education in some older persons who did not speak Portuguese did not understand how to vote;
- There were too few candles at some stations to last throughout the counting of the votes.

Unprocessed Tally Sheets

A large number of tally sheets from the provinces were sent to the National Electoral Commission (CNE) in Maputo for review by two CNE members, one from each party. Observers were allowed to observe the incoming tally sheets, but not permitted to inspect the unprocessed tally sheets. Although the lack of transparency was brought to the attention of the President of the Commission, no action was taken to remedy the situation. The opposition, Renamo, party claimed that most of the unprocessed tally sheets came from the areas that were stronghold provinces, particularly Zambezia, Sofala, and Nampula, and charged that the elections were being rigged by the CNE and the ruling Frelimo party. When the final results were announced, the ruling party's candidate Joaquim Chissano, was declared the winner by 52.29 percent of the votes, and the losing party, Renamo and its candidate, Dhlakama, 47.71 percent. The matter went to the Supreme Court where Renamo alleged that 938 tally sheets were not included in the count. The Supreme Court ruled against Renamo. It found that 550 tally sheets excluded represented 377, 773 potential valid votes—a number of votes significantly larger than the margin of victory by Chissano, the declared winner.

Independence or Integration? East Timor Election 1999 August 30.

The consultation process leading up to the vote was punctured by violence and intimidation. The volatile environment exploded into open violence when the results of the August 30 poll were announced on September 4th by the United Nations Mission to East Timor (UNAMET) had voted overwhelmingly for independence. The pro-integration militia immediately resorted to burning of property and looting on a large scale throughout the territory of East Timor. Expatriate election workers and observers had to be evacuated to Indonesia and Australia.

'Dawn Attacks'—Indonesian Legislative Elections June 7 1999.

There were widespread rumours that on polling day persons would menace prospective voters and offer money to them to vote for particular political parties. Those fears were expressed in respect of remote rural areas where there would be few election observers. The stories remained as mere rumours, as no evidence emerged on polling day to support the rumours

Irregular Election Practices

The Indonesian legislative elections of 1999 revealed some irregular practices, including the following:

- Late delivery of election materials, as well as shortages of materials;
- Insufficient training of election officials at polling stations;
- Breach of the procedure at the commencement of the polls in not keeping a proper check of the amount of ballot papers received;
- Omission to check the fingers of persons for traces of indelible ink before allowing them to vote
- Failure to use and mark the voters' lists; and
- Ballot papers were signed and piled up ahead of delivery to voters for voting.

Corrupted Ballots

During the legislative elections in Indonesia in 1999, the chairman of a polling station marked the name of the voters on the ballot paper given to them. When the irregularity was discovered by the provincial Election Oversight Committee (Panwas), it intervened. The entire team of officials at the polling station was replaced with volunteers from among voters, and the Panwas supervised the station throughout the process. The Panwas invalidated the corrupted ballots and extended the voting hours. The Panwas also afforded an opportunity for the voters, some 60 of them, affected to vote again.

Flawed Election Campaign

The stakeholders in 2000 Peruvian elections complained of serious deficits in the election campaign, in particular:

- The lack of access to the media by opposition parties candidates;
- Pro-government media bias;

- Smear campaigns in the tabloid press against opposition candidates and others critical of the Government;
- Incidents of intimidation of opposition candidates and their supporters by the national tax agency (SUNAT);
- Harassment and intimidation of opposition candidates by the security agencies;
- Misuse of state resources by the ruling party;
- Falsification of signatures to qualify one of the parties the Peru 2000 alliance;
- Immunity for the perpetrators of electoral violations; and
- The perception that the electoral authorities were not neutral.

The Dirty War Third Term Environment

When President Fujimori announced that he would submit his candidacy for a third term towards the end of 1999, the election environment was already cloudy, and many of the prospective candidate feared that the playing field would not be level. The supporters of candidate Fujimori were already accused of waging a dirty tricks war and harassment and intimidation against the supporters of leading opposition candidates. The election process attracted widespread complaint of harassment by opposition candidates and their supporters. There were violent counter demonstrations, mysterious blackouts at opposition rallies, organised assaults by 'common criminals', surveillance by intelligence agents. The authorities often failed to investigate those incidents and the absence of any prosecutions with respect to those responsible added to the electoral environment of fear. Further, there were persistent attacks in the media on those who spoke for the opposition and that served to impinge on the integrity of the electoral process and erode confidence therein. Also opposition media houses that investigated irregularities in the electoral process were subjected to judicial investigations or attacks in the media generally.

Examples of Misuse of State Resources—Peru 2000 Elections

The 2000 Peruvian presidential elections attracted widespread misuse of state resources, for example, the law preventing the under-mentioned activities was not enforced:

- Campaign during the inauguration or inspection of public works;
- Distribution of public resources or property to individuals or private entities;
- Several examples of the President's campaign linking to the inauguration of a public site to the re-election campaign;
- Threats against local leaders of poverty alleviation programmes to with hold food aid, if their community voted against the President.

A Bundle of Irregularities

Observers and other stakeholders reported widespread election irregularities during the conduct of the April 9 Peruvian presidential elections. Among the most glaring irregularities were:

- Improper election propaganda in and around polling stations;
- Irregularities in voting materials;
- Intimidation of political party agents by security officers;
- Unauthorized participation by government officials in the voting process;
- The results put out by the National Office of Electoral Processes (ONPE) showed a million more votes cast than voters who went to the polls

Despite the irregularities, the results announced on April 28 showed President Fujimori got 49.87 percent and Dr. Toledo 40.24 percent of the votes, and so a run-off election was set for May 28 2000.

An EMB under Scrutiny

Subsequent to the April 9 presidential elections in Peru, the National Office of Electoral Processes (ONPE) presented the election results to the Jurado Nacional de Elecciones (JNE) National Elections Board without first giving all the necessary information to the political parties so that they could present challenges, or lodge complaints as necessary. Further, the ONPE did not release the results of the congressional elections, which were held on 9 April, until the second week in May. Party leaders complained that they did not receive precinct by precinct information which would facilitate analysis of the results and aide the determination as to whether or not to make challenges. Some stakeholders were not satisfied with the calculation of the parties' proportional allocation of seats according to the congressional elections results. They pointed out that there was a discrepancy with respect to 120,000 votes in the official ONPE results between the number of people who voted in the presidential and congressional elections, the presidential numbers being higher. More compelling, was the fact that one party received a total of 752,452 votes when 99.97 percent of the precincts counted, and only 715,384 votes when100 percent of the precincts were counted.

Damaged Electoral Machinery

The date of 28 May 2000, which was set for the run-off presidential election in Peru became rather controversial. This was due in part to the fact that many stakeholders in the April 9 elections were aware of the shortcomings of those elections and had lost confidence in the National Office of Electoral Processes (ONPE) and National Elections Board (JNE). They feared that the time was too short to prepare properly for the run-off elections, in the light of the weaknesses revealed at the April 9 elections. Many election observer groups and other stakeholders requested that the date be deferred by a few weeks in order to give more time to the ONPE to remedy the shortcomings and allow the tallying computers to be checked. The JNE refused the request. The opposition candidate, Alejandro Toledo, indicated that he would not contest the run-off election on the date of 28 May. Upon that announcement, some domestic observer groups announced that they would not observe the election if both candidates were not contesting. The Organization of American States (OAS) indicated that their mission would withdraw from observing the election. That was followed by the European Union's observer mission, which also withdrew. The National Democratic Institute (NDI) and the Carter Center decided against strengthening their field team in Peru for the run-off election. The reason put forward for those actions was that genuine election in Peru was no longer possible.

Crisis of Legitimacy

The presidential run-off elections in Peru took place on May 28 2000 in spite of numerous calls for their postponement by stakeholders and observers. The vast majority of impartial observers and opposition poll workers did not take part in the elections. The National Office of Elections Process (ONPE) reported the election results as follows: 29.93 percent of the voters spoiled their ballots; 51.2 percent voted for President Fujimori, and 17.68 percent voted for Dr Toledo who did not participate in the contest. There was lack of confidence in the results and the mandate given to President Fujimori. There were demonstrations against the results across the country. The re-election of President Fujimori in the disturbed electoral environment was widely regarded as triggering a crisis of legitimacy. The election had failed to meet international standards for a genuine multiparty democratic election.

Venezuelan Elections 2000 under a New Constitution

Audit of Voting Machines

A private audit firm was contracted to audit the voting machines used in the 2000 elections in Venezuela and it reported a confidence rate of 95 percent in the electoral process, with a 2.5 margin of error.

Last Minute Suspension of Elections—Venezuela 2000

The Venezuelan mega-elections of 2000 were called under the new Constitution and it faced considerable difficulties. There were allegations that there was failure to educate voters on the voting procedures; and there was a general perception that the election machinery was not ready. Two non-governmental organizations petitioned the Supreme Court to suspend the elections to ensure that better preparations could be undertaken. The National Electoral Council admitted that the preparations for the elections were behind schedule. The Supreme Court suspended the poll three days before the mega-elections were due, an event that some stakeholders called mega-fracaso, mega-failure. A new date was set for polling, July 30 2000.

The Mega-Elections, Venezuela 2000

The mega-elections earned that label because they included elections for all the major elective positions in Venezuela, that is to say, presidential governors, federal legislature and local community council members, among others. The mega-elections were intended to usher in the changes brought about by the new Constitution which was approved in 1999. The mega-elections attracted 33, 000 candidates for 6, 000 positions and with some 1370 ballot types.

Privatizing Core Election Activities

Faced with the organizing of the mega-elections in 2000, the National Elections Council (CNE) contracted a number of companies, mostly foreign-based, to carry out the election organization tasks—one company was given the task of placing staff at voting centres, totalling results and disseminate final results; another company was hired to maintain voting machines and ensuring ballot production quality, and programming the electronic memory card; a third company was contracted to manage all of the candidates' (nomination) registration to contest the elections; and a fourth company was hired to print over 1200 unique ballot papers for a total of more than 40 million ballot papers. When the mega-elections were postponed on the 25 of May 2000, many of the foregoing arrangements were either changed or modified.

President in Breach of Campaign Rules

The National Elections Council (CNE) set rules for the campaign period which ran from May 2 to May 27 2000. The campaign rules were considered to be liberal in that only direct canvass for votes was categorized as campaigning. However, when President Chàvez used the state-owned TV station and the national radio for the transmission of a meeting on March 16, the president of the CNE held that it was in breach of the campaign rules and fined Chàvez in the sum of the cost of the broadcast to be paid for out of his campaign funds.

Trouble with Voting Machines

The mega-elections in 2000 ended in failure, when the Supreme Court suspended the date of the 28th May 2000. A new date was subsequently set for a scale-down set of elections on the 30th July 2000 and the other elections were set for a different date. When the 30th July elections, including the presidential, were held, the voting machines proved unreliable in several places, experiencing problems ranging from failure to accept ballot papers, which had to be fed several times; inability to accept any ballot at all; and machines that otherwise failed to work.

High Price of Distrust-Mexico Elections 2000

The Federal Electoral Institute had a budget of approximately $900 million for the 2000 elections. The expenditure ceiling, public and private contributions was set at US$51 million for presidential candidates each; US$ 77,000 for Federal Deputies each, with a varying ceiling for senators, according to the state they represented, ranging between US$314,000 and US$ 3.14 million. The ceiling for individual donors was US$79,000. The total public expenditure for all the campaigns for 2000 was put at US$315 million.

Legendary Fund-Raising Dinner-Mexico 1993

The incumbent President of Mexico, Salinas de Gotari in February 1993 was alleged to have organized a fund-raising dinner for 30 special guests who paid US$25 million a plate.[29]

China Village Committee Elections

During the village elections campaign in Quanwang Village in 2001, an elderly villager challenged the Village Committee Chairman as to why he was promising 16 new toilets when the old ones were not even replaced.

Zambia Elections 2001—Third-Term Issue

President Chiluba and his Movement for Multiparty Democracy (MMD) party wanted to amend the Zambian Constitution to enable the President to contest the elections for a third term. They were met with strong opposition from a collection of civic groups, including churches, the Law Association of Zambia, and other non-governmental organizations under the banner of the Non-Governmental Organizations Coordinating Committee (NGOCC). Popular opposition to the third term grew, and when the MMD party changed its constitution to allow for a third term for Chiluba, there was a great split in the MMD party and 22 senior members were expelled. Chiluba subsequently stood down due to the strength of the opposition to the third term issue both inside and outside of the MMD party.

---

[29] Carter Center Report, Observing the 2000 Mexico Elections, Note 13, p.17, citing Andrés Oppenheimer, '*Bordering on Chaos*'; (Boston: Little, Brown & Co, 1996): 87. Some guests paid up to $50 million for a total of $750 million gathered that evening.

Untimely Funding of an EMB

Stakeholders found that the Electoral Commission of Zambia (ECZ) was not perceived as independent in 2001. That perception was due largely to the lack of timely funding as the government was always late in disbursing funds for the conduct of electoral processes. The delay in funding the ECZ undermined its ability to adequately administer the preparation for the elections and adversely affected its credibility. The erosion of the ECZ's credibility with stakeholders was not helped by the fact that the President had the constitutional right to make appointments to the ECZ in his sole discretion, without consultation with other political parties, or other stakeholders.

National Registration Card (NRC) and Voter's Registration Card (VRC)

In Zambia in 2001, the national registration card (NRC) served as a condition precedent to obtaining registration, and hence holding a voter registration card (VRC). That dual requirement eventually led to the disenfranchisement of many youths who reached voting age, but who did not qualify to register, because they did not possess a NRC. Many stakeholders considered that the linking of the NRC with the registration process was in appropriate and was done to disenfranchise young voters who were believed to favour the opposition

Over-Priced Voters' Lists

At the price of Z$55 million kwacha (approximately US$20,000) to purchase the voters' list, stakeholders considered that the price was exorbitant, perhaps in part, because previously, the voters' list was free of charge. The high charge was believed to be unjustified and a hindrance to many stakeholders obtaining copies and inspecting them in detail. The lists were not on public display and were not easily obtainable at the local level. Those difficulties were seen as deliberate obstacles to inspection of the voters' lists by stakeholders. Opposition parties accused the ECZ of trying to discourage public access to the voters' lists.

Code of Conduct That Exempted the Chief Offenders

The Zambian Code of Conduct dealing with political parties and candidates of 1996 exempted the president and the vice president, in that they were not bound by the provisions that forbade persons to use government transport or facility for campaign purposes or to carry voters to polling stations. Thus, the basic purpose of the Code, as it related to incumbency was frustrated and its goal of creating a level playing field thwarted.

Onerous Conditions on Observers

The Zambian authorities imposed stringent conditions on election observers of the 2001 elections just prior to polling day. The Electoral Commission of Zambia introduced an accreditation fee and a new requirement for sworn affidavits for each individual observer, which created considerable logistical and financial burden on domestic observer organizations just prior to polling day. As a consequence, it was not possible for some organizations to obtain accreditation for all of their observers, due to the inability of the ECZ to issue accreditation cards to all of the observers in time for the polling. Some stakeholders and observer groups concluded that the ECZ created excessive barriers for domestic observers through the accreditation fees and other new requirements.

Logistical Difficulties

The Zambian elections of December 27 2001 experienced considerable logistical and administrative difficulties, including late opening of polling stations, late delivery of election supplies such as ballot boxes, ballot papers and voting booths. The secrecy of the vote was often compromised because of the faulty construction or lay out of the voting booths. There was no electricity at many polling stations, and communication and transportation capacities of the ECZ were limited. The closing of the polls was haphazard as, due in part to late opening, the ECZ decided to extend the polling until all persons in the queue had voted. However, the ECZ was unable to communicate adequately the decision to extend the polling and so presiding officers were forced to act arbitrarily, with some allowing polling to go on far into the evening and others stopping at the precisely at 17.00 hours as scheduled.

Improper Release of Elections Results

The manner of announcing the results of the Zambian elections of 2001 triggered complaints by a wide section of stakeholders. The results were delayed or released sporadically in a manner which appeared to be biased, as in the early release of results the Electoral Commission of Zambia (ECZ) and the state-owned TV announced mainly the results of constituencies won by the Movement for Multiparty Democracy (MMD), notwithstanding that the results for other political parties were also available.

Election Results Not Credible

The Carter Center, in its final statements on the Zambian 2001 elections concluded that the Electoral Commission of Zambia (ECZ) and the government failed to administer a fair and transparent election and failed to address electoral irregularities that clearly could have affected the outcome of a close race. The statement went on to say that the December 27 presidential, parliamentary, and local government election results were not credible and could not be verified as accurately reflecting the will of the Zambian voters. The statement pointed out that as a consequence, the legitimacy of the entire electoral process was questionable. The Center gave as the basis of its conclusion the following:

- Uneven playing field in the pre-election period-problems with voter registration, misuse of state resources, and unbalanced reporting in the media;
- Lack of political will on the part of the ECZ and government to effectively and transparently manage the elections;
- Inadequate logistical arrangements for the polls and lack of procedures to ensure transparent vote counting at the polls;

- Lack of transparency in tabulating the vote at the constituency level and in relaying the results to ECZ;
- Failure by the ECZ to release polling station results in a timely manner; and
- The ECZ failed to implement a transparent verification process open to the political parties and observers.

High Security Fees for Costs

The experience of Zambia in 2001 showed that, if the required security-for-costs fees are too high, given the local circumstances, the overall fairness of the election process concerned could be adversely affected. The Electoral Act of Zambia required petitioners to pay into court with respect to the presidential elections ZK, 5,000,000 kwacha (about US$1,500.00), and for a parliamentary petition, the petitioner had to pay ZK1,000,000 (aboutUSD$300.00). The upshot of the high security fees was that many prospective petitioners failed to make the payment on time, and often had to apply for an extension of the time period within which to pay the security for costs.

Guyana Elections 2001

Voter Identification Card Violated Constitution

In January 2001, the Guyana High Court ruled that the 1997 general elections were invalid, because the statutory requirement of using voter identification cards violated the Constitution. The Court went on to hold that in order to uphold the rule of law and prevent the creation of a legal vacuum, the sitting government elected in 1997 should remain in power until March 2001. During the interim period, the High Court restricted the government's powers to those necessary for day-to-day operations and for elections preparation.

Irresponsible Partisan Media

During the election campaign in Guyana 2001, many stakeholders and observers felt that the media, particularly talk shows and campaign commercials were unbridled in their contents and utterances. The state television was largely pro-government. Voters were often given inaccurate information, which was not objective and which served to whip up political and ethnic tensions. The seemingly unbridled media environment led to a media code of conduct 2000 to lay the ground rules for the political campaign of 2001. Further, an independent panel of media referees was set up to monitor the media environment. Those valiant efforts yielded only a lukewarm attempt by the publicly owned media to accommodate the opposition platform, and the private media made even less effort to curb their partisan exuberance and excesses

Voter Education Caravans

In the lead up to the March 19 2001 elections in Guyana, voter education caravans travelled around the country on scheduled visits with groups of performers to demonstrate parts of the voting process. However, the schedules were not always followed, and there was often lack of proper organization, which resulted in the programmes not conveying a clear and coherent message. Some stakeholders felt that problems with the voter education programmes ultimately reflected in the relatively large numbers of rejected ballots on polling day in the remote areas.

Errors in Computing Election Results

In the Guyana elections of 2001, after the Elections Commission had published the elections results and the parliamentary seats were allocated, a supervisor from Region 4 discovered that she had omitted to include results from some stations, and she immediately notified the omission to the Commission. Although the elections results were publicised, they had not yet been gazetted and legal opinion that was sought indicated that the results could be amended. The results were accordingly revised, and that led to a change in the seat allocation. The change in the seat allocation reduced by one the seats given to the ruling party.

Commissioner Attacked

In the immediate aftermath of the 2001 elections in Guyana, the supporters of the losing main opposition party, the People's Nation Congress Reform (PNC/R), attacked one of the party's representatives on the Guyana Elections Commission (GECOM), apparently because he supported the unanimous decision of GECOM approving the election results.

Recertification of Statements of Poll

Following the results of the Guyana poll in 2001, an action was brought in the High Court to delay the swearing in of the successful presidential candidate, because of deficiencies in the counting procedures. The Chief Justice dismissed the action, but ordered the Guyana Elections Commission (GECOM) to ensure that the procedural shortcoming complained of be remedied. Thereupon, GECOM ordered the returning officers to re-certify the statement of the poll in front of the party agents as required by the electoral law and which had not been done at the counting of the votes in the polling stations.

Lack of Trust in the Electoral Process—Bangladesh 1996

In 1996 a constitutional change was passed in Bangladesh providing for a caretaker government (CTG) at the end of the elected government's term of office to over see the pending elections. That approach was frequently used to manage transitional elections for a one party or military regime to a multiparty democracy. In Bangladesh, the device was intended to be a permanent feature of the electoral system. The approach was that following the achievement of a maximum of five years from the date of a government being sworn in, it passed control to a Chief Advisor, in the person of the most recently retired Chief Justice of the Supreme Court who will govern the country and administer the elections with the assistance of up to ten advisers appointed by the Chief Advisor, and who perform the job of temporary Cabinet ministers. The CTG serve for a maximum period 90 days.

'Tolls' Imposed by Political Activists

In the lead up to the 2001 polls in Bangladesh, the youth wing activists of the ruling party took it upon themselves to levy 'tolls' at bus stations, ferry terminals, on some roads and in university residences, for the support of the party's campaign.

Deadly 'Hartals'

The 'hartals' of Bangladesh are politically inspired strikes. They are usually accompanied and or preceded by warnings to people who are not involved to keep off the streets. Motorized transportation is not permitted to participate. The economic cost could be high, as markets and banks are often advised to close. Hartals are enforced through violence, sometimes resulting in deaths, intimidation, and often resulting in severe economic disruption. Although perhaps more frequently used by the Awami League (AL) and its allies, the Bangladesh Nationalist Party (BNP) and its allies also resorted to hartals when in opposition.

Father of the National's Family Members Security Act 2001

Shortly before the 2001 elections was due in Bangladesh, the governing party piloted an enactment through Parliament called the "Father of the Nation's Family Members Security Act 2001" which allowed the leader of the ruling party, Sheikh Hasina, and her sister, Rahana, life long government security and housing. (That Act was repealed by the incoming administration after the 2001 elections.)

Fading Minutes of an Elected Government

The caretaker government (CTG) was popular with the Awami League (AL) government whose leader, Sheikh Hasina, had spearheaded the drive for a constitutional change in 1996, but was unpopular with the Bangladesh Nationalist Party (BNP) which dubbed it 'Hasina's child'. When the time came for the AL government to hand over power to the CTG in 2001, the Parliament sat until the last minute on the last day, before being dissolved in preparation for the transfer to the caretaker government on the 15th July 2001.

The 2001 Bangladesh Caretaker Government in Action

In order to smooth the path to non-partisan election environment, the Caretaker Government transferred dozens of bureaucrats; particularly those who had controlled elections in the districts—over 1500 civil servants were moved around in departments or relocated to other parts of the country. The CTG ordered raids against perpetrators of political and criminal violence, and cancelled several large contracts that had been signed by the outgoing government, just before it demitted office, on the ground that the contracts were politically motivated.

Inter-Party Election Campaign Violence

The 2001 Bangladesh elections campaign was noted for inter-party violence. The clashes intensified when the Caretaker Government took office. The activists of the opposition parties felt that they had greater freedom to operate and clashed frequently with their rivals at rallies. There were many deaths caused by injuries by knives, machetes, and fatalities from beatings. There were less injuries or fatalities from firearms.

Candidates May Run in Multiple Constituencies

In the 2001 elections in Bangladesh, a candidate could run in up to five constituencies. That approach was expensive as it led to by-elections immediately following the parliamentary elections.

Trouble with Vote Tabulations—Nicaragua Elections 2001

The Nicaraguan election of Sunday 4 November 2001 experienced trouble in conducting the vote tabulation which led to the suspension of the process. The decision to suspend was taken because of suspicions of deliberate, politically motivated obstruction of the typing of training polling station (Junta Receptora de Votos or JVR) tally sheets into the Supreme Electoral Council's (CSE) computers. The major political parties had agreed to replace trained CSE data entry clerks with untrained people from their ranks. The new people were still being registered and given passwords at the close of the polls, which led to the slowing down of the process of posting of the tally data.

A Positive Example of Electoral Transparency

The East Timor elections of 2001 and 2002 have been cited as a good example of electoral transparency. The Independent Electoral Commission (IEC) was set up by the United Nations to run the Constituent Assembly election in 2001 and the presidential elections in 2002 and both elections were described by stakeholders as well organized and conducted. The IEC had been credited by stakeholders with having conducted its work in a transparent manner, keeping the public informed of the progress and important issues by holding public briefings. It functioned in a participatory and inclusive manner, working with all the players and conducting effective voter education programmes.

Pact of National Unity

Prior to the constituent assembly election of East Timor in August 30 2001, the political parties agreed on a pact of National Unity. The Pact provided for a commitment to defend multiparty democracy, respect the rights of all legally established parties and discourse between parties in a non-violent environment. The parties and their nominated candidates respected the principles of tolerance set out in the Pact of National Unity during the presidential campaign in 2002.

Ballot Paper Design East Timor Presidential Election April 14 2002.

Candidate Xanana Gusmao desired to maintain his political independence, and did not wish to have the logos of each of the political parties that had nominated him placed next to his photo on the presidential ballot paper. In early March 2002, Gusmao announced that he would withdraw his candidature for the election, if the ballot paper was not re-designed. The Board of Commissioners could not remove the design of the ballot paper, because some parties did not agree. Eventually, all the political parties agreed to a re-designing of the ballot paper as requester by Gusmao and the Board of Commissioners agreed.

Mali Presidential Election 2002

The first round of the Mali presidential election of 2002 was marred by a number of irregularities such as:

- Polling stations were without voters' cards for distribution on polling day;
- At some polling stations voters' cards inadvertently locked away and were not available for timely distribution;
- The voters' lists were unavailable at some polling stations, and so were other essential election materials, such as ballot papers, voting booths and indelible ink;

- Proxy forms, signed by the appropriate officials, but not by the voter contrary to the legal requirement, were seen in the polling stations.

Vote Tabulation with Limited Transparency

The vote counting and tabulation processes of the 2002 Mali presidential elections experienced considerable difficulties, in particular:

- Poor lighting at many of the polling stations adversely affected the counting of the votes;
- The tabulation process, which was conducted at multiple levels, was carried out manually and took several days;
- This process was carried out at the local, regional and national levels;
- Some stakeholders and observers had only limited access to the tabulation process, with the process at the national level not always open to observers;
- The work of the national tabulation committee was split up into several strands, collection of results by radio, telephone, fax, communications from embassies and consulates, and liaison between the commission and the database operations;
- Some observers could not adequately monitor all the above channels satisfactorily;
- Some observers were not given access to some of the components and communication channels conveying tabulation information; and
- There were complaints from political parties and candidates about the slow pace and apparent lack of transparency of the tabulation.

An Unusually High Level of Invalid Votes

The Constitutional Court of Mali has the responsibility of announcing the election results and on May 9 2002 the official results of the first round were announced. The Court had undertaken its own review of the results and taken account of some 30 complaints received from political parties and other stakeholders. It invalidated a total of 541,019 or 24.6 percent of the votes cast. Further, 4.3 percent of the ballots were declared void. Thus, nearly 30 percent of the votes cast during the first round were unable to be taken account of in the results. The process by which the Court narrowed the results between the candidates was not witnessed by any observers.

Election Campaign Ban in Some Constituencies—Jamaica General Elections 2002

Shortly after the campaign period opened in the beginning of October 2002, campaign events were marred by complaints of gunshots, stoning of cars and buses in motorcades, and the occurrence of general violence. The situation threatened to get out of control in some areas and the electoral authorities requested a ban on campaigning in 6 constituencies, where the ban was enforced.

Political 'Dons' and 'Turf War'

During the election campaign leading up to the 2002 elections in Jamaica, violence erupted in the area of Western Kingston. There had been a long history of an on and off 'turf war' in many violence prone areas of Kingston and St Andrew, among them Western Kingston. In some of those areas, the phenomenon of the 'dons' or community leaders was born. These 'dons' allied themselves to one or other of the two main political parties, the then ruling People's National Party (PNP) and the then main opposition party, the Jamaica Labour Party (JLP). Many of the 'dons' had antecedent of a mixed bag of community services masking misdeeds such as instigators of violence (political and criminal), as well as drugs dealing. In 2001 a notorious 'don', believed to be a PNP supporter, was assassinated by persons who were believed to be JLP supporters. That incident triggered gun battles between gangs and between the police and the armed gangs. Many citizens were caught up in the shootings and lost their lives.

Attempts to 'Take Back' the Elections in Troublesome Constituencies

Faced with some 15 of the 60 constituencies of Jamaica having a history of election irregularities, the election management body of Jamaica designed a scheme to 'take back' the elections in those constituencies. Of the 15 constituencies identified, 8 were categorized as capable of responding to standard remedial measures of proper re-focussing to deliver free and fair elections. The remaining 7 however were in need of stiffer measures and so the electoral authorities communicated with the party leaders and prospective candidates for each of these constituencies warning them of the extra scrutiny that was placed on those constituencies. The group of 8 constituencies was warned that election irregularities would be published to their embarrassment. The group of 7 constituencies were singled out for a visit to their political party representatives by the Chairman of the Electoral Advisory Committee (EAC) and the Director of Elections to convey the message that they would be under the microscope and would be prime candidates for a petition to the Electoral Tribunal to void the election results. In addition to the foregoing measures, the EMB placed full-time employees at the polling stations with a history of over-voting and fraudulent activities. Special police presence was strengthened in those areas.

Kenya Elections 2002-EMB Reversed Itself

The Electoral Commission of Kenya (ECK) announced a week before the December 27 2002 elections that presiding officers would have the discretionary power to allow voters not appearing on the 2002 roll to vote. Two days before the polling, the ECK, reversing itself on the issue, announced that only voters on the 2002 roll would be permitted to vote.

Chaotic Formal Nomination Proceedings

The registration of candidates to contest parliamentary elections in Kenya is subject to a two-staged process. Firstly, the political parties conduct party primaries at which each party select its nominees. The names are submitted to the Electoral Commission of Kenya (ECK). Secondly, the prospective candidates submit their nomination papers and stipulated fees to the returning officer of the respective constituencies, in which each candidate intends to contest the elections. In the 2002 elections, the both stages were marred with confusion and violence. The intra-party competition was fierce and led to defections, complaints and violence. The confusion led to double allocation of nomination certificates, and even to attacks on rival aspirant candidates, as well as, in one reported case, attack on a returning officer. In some cases, nomination papers were destroyed or mislaid, and many prospective candidates lost out, either by delays or loss of paperwork.

Stakeholders and Observers Commended EMB and Staff

Notwithstanding the many problems with the nomination process, the 2002 elections in Kenya earned the Electoral Commission and its staff commendation from stakeholders and observers for well-run elections. The stakeholders were pleased with the professionalism and impartiality displayed by the Commission and staff. They noted the strong presence of party agents and non-partisan observers at most polling stations. They express satisfaction with the Commission in its readiness to enforce the Electoral Code of Conduct.

EMBs Members Accused of Corruption-Sierra Leone 2002

Prior to the Sierra Leone elections of May 14 2002, the Sierra Leone Anti-Corruption Commission issued indictments against three (including the chairman) of the five members of the Electoral Commission. However the indictments were not pursued before the elections. Some observer groups called for the completion of the investigation into the corruption allegation in their report on the election organization and conduct. An interesting twist concerning that incident was that the Attorney General and Minister of Justice, who should prosecute the case against the Commissioners, became the running mate of the President in 2002 elections.

Insufficient Voter Education Programmes

In the post-conflict Sierra Leone of 2002, the electoral environment was less than ideal and it showed up in many aspects of the organization of the 2002 elections. One such area was the voter education programmes mounted prior to the elections where the deficiencies showed up in the following ways:

- Incidents of multiple voting;
- Underage voting;
- Unsolicited interference by polling officers in the marking of the ballot by voters;
- Polling procedures not properly understood by voters;
- Compromise of the secrecy of the ballot;
- Need for on the spot instructions to voters how to fill out ballot papers;
- Need for some election officers to accompany voters into polling booth to assist them; and
- High percentage of spoiled ballot papers.

Special Needs Provided For

The 2002 Sierra Leone elections offered good examples of an election management body making an effort to accommodate voters with special needs at the polls, for example:

- Special procedures to register internally displaced persons (IDPs) and transfer their votes, were put in place;
- In order to facilitate voters with limited literacy, political parties logos, and not only names of parties or candidates, were put on ballot papers;
- The electoral authorities allowed a pilot scheme of Tactile Ballot Guide enabling blind voters to cast their ballots without assistance, and in secret;
- Amputees who had both hands removed were taught to vote with their feet, after being given several weeks of training-the voters left a print of their big toe on the ballot paper.

Guatemala Elections December 28 2003—Vote Buying

Stakeholders in the Guatemala elections of 2003 reported voting-buying incidents at the local elections level in certain departments. The vote buying appeared to be planned strategies pursued by some of the political parties. Voters were offered money, agricultural tools, housing construction materials, and credits to vote for particular parties or candidates. The practice of vote buying preyed on the indigenous population custom of being bound by the maxim 'my word is my bond', whereby a prospective voter felt bound to vote for the party or candidate who gave consideration in cash or kind in return for the vote. Stakeholders began to make inroads into the practice of vote buying through direct voter education against the practice, and by teaching voters to breaking the link between the rewards and vote. The sanction against vote buying in Guatemala at that time was not clear cut.

Nigeria Elections 2003—Voter Registration30

The voter registration process was punctuated by delays and computerization problems which caused multiple postponements of the local elections. Then when the exercise finally got going, the inevitable reports of irregularities on a wide scale began to consume the Independent National Electoral Commission (INEC). The reported irregularities included the following:

- Partisan election officials;
- Hoarded voter registration materials resulting in shortages;
- Buying of voters' cards;
- Multiple registration;
- Underage registration;
- Registration of non-nationals;
- Inadequate training of registration officials;

---

30 The author was a short term consultant to Department for International Development (DfID), Nigeria, prior to the 2003 elections.

- Misbehaviour by party activists in intimidating qualified persons; and
- Logistical problems.

Mozambique—Local Elections November 19 2003

Observer Team's Logo

The local elections in Mozambique in November 2003 were pronounced by stakeholders to be relatively well organized and peaceful. However, in several provinces the logo of the Carter Center triggered adverse reaction, as the resemblance of the Carter Center's logo to that of the opposition party, Renamo-UE's party, raising allegations of partiality, although perhaps more fear of confusion than bias. The Carter Center observers were advised to remove their logo in the event that the perceptions were raised and to prevent conflict with any stakeholder.

Tabulation Problems

Three days prior to the local elections in Mozambique in 2003, the methodology to carry out the intermediate count was undecided and when it was settled on the following day, the preference of the opposition for a manual count was agreed. The role of observers and party agents was not clear for the intermediate tabulation in some areas, it was considered sufficient to have the presence of the commission members and or the agents of the two main political parties. In some provinces, national, but not international, observers and agents, were allowed to observe the intermediate count. In some places, international observers were allowed to observe freely. The count tally sheets contained multiple errors which were confirmed by stakeholders.

Indonesian Elections 2004—Improvements, but Irregularities Abounded

Amidst the turbulent period of transition in Indonesia in the late 1990s from a long-standing autocratic administration to a multiparty democracy, substantial improvement toward democratic governance was achieved. The legislative and presidential direct elections of 2004 tested the new constitutional and electoral structures to their limits. In the evolving electoral process that was in place in 2004 much progress was discerned, but not unexpectedly stakeholders chronicled a large number of election irregularities including:

- Inadequate allocation of resources for the training of polling and tabulation officials;
- Poor training of tabulation officials, which led to large numbers of incorrectly filled out, and which in turn led to opportunities to commit tabulation fraud;
- Incidents of election officials committing fraudulent acts in accepting bribes to tamper with the count during the tabulation process; and
- Election officials who behaved in a partisan manner towards a particular political party or candidate.

Indonesian Election 2004—Irregularities in Preparing the Voters' Register

In order to vote a person was required to be listed in the voters' register, being in possession of a voter's card and a letter from the village level election committee (PPS). The distribution of the ID cards and invitation letter was not even. An audit of the voter registration in March 2004 found that the voter register achieved 91 percent, but that the accuracy and completeness varied among the regions and among ethnic groups. There was evidence of 'ghost voters' and the procedure for registering persons from disadvantaged groups were not as efficient as it could be.

Self Training of Poll Staff

Self training through watching instruction videos, or reading leaflets describing particular election tasks, was used in place of the more widely used 'cascade' methodology. The experiment in training methodology was less than successful as was evidenced in widespread incorrectly completed tabulated forms in the legislative elections.

Candidacy and Disability

The Constitution of Indonesia dated November 2001 contained a provision that stated that certain disabilities were not compatible with legislative office, or with the office of the presidency. The constitution provision was passed after a former President, Abdurrahman Wahid, who was partially blind, was apparently intending to run for office again. Indeed, Mr. Wahid, on May 22 2004 sought to file papers for his candidacy for the presidency, the Electoral Commission rejected his application after he failed a medical examination conducted by the Indonesian Doctors' Association. Wahid filed several legal actions in the courts challenging the decision to disqualify him for candidature for the presidency, but they failed.

Double Punching of Ballots

During the first round of the presidential elections on July 5 2004, as the counting of the votes began it became clear that many ballots were invalid because they were marked more than once. This happened because many ballot papers were folded in a way that allowed voters to punch their vote on one side without opening the entire ballot sheet causing many voters to unwittingly puncturing both sides of their ballot. To cure the resultant defect, the Election Commission issued a set of directives which required election officers to re-check and review invalid ballots and treat them as valid. Some party witnesses who were to be present during the re-checking did not turn up on time. Limited field tests of the ballot indicated that double punching could have been a problem, but the design of the ballot paper was not changed.

Prosecutions for Election Misdeeds

Although the irregularities occurred at all levels and in various geographical locations, the election authorities, during the first round of the presidential elections in July, successfully prosecuted some of the miscreants, for example, at four polling stations in Kwamki Lama, Mimika, West Papua, election officials illegally punched more than 3200 ballots in favour of a candidate. They were tried and sentenced to a three months suspended sentence. The votes were cancelled and a re-vote was conducted

Second Round Run-off Election September 20 2004

Though the organisation was improved and there was calm and peaceful atmosphere, a number of weaknesses were complained about by stakeholders during the run-off presidential election in Indonesia in 2004. The main problems were:

- Polling officials did not consistently the administrative procedures;
- There was multiple voting and voter's fingers were not often marked;
- Voter's card was not always produced and names were not crossed off the voters' roll;
- The Commission (KPU) issued directive allowing stations to close as early 11.30 a.m., but it was not uniformly applied or conveyed, and resulted in confusion;
- Some stations closed early, even though all eligible voters had not voted, as required;
- The tally sheet had a serious design flaw, as the signature page stood alone, and so could be easily detached, paving the way for fraud.

Mozambique Elections December 1-2 2004—Improper Use of Public Resources

The series of goodbye trips by the outgoing President Chissano to all the provinces, where he presented his candidate, Guebuza, was seen by stakeholders as political campaigning using public resources. In addition, stakeholders pointed to numerous cases where official vehicles were used in party rallies and convoys. In a similar vein, there were reports of some political parties using the tax exemption given to political parties to import goods for official party use to engage in commercial activities unrelated to party activities. Such illegal activities included the following:

- Importation of tax free motor vehicles for purposes unconnected to parties' political activities;
- Importation and re-sale of goods on the local market;
- Allegation that the ruling party imported 300 tons of paper for party purposes, but the materials were later sold on the local market.

Mozambique Presidential & Legislative Elections of December 1-2 2004

The December 1-2 2004 presidential and legislative elections of Mozambique earned high marks from stakeholders for thorough preparation and good conduct. As one observer team put it-multiple evaluations suggested that the organisation passed both the objective test, for example, the polls were opened on time; and the subjective test, and that the polling went well. In other words, polling stations functioned well and the elections were generally well organised. The polling procedures were properly applied. Perhaps the low turnout, 36 percent facilitated the overall organisation. However, the tabulation process was delayed and not considered by stakeholders to be wholly transparent. Some observer teams were not completely satisfied with the accuracy of the tabulation results, as they were not accompanied by the required district-by-district map results. Furthermore, the results excluded about 699 presidential tally sheets and 731 legislative assembly tallies and no explanation was given for the exclusion.

The Recall Referendum of Venezuela August 15 2004

There was widespread distrust of the ruling party and the opposition, as well as of the National Electoral Council (CNE) by many stakeholders. At first, there were disputes regarding the validity of tens of thousands of signatures to count towards the stipulated required number of signatures to allow the recall referendum to be held. When the recall referendum was held on 15 August 2004 and it went in favour of the President, the losers (the opposition) called fraud on a number of grounds, namely, that:

- That the voting machines were programmed to alter the results;
- Communication from the central computer during the voting day altered the electronic result of individual machines.

These grounds were discounted by tests carried by stakeholders and observers. Some observers did record that irregularities did take place during the recall referendum. Such irregularities included the lack of transparency of the CNE in its decision making; and issuance of late regulations which were often incomplete or unclear.

'Repentant' Signer

During the lead-up to the re-call referendum in Venezuela in 2004, the question of who could withdraw a signature and when, became controversial. The opposition contended that only persons who had not signed in the first place could withdraw a signature during the reparos period. Some pro-Chávez supporters argued that 'repentant' signers could withdraw their signature. Observers from the Organization of American States and the Carter Center supported the view that only those persons alleging that they had not signed could withdraw their signatures. They equate the position to that of a voting exercise in which one casts a ballot and then cannot withdraw it, and so a signer should not be able to simply change his or her mind after exercising the right to sign.

Reported Voter Migration

During the lead-up to the Venezuelan re-call referendum in 2004, many voters complained that they had been involuntarily placed in a new voting centre, or were omitted from the register. The National Electoral Council acknowledged that some of the reported problems did exist.

Ethiopia Parliamentary Elections—15 May 2005, Post-Elections Violence

The report of stakeholders and observers suggested that the preparation and conduct of the elections went relatively well. However, with the release of the early results from the urban areas showed the opposition parties gaining a big victory in those areas. The rural areas were slower to yield their results. The upshot was that both opposition and the ruling parties claimed victory. The opposition accused the government of fraud and vote rigging. The students of the University of Addis Ababa took up the opposition cause of vote rigging and demonstrated. Several hundreds of the students were arrested. A day or two later on June 8 a transport strike spread throughout the city and violence accompanied by shooting that left more than 37 people dead.

Liberia Election 2005—The Court and Election Calendar31

The Supreme Court of Liberia showed little regard with respect to the election deadlines which were set in order to meet the date mandated by the Comprehensive Peace Agreement (CPA) of August 2003, which brought peace to Liberia. In the first place, the Court ruled quite late that voters may mark two choices on their ballot papers in Senate elections. The timing of the Court's decision gave the National Election Commission

---

[31] The author was Election Consultant for the European Commission in Liberia 2004 -2005

(NEC) little time for implementation. In another case, the court held that a number of candidates who were rejected by the NEC should be given the opportunity to correct deficiencies in their applications. The full implementation of the Court's decision would most certainly mean that the election date would be adversely affected. The conflicting position between the internationally and nationally agreed election date and the ruling of the Supreme Court was avoided by the candidates, who had won the case in Court, withdrawing from the elections, after a good deal of mediation within the framework of the CPA. This event illustrated the potential problems in the legal framework respecting dispute settlement and the need to avoid disruption of the electoral process that is in motion.

Palestinian Presidential Elections—January 9 2005

The January 9 2005 presidential election in Palestine was well organized in an orderly and peaceful atmosphere. In the view of the stakeholders and observers, the organisation and conduct of the elections met international standards. There was a relatively strong participation of women voters, while there was also evidence of women activists of political party, as well as women election officials. There were reports of poor management at some polling stations where there appeared to be larger numbers of persons claiming to be in need of assistance to vote. Some stakeholders complained that a series of late decisions taken by the Central Election Commission (CEC) on polling day were taken under duress and to assist the Fatah faction. Voting at designated post offices in East Jerusalem was restrictive and disorganised, resulting in a good many voters being disenfranchised. Generally, the numerous check points operated by the Israelis adversely affected freedom of movement during the campaign period and on polling day.

Election in the Democratic Republic of the Congo-July 30 2006

The post-conflict transitional elections of 2006 in the Democratic Republic of the Congo took place in difficult circumstances. There was certainly no guarantee as to how the Independent Electoral Commission (CEI) would perform in terms of its non-partisanship and overall competence. Its ability to ensure a level playing field respecting access to the media and moderating the excesses of incumbency was untried. Its oversight reach over its officers in distant parts of that vast country was all in doubt. However, stakeholders confirmed that many of their worse fears did not materialize. Firstly, voting on the 30 July was relatively peaceful and orderly. Secondly, polling staff for the most part were competent and managed polling stations competently. However, not unexpectedly, there were some important administrative set backs occurred, for example, last-minute changes to voters' lists and polling stations impact adversely on the smooth conduct of the process. In a similar vein, the CEI did not succeed in eliminating the excesses of incumbency during the election campaign, for example, hindering free campaigning by the opposition candidates, and orchestrating delays at ports of campaign materials for opposition parties.

Election Transparency and Credibility

Although not all aspects of the polling and counting processes were open and transparent, the Independent Electoral Commission (CEI) in the elections of July 30 in the Democratic Republic of Congo earned high marks from stakeholders, when they presented the election results on their Web Site for every polling station across the country and posted up at the local tabulation centres (CLCR). It demonstrated to stakeholders the assurance that the numbers witnessed at polling stations were accurately reported in the final results. This procedure enabled the CEI to defend its credibility against claims of manipulation. However the issue of transparency did not end there, for a number of ballot papers were unavailable, through being lost or mislaid, and so would not be forthcoming if needed in a court case for verification. Further, stakeholders pointed to many cases where transparency was obscured:

- Unexplained last-minute changes to the number and location of polling stations and to the official voters' list hindered political parties and observers to verify that all the polling stations were open to scrutiny, and dispel rumours about ghost stations;

- Information about the location of the lists of voters could not always be verified;
- Last-minute changes to the criteria for voting by 'delegation' made monitoring difficult; and
- Communications problems reduced the timely implementation of decisions.

The Palestinian Legislative Council Elections-26 January 2006

With mounting tension in Gaza and lack of freedom of movement to campaign freely in East Jerusalem, stakeholders in the Palestinian Legislative Council (PLC) elections 2006 were apprehensive about the conduct of free and fair elections in an atmosphere that was not nearly ideal for purpose. However, the Central Election Commission (CEC) and staff were confident and professional. The CEC enjoyed a high level of confidence among election stakeholders. The election campaign was largely peaceful, and so was the Election Day itself. The turn out of voters, including women, was good. The election was witnessed by a large number of agents of political parties and candidates, as well as non-partisan election observers. However, there were some problems were encountered during campaigning and on polling day, particularly with respect to:

- Voting in East Jerusalem at post offices where the secrecy of the ballot was often compromised by the prying eyes of the postal workers;
- Candidates and parties did not always observe the rules which prevented campaigning on Election Day;
- Checkpoints hindered freedom of movement on polling day;
- Some media outlets varied their charges for paid campaign advertisement;
- The Fatah candidates were reported to benefit from the use of public resources; and
- The Islamic Resistance Movement (Hamas) was reported to extend their campaign to mosques.

The Presidential Election, Ukraine—31 October, 21 November and 26 December 2004

"Technical Candidates"

The phrase 'technical candidates' popped up during those elections to describe the unusual situation when a large number of candidates were registered, but who did not enjoy significant popular support. The upshot was that they formed a majority block with one party's (Mr. Yanukovych's) representatives on the Territorial Election Commissions (TECs) and Polling Station Commissions (PSC). Many stakeholders felt that the technical candidates were helped by the state administration to 'manufacture' signature sheets in order to get the required 500,000 valid signatures to support their nominations. The verification procedure for signatures was unclear and lacked transparency.

Mobile Ballot Box

The electoral law of Ukraine during the 2004 elections (section 78) imposed harsh penalty on the voters using the mobile ballot box in so far as it stipulated that all ballots in a mobile ballot box be invalidated if the number of ballots found in the box exceeded the number of ballots stated on the control sheet. That procedure was considered unbalanced, as there was no similar requirement in respect of ballot boxes in polling stations. It may be said that a ballot too many was not a sound reason to nullify the franchise of many other persons.

Absentee Voting Certificates (AVCs)

The Election Law of Ukraine allowed a polling station commission (PSC) to issue an AVCs to a voter registered to vote in that PSC to enable the voter to vote elsewhere, if the voter were going to be away from his/her residence on Election Day. The name of that voter would be deleted from the PSC's voters list, and on Election Day should be added to the voters list of the polling station where the voter votes. The procedure governing the issuance of AVCs and particularly controls over their use was unsound.

Stakeholders complained that there was widespread misuse of AVCs leading to large scale multiple voting. There were reports that public employees were coerced into applying for AVCs for onwards transmission of blank AVCs to their work supervisors. There were also reports that persons were bussed from one polling station to another and voted on multiple occasions with the use of AVCs.

Registration Inaccuracies (Ukraine)

In the lead up to the first round of voting, large-scale inaccuracies were found in the voters' register. There was the inclusion of names of deceased persons, changes in addresses were not recorded, multiple registrations were undetected, and misspellings of names and addresses were uncorrected.

Election Day Weaknesses

On Election Day, 31 October 2004 in Ukraine, observers assessed the voters' lists as bad or very bad in about 20% of the polling stations visited. Many voters were turned away from polling stations because of misspelling of their names in the voters' lists. It was noted that the secrecy of the vote was not assured in about 28% of the polling stations visited by observers. Group voting was allowed in about 13% of the stations visited by observers. The transparent ballot boxes exposed how people voted, as the law did not require voters to fold their marked ballots and that further compromised the secrecy of the ballot.

Large-Scale Dismissals

Notwithstanding that the Central Electoral Commission (CEC) in Ukraine issued, on 10 November 2004, clarification to Territorial Electoral Commissions (TECs) regarding the circumstances in which Polling Station Commissions members could be relieved of their duties, on the eve of the second round of elections, TECs in nine regions apparently erroneously dismissed hundreds of opposition-nominated PSC members.

A Broken or a Fraudulent Process?

Immediately after the Ukraine elections on 31 October 2004, the Central Electoral Commission (CEC) started posting up results on its Website on 1 November. The next day when 97.6% of the results had been processed and the candidate of the ruling party had a slender lead, the system went down. The CEC blamed it on technical malfunction and deny that there was any fraudulent activity involved, and dismissed the Head of the IT Department. However, the opposition claimed that it was a ploy to deny Mr Yushchenko, the opposition candidate the leading position, and that the partial results that were announced were false. No candidate secured the majority of the votes required to claim victory at the first round and so a run-off election was set for the 21 November 2004. The run-off election on 21 November resulted in victory for the ruling party's candidate, but the opposition refused to accept the results and took the matter to Court which blocked the inauguration of the new president. Thereafter, mass demonstration followed and on 27 November, Parliament adopted a resolution invalidating the election results announced by the CEC. On December 3 2004, the Supreme Court held that a repeat second round should be held and the date was set for December 26 2004.

The Kenya General Election—2007

Novel Treatment of Double and Multiple Registrations

The incidence of high levels of multiple registrations came to the attention of the Electoral Commission of Kenya (ECK) before the 2007 elections took remedial action, but nevertheless some 400,000 duplicated names remained on the register. The names were identified and a special list was created and sent to each polling station. Some of the cases of multiple registrations were caused by failure on the part of the officials of the ECK who failed to cancel original registrations of persons who were transferred. With respect to the treatment of the 400,000 duplicates that remained on the register, the ECK formulated a novel procedure whereby the following steps should be taken:

- Voters who had registered twice (that is to say, double registered voters) were to be allowed to vote provided that the following conditions were met:
- the voter was to surrender to the presiding officer both elector's cards; the presiding officer or deputy presiding officer was to emboss both cards as if he/she voted with both of them and retain the cards;
- the presiding officer or deputy presiding officer was to interview the voter first, to ascertain whether or not the voter had registered twice as a result of the Electoral Commission's failure or default to delete one of his/her registrations;
- the voter was to fill a form entitled "Declaration by a doubly registered voter" which the District Election Coordinator was to supply to the returning officer, who in turn was to supply it to the presiding officers; and
- the presiding officer or deputy presiding officer should firstly, make a record showing the names and serial numbers of the voters' cards and registration centres they originated from, and secondly, retain the form "Declaration by a doubly registered voter".

Voters who had registered more than twice were prohibited from voting, and faced possible legal sanctions if they attempted to vote.

Abuse of Incumbency

During the campaign period leading up to the Kenyan general election of 2007, stakeholders drew attention to the large scale abuse of the incumbent government and the members there of, including use of state resources for the political purposes of the ruling party, the use of official vehicles during campaigns, government granted land tenure to a number of Kenyans, and made adjustments to the salaries of public servants, during the campaign.

Anonymous Advertisements Allowed

During the campaign period of the 2007 general election of Kenya, anonymous advertisements popped up in support of one party or another. Stakeholders complained that there was no limit on the amount of money that could be spent on political advertising, and no clear rules governing the standard of election advertising.

Disappearance of Returning Officers

Serious post-election violence in Kenya in 2007 which continued into 2008 was triggered in part after the Chairman of the Electoral Commission, two days after polling, announced that he was unable to trace returning officers in 21 constituencies, and that in one instance a set of election results was voided as it showed a turnout of over 100%. As if to make matters worse, both the leader of the ruling party and the leader of the opposition, at separate press conferences, claimed victory and brandished figures in support of their claim.

Short of Acceptable International Standards

The announcement of the results of the general elections in Kenya in 2007 gave victory to the ruling party's candidate and sitting President, Mwai Kibaki by a narrow margin of votes. The results were immediately disputed by the opposition and many stakeholders and observers. Widespread riots and ethnic violence erupted during more than a thousand lives were lost and many people forced to flee their homes. The Commonwealth Observer Team stated that the events that unfolded since polling day had eroded the confidence of the people of Kenya, that the manner in which the results were announced had raised suspicion about and caused widespread mistrust. The Observer Team concluded that the election process following the closing of the polls fell short of acceptable international standards.

The Russian Gas Vybori System

Stakeholders and observers reported that the Gas Vybori System performed to satisfaction in the 2003 Russian Federation elections to the State Duma. The Gas Vybori System was designed to facilitate election-related activities and to furnish the election administration with internal information. The principal tasks of the system were to aggregate the election results, assist in maintaining the voters register, and make available financial information to parties and candidates. The network operates autonomously. It aided transparency and improved efficiency in the tabulation process.

Abuse of Incumbency Advantages

Stakeholders reported high levels of the use of administrative resources by the machinery on behalf of United Russian candidates in the 2003 Russian Federation elections to the State Duma. The distinction between the party and the executive administration was blurred. The abuses of the executive authority created distortion in the electoral process and impinged on the integrity of the democratic elections. Many officials openly flouted the rule to suspend their official functions while they were running as candidates. Election observers noted many individual instances of abuses by candidates of the United Russia party, such as the provision of free transport services to United Russia-organized events in the local administration in Khabarovsk. Many opposition candidates complained that they were denied suitable spaces for meetings and rallies, and were also denied equal conditions to hold campaign meetings with employees in public institutions.

Media Treatment-A Mixed Bag

The behaviour of the publicly owned presented a mixed picture. The State TV channels complied with the requirement with respect to free airtime for all contestants. The state-funded newspapers also met the legal requirements with respect to free space for each party. Both arms of the media also assisted with voter education programmes. However, a part from the provision of free time, State broadcasters mainly supported and even promoted United Russia. Some broadcasters even went as far as producing news items which tended to discredit the opposition. A similar pattern in behaviour was observed with the State-funded newspapers, which while giving overwhelmingly positive slant to the United Russia party gave mainly negative coverage to the opposition candidates. Private broadcasters, on the whole were observed to be more balanced in their reporting of election coverage. Private newspapers supported one side or another. In the regions, there were reports of privately owned media houses being subjected to unwarranted inspection by local authorities or on orders of the Fire Inspectorate. In some areas, discriminatory media charges for political advertisements were reported.

Toy Donation—A Bribe?

The competition for registration of candidates proved to be fierce during the Russian Federation elections to the State Duma in 2003 that some contestants sought to remove others through fair of foul means by de-registration. Thus in one case in Moscow a United Russia candidate sought to deregister another candidate, Mikhail Zadornov, his Yabloko opponent, on the ground that Mr. Zadornov's agent had donated a toy to an orphanage, and had thereby sought to bribe voters. The Court dismissed the application as groundless.

Open Voting

Opening voting, where voters do not vote in private, is contrary to the Duma Election Law. Nevertheless, many cases of open voting were reported during the 2003 Duma elections. There were also instances of group or family voting, where two or more voters mark their ballots together. In some cases, open balloting was believed to be caused by insufficient number of polling booths in many polling stations or through defective polling booths. There were instances, albeit few, of polling stations where there were no voting booths, while in other cases there were reports that precinct election commissions (PEC) members encouraged voters not to use voting booths.

Mobile Ballot Box

During the polling in the State Duma election of 2003, stakeholders reported that control over the use of mobile ballot boxes was often lax. The disabled and infirm voters who voted outside of a polling station used a mobile ballot box. A number of those voters voted openly, the mobile ballot boxes that were taken to hospitals were often supplied with ballot papers for all patients regardless of whether or not they had requested a mobile ballot.

Belarus Presidential Election 19 March 2006

Election Campaign not Covered by the Election Code

The "za Belarus" campaign was not related to a specific candidate and so was not covered by the provisions of the Election Code. There was little doubt however that the main beneficiary was the incumbent President, as many speakers at "za Belarus" events openly urged citizens to vote for Mr. Lukashenko. The "za Belarus" campaign concentrated on promoting the country's achievements. It featured concerts and advertisements on billboards all over the country. The events got wide coverage on television throughout the country.

A Pattern of Intimidation

The Belarus presidential campaign in 2006 exhibited an example of a pattern of intimidation against opponents. The opposition's campaign activity was highly restricted and the environment was such that there was fear of loss of jobs or arrest inhibited free campaigning. There was suppression of independent print media and failure to tolerate political competition. Opposition campaign workers intimidated or harassed and impediment put in the way of meeting voters. Campaign venues designated by local authorities were often too small and located outskirts of town and cities where they were difficult to reach. Police frequently confiscated opposition campaign materials. Leaflets were restricted and routinely disrupted, and courts fined some campaigners who had been distributing leaflets for littering offences. The upshot of that systematic harassment, it became increasingly difficult for the opposition to recruit volunteer and campaign staff. The climate of fear and insecurity was extended to public workers where some senior members of executive committees and senior management at factories and universities campaigned for the incumbent. Many senior campaign figures of the opposition were detained or arrested and the campaign efforts were severely disrupted.

Closure of Media Houses

Belarus boasts of 1,222 print media outlets, 8 information agencies, 54 TV and 154 radio channels. However, many non-State national and regional print media have been closed. During the presidential election campaign, no independent daily newspaper existed. Some titles, such as *Narodnaya Volya* and *Tovvarisch* were printed in Smolensk in the Russian Federation. Those papers were considered to be sympathetic to the opposition. In March, on several occasions the police seized either the entire print run of those papers, or copies from vendors. During the election campaign, many journalists were detained by the police, or subjected to violent apprehension while carrying out their professional duties.

Shortcomings in the Tabulation of Election Results

The Election Code provides that polling results be publicly posted at polling stations. However, there is no legal provision in place that allows election stakeholders to follow the processing of the results from polling stations to the central level, and has the potential to reduce transparency. The legislation does not provide for observers to receive official copies of election results protocols. The Code does not provide that the calculation of the election results from all levels of the election administration is made publicly available. The tabulation process at the Precinct Election Commissions (PECs) and the Territorial Election Commissions (TECs) was not fully opened to observers, and in some cases observers and stakeholders were obstructed in their efforts to get information on the process at those levels. The severe limitation at those levels had undermined the transparency of the process.

Cambodia National Assembly Elections July 2003

Post-Election Recommendations

A group of about 170 stakeholders who at a conference in early 2004 examined and evaluated the elections conduct in 2003 recommended that the electoral register needed to be improved. Indeed, the conference proposed that the then existing electoral register should be nullified and a new register be created based on Khmer identity only. The recommendations of the stakeholders extended to the scrapping of old voters' cards and other registration documents. In the proposed new arrangements, persons who were of Khmer origin or who became a naturalized Khmer citizen should have their citizenship approved by a royal decree consistent with the requirement of the law.

Vote Buying and Related Election Irregularities

During the election campaign for the National Assembly Elections of 27 July 2003, stakeholders complained about the bad behaviour of political parties and candidates of all sides. The untoward activities ranged from the distribution of gifts by political parties in the name of associations and charitable organisations, to vote buying on a large scale throughout the election campaign period. In some cases, candidates were reported to have entered into commitments to voters to pay monies after the elections.

Post-Election Deadlock

The July 2003 elections of Cambodia joined the ever-growing list of elections that end in governance deadlock in the country as a result of the elections. In this case, the deadlock was due to the Constitutional provision which required a two-thirds majority to constitute a government. That requirement was aimed at encouraging reconciliation in post-conflict Cambodia subsequent to 1993. However, the formula was not successful in producing a government of national unity within a reasonable period of time after the elections, because the political parties could not agree on the formation of a new government.

A King without Power

Some stakeholders in the Cambodian elections felt that the Cambodian Constitution did confer enough powers on the King to facilitate the resolution of political deadlocks of the kind that occurred after the 2003 National Assembly elections. The Constitution requires the King to be the symbol of national unity, and to reign but not govern. The King's role to act as an arbiter to ensure the regular functioning of powers is considered to fall short of the powers that would enable the King to solve political deadlocks in a timely manner.

Flawed Election Management Structure—Philippines

Many stakeholders lamented the weak electoral management structure of the Commission on Elections (COMELEC), which existed during the lead up to the 2004 Philippines national election, despite the fact that the Constitution of 1987 mandated a strong Commission independent of other branches of government. The basic management concept envisaged a Commission which made policy through the issuance of resolutions, and an operational arm which implemented policy and conducted the daily electoral affairs through civil servants managed by an executive director. In practice, however, what emerged was a system in which the Commissioners divided up all areas of responsibilities among themselves, resulting in different regions falling within the competence of individual Commissioners with little regard for, or coordination of, operational issues. The concept and role of the executive director was deemphasised and experienced diminution of authority and central control over operations. The Commission in charge (CIC) system, as it was called, facilitated the growth of influence, control and power in the hands of Commissioners, where it never belonged, at the expense of the responsibility and authority of the executive director. The CIC system fell short of the level of electoral management envisaged, or indeed required to deliver free and fair elections

Electoral Staff Professionalism Wanted

Stakeholders in the Philippines 2004 national elections complained that the need for greater professionalism among the electoral staff of COMELEC was urgent. They drew attention to the relatively large number of headquarters and field staff-over 5,000 in all—who were often recruited pursuant to unclear or uncertain rules regarding qualification, an absence of proper operating procedures and little or no staff-development programmes in place in COMELEC. Staff responsibilities were not clearly assigned and the execution of election tasks was not properly supervised.

Weaknesses in Strategic Areas

The preparatory processes for the Philippines 2004 national elections revealed a number of weaknesses in strategic areas, among which were;

- An absence of reliable communications inside headquarters, as well as with the field offices;
- The office was poorly equipped with computers and little or no on-line capacity;
- Shortages of office materials and even of election supplies such as ink and paper to print sufficient voters' lists for exhibition in all areas;
- Manifestly poor relationship between field offices and headquarters staff of COMELEC;
- Inadequate budgeting for the election, coupled with the late disbursement of allocated funds;
- Stakeholders widespread lack of confidence in the impartiality and competence of the COMELEC; and
- COMELEC reluctance to work with and openly embrace civil society organizations and the media.

Procedural Misstep

The Republic Act No. 8436 of the Philippines in 1997 conferred powers on the COMELEC to use an automated election system for the process of voting, counting votes and announcing election results. COMELEC, in its efforts to implement the law with respect to the automated system, apparently did not follow the public bidding procedure in awarding the contract for the acquisition of the voting machines and related equipment. COMELEC's action in circumventing the public bidding requirement was challenged in the Supreme Court which nullified the contract for the purchase of the voting machines. The programme for the automatic count and announcement of election results failed as a result of the Court's ruling.

A Further Procedural Misstep

COMELEC encountered a further procedural setback when the Supreme Court of the Philippines struck down its proposal to transmit the election results electronically, apparently because the parties had not been informed.

Reforming Voter Registration

In August 2003, COMELEC embarked on an ambitious programme of reforming the process of voter registration in the Philippines, which entailed the collection of biometric data, production of a centralized voters' list, and issuance of identification cards. The process was referred to as the Voters Validation System (VVS). The aim of the VVS was to facilitate the identification of duplicate entries. COMELEC was only able to validate a small portion of the electorate under the new system and there was not enough time to produce a centralized list in time for claims and appeals to be dealt with. The upshot was that a large number of voters remained on the decentralized system. In short, the VVS failed to meet its objective of producing a clean centralized list of voters.

Failure to Distribute Voters' Lists in Precincts

The woes of the COMELEC deepened when it was unable to distribute the voters' lists in every precinct in the Philippines. Moreover, the voters' lists that were produced were flawed and unusable on Election Day and COMELEC had to ask election officers to use the decentralized lists and records, which had become out of date. The consequence of the flawed voters' lists was the disenfranchisement of many voters on polling day.

Republic of China (Taiwan) Presidential Election 2004

Election Campaign Offices

A senior member of the Kuomintang/People First Party (also called the Pan-Blue Coalition Party) of Taiwan attempted to establish four campaign office branches on mainland China with the aim of persuading Taiwanese businessmen on the mainland to support that party. When the news about that development broke in Taiwan, it caused an uproar, which was aggravated by accompanying photograph of the Mr. Cheng-hao, a former Justice Minister and the party official behind the move to establish the branches on the mainland, with several fugitives from Taiwan. The leader of the Pan-Blue Coalition quickly distanced himself from the action and the former Minister wrote an essay indicating that his activities were not authorized. Shortly after the incident, the People's Republic of China issued instructions to local officials not to allow Taiwanese businessmen to openly campaign on the mainland.

A Shooting Incident

On the 19th March 2004, the day before polling in the presidential elections, President Chen Shui-bian and Vice President Annette Lu were shot while campaigning in Tainan. They were travelling in an open convertible jeep in the presidential motorcade, when one bullet struck the President in the stomach and lodged in his clothes. The reports suggested that the President suffered a wound 8 cm long and 2 cm deep. Another bullet grazed the knee of Vice President Lu and was found in the jeep. Their injuries were not life-threatening, and both were treated at the Chi-Mei Hospital and released the same day. The police quickly announced that they were certain that the crime was not political and that mainland China was not involved. In the meanwhile, chat rooms on the Internet, talk radio shows, and Pan Blue supporters theorized that the incident was faked in order for the President to gain sympathy votes.

Disputed Election Results

The election returns from the March 20 polls in the Taiwan presidential election show the incumbent Chen as re-elected. The opposition immediately denounced the vote as unfair and called for a recount. They demanded a full inquiry into the assassination attempt on Chen that happened the day before, describing it as surrounded by 'clouds of suspicion'. The opposition filed several lawsuits and led marches against the election results. The Central Election Commission confirmed the victory of President Chen on March 26, and the result was further confirmed by a small margin (25,563) after a judicial recount in May 2004.

Armenia Parliamentary Elections May 2003

Lack of Transparency

Despite the fact that formal sessions of the Central Election Commission (CEC) are open to proxies, accredited observers and the media, most of the decisions of that body were taken by its executive officers and secretariat outside of formal sessions. Further, there were frequent informal private meetings between the Chairman and Deputy Chairman and individual Territorial Election Commissions.

Uneven Rules Regarding Registration of Candidates

The Electoral Code (Article 97(2)) of Armenia prevents any person holding public office from contesting an election as a candidate in majoritarian constituencies, unless that person resigns prior to registration. However, there is no such restriction with respect to contesting the proportional election. The differences were highlighted in the lead up to the parliamentary elections in 2003 when two nominees were refused registration as majoritarian candidates for having failed to resign as

Community Heads, while the Mayor of Yerevan and the Minister of Defence registered as proportional list candidates while continuing in their official position during the campaign.

Refusal or Deregistration of Candidates

The parliamentary elections of Armenia in May 2003 experienced an unusually high level of refusal and or attempts at deregistration of candidates. Stakeholders reported many instances of refusal to register candidates on ground of failure to declare fully their personal property. One reason for this confused state of affairs was that the definition of property for these purposes was unclear and seemed to have included elements of constructive ownership, as in the case of family property where candidates were often deemed to possess an equitable interest in property belonging to other family members. The Central Election Commission (CEC) had no guidelines and did not give clear instructions on the issue. Stakeholders reported that there were instances of discriminatory practices in the manner in which property checks were made with local authorities—mainly against opposition candidates. Some refusal to register candidates was based on invalid or false signatures and no opportunity was afforded the prospective candidate to take remedial measures. There were cases where constituency boundaries had been changed recently and nominees who had obtained signatures of voters who were previously, but no longer, resided within the constituency. A substantial number of the refusal to register prospective candidates were overturned by the courts which held, in a couple of instances that valid signatures were wrongly declared to be false. One candidate who had been deregistered by the CEC on the grounds of failing to declare fully his property for the purposes of a party's list, was reinstated by the court, but that same person was denied registration as a majoritarian candidate on the same grounds by a Territorial Election Commission and upheld in another court.

Election Gifts and Promises

During the election campaign of 25 May 2003 in Armenia, many political parties, contrary to the stipulations of the Electoral Code, provided or promise to provide free goods and services to citizens during the pre-election period. Stakeholders complained of the distribution of gifts of fuel, food and computers to individuals, while the asphalting of roads and repairs to apartment buildings were carried out by some parties and or candidates.

Falsification of Results

Many instances of falsification of election results were reported by stakeholders during the counting of votes in the May 2003 parliamentary elections in Armenia including:

- Falsification of the result protocols in nine precinct election commissions;
- Destruction of valid ballots to achieve tally balance;
- Falsification of signatures on the voters list;
- Ballot stuffing was seen in many polling stations and even during the count at some stations; and
- Irregularities short of falsification, such as interference with ballot materials, overturning an open ballot box, reopening sealed envelopes of counted ballots, not invalidated unused ballot papers.

France, Presidential Election April-May 2007

Proxy Voting on the Rise

According to the report of the *Conseil Constitutionnel (*Constitutional Council*)* proxy voting increased by one million, to three million, in the 2007 elections over the previous presidential elections in 2002. Proxy voting offers wide and easy access to voters in France—anyone who is registered to vote may apply on grounds of professional obligations, health, education or holiday, to vote by proxy, if he/she is unable to vote at the polling station where he/she is registered. The voter is only required to sign a 'declaration of honour' to support the absence. The proxy facility is often used by the military, prison inmates and the sick. The procedure allows a voter to apply to vote by proxy at any time up to the day before polling. The proxy-voter is required to be registered in the same commune (municipality) as the principal, but is not required to vote at the same polling station. A proxy's mandate may be revoked at any time by the voter who issued it.

Gens Du Voyage (Travellers) (France)

This phrase applies to a general group of persons who undertake itinerant work. The law required anyone falling into the category of *gens du voyage* to be attached to a commune for at least three years in order to register on the voters' list in that location. Upon registration, a person is given an identification card, which should enable the holder there of to vote on polling day, but there was uncertainty as to the true status of the identification card issued with respect to the *gens du voyage.* Stakeholders complained about the long period of attachment in a commune before registration could be achieved and sought changes to the procedure. Although a National Consultative Commission was established to improve the application of the law relating to *gens du voyage,* the performance of the Commission in the years leading up to the 2007 presidential elections was considered unsatisfactory by stakeholders

Electronic Voting in the 2007 French Presidential Elections

The introduction of electronic voting in France has been gradual and a considerable amount of preparatory work had been done through pilot schemes in many communes. The electoral and legal framework had also witnessed considerable efforts to strengthen the electoral environment to cope with wide scale use of electronic voting. However, the plans for use of electronic voting in the 2007 presidential elections were modest—use in 83 cities involving a mere three percent of the electorate. The technical specifications for voting machines were in some cases imprecise and unclear, and so were the precise functions to be performed. One interpretation suggested that the voting machines could only be used for automating the voting and counting processes, which might not include voter identification and list checking. The specification did not require the voting machines to produce a 'voter verifiable paper audit trail', which would have enhanced the voters' confidence in the new system. After the first round of voting in the 2007 presidential elections, a small number (4) communes decided to revert to the old paper ballot system and not to continue using the voting machines. Although the use of the system improved in the second round, many voters were still unfamiliar with the system.

Sponsorship Auction

French electoral law requires, among other things, a prospective presidential candidate to have at least 500 elected officials from at least 30 different districts, departments or overseas collectives in France with a maximum of one tenth of the sponsors coming from any one district. The elected officials include member of French Parliament, the European Parliament, regional and local councils, elected bodies of overseas territorial units and mayors. The method of securing sponsors was not well regulated or organized. There complaints by stakeholders that potential sponsors were pressured by candidates or by their parties to give or refuse their support for particular candidates. One Mayor reportedly publicly auctioned his sponsorship for 1,550 Euros to a potential candidate who ultimately failed to secure the required 500. The sponsorship issue is unclear and controversial in some respects, for example, it is not clear whether the names of all the sponsors of a particular candidate, or only those up to the required 500, should be published.

A Conundrum—Ballot Box versus Voting Machine

On polling day during the 2007 French presidential elections, polling officials had to deal with the application of the electoral law relating to ballot boxes—was a voting machine the equivalent of one or more ballot boxes? The law allowed only one ballot box per polling station. The *Conseil Constitutionnel* indicated that multiple voting machines could be considered as a single ballot box only if linked in an internal network. However, there was no clear instructions given and there were many instances of the use of multiple voting machines in a polling station which were not linked in a network.

The Incidence of 'Under Voting'

The use of voting machines-three types of voting machines were used-threw up the incidence of 'under voting', which occurred when a voter does not complete the voting process required by the machine. One type of voting machines used during the French presidential elections of 2007 produced a risk of not finalizing the voting process where a voter left without completing the process and the president of the polling station had to decide if a vote should be cancelled or confirmed. If the president cancelled the vote, the final printout would include an under vote, and there were no clear rules dealing with how an under vote should be recorded in the results protocols.

Canada Parliamentary Elections January 2006

Good Record of Conducting Free and Fair Elections

Canada had a good record of organizing and conducting free and fair democratic elections. Stakeholders generally agreed that the conduct of the 2006 parliamentary elections was in keeping with that tradition. The credibility of the election process was well established in Canada. The process was generally transparent and had inbuilt accountability to stakeholders. Public confidence was good, although the voter turnout was, at 64.9 percent, was modest.

Constituency Boundaries

In Canada, the boundaries of constituencies (electoral districts) are constructed by an Electoral Boundaries Commission which was established in each province, and consisted of three members. In theory, the commission should divide the province into constituencies with equal population, but allowance is made for deviation from the average population size of constituency in the province to accommodate situations of minority concentration or sparse population distribution. The deviation allowed may be up to or below 25 percent of the average population size of constituencies in the province. At the time of the parliamentary elections of 2006, the average size of a constituency was 74, 067 voters, although the 2001 census in Canada showed the smallest constituency has well below the average, 26,745 voters, while the largest constituency had 124, 572 voters, again considerably above the average.

Campaign Period Too Long

Some stakeholders complained the campaign period for the 2006 parliamentary elections was too long. It lasted 56 days, while the minimum campaign allowed under Canada Elections Act was 36 days. That long period seemed unusually long as for several decades the campaign period in Canada had not exceeded the minimum period. The focus of the complaint of some stakeholders was on the running a longer campaign with existing contribution and spending limits.

Canadian Aboriginal Peoples and 'Visible Minorities'.

According to the 2001 census of Canada, there were 976, 305 persons who described themselves as aboriginal. The Canadian Indian Act of 1985 conferred certain guaranteed rights on the aboriginal people and Elections Canada had been implementing several of the electoral requirements. The Chief Electoral Officer of Canada consults and maintains regular contact with representatives of national and regional Aboriginal organizations. Prior to the 2006 elections, a strong voter education programme was mounted to encourage the Aboriginal people to vote.

In Canada, ethno-cultural communities were sometimes called 'visible minorities'. The Employment Equity Act defined them as 'persons other than aboriginal people, who are non-Caucasian in race or non-white in colour'. The 2001 census recorded some 4 million persons who identified themselves as visible minorities. Many of those communities participate actively in politics and form a significant political force in their communities. The general perception, although not supported by reliable data, is that the 'visible minorities' turn out in lower numbers to vote than other Canadian born citizens.

USA Presidential Elections 2000

Focus on Florida

It is perhaps the general consensus inside and outside of the United States of America that the 2000 presidential elections threw up serious shortcomings in the election administration in Florida. There were problems with voting equipment, inadequate training of election personnel, and inaccuracies in voters' register, multiple ballot design and counting procedures, unclear regulations with respect to overseas voting, and poor voter education programmes.

Post-2000 Presidential Elections

Electoral Reform in Florida

The breakdown of the electoral system in Florida affected the credibility of the presidential elections not only in Florida but also in the whole United States. The Governor, Jeb Bush, quickly appointed a bi-partisan task force to look into the election procedures, standards and technology in Florida. The *Task Force on Election Procedures, Standards and Technology* reported in March 2001 and made a number of recommendations which included the following:

- Florida should establish a uniform and standardized state wide voting system for the 2002 elections;
- There should be adequate state and county funding for better voter education;
- More qualified poll workers should be recruited;
- Uniform state wide standards should be established for counts and recounts for each type of voting system;
- The development of an on-line voter registration system; and

- The adoption of uniform closing times in all time zones throughout the state.

Implementation of Electoral Reform in Florida

The Florida Reform Act was passed in 2001. It included many recommendations made by the Task Force of which the most significant were:

- Changes with respect to administrative practices regarding voter registration and the creation of a state wide voter register;
- The abandonment of punch card voting, optical scan with centralized tabulation and lever machines voting methods;
- The establishment of guidelines to ensure greater uniformity in ballot design;
- Introduction of 'provisional voting' to mitigate errors in or omissions from the voters' register;
- Formulation of improved procedures to deal with recounts and undertaking of voters' intention during manual review of under-voted and over-voted ballots;
- Provision of stricter requirements for the training of polling station staff; and
- Establishment of minimum standards for planning and implementation of voter education programmes.

USA-General Elections November 2002

Focus on Florida

The Florida Reform Act of 2001 set the stage for improved election organization in that state in the 2002 general elections, and many stakeholders and international election observers showed an interest regarding the application of the electoral reform package. As an important part of the reform package, many new technologies were introduced for use in the November elections. Touch screen voting and optical scanning systems were introduced and served to overcome the incidence of under and over voting that caused serious problems in the 2000 presidential elections. The touch screen machines did not allow for voting for more than one choice, while the optical scanning machines were programmed to reject a ballot containing more than one choice in the same contest. The new systems were user-friendly and gave voters, including elderly voters, a higher level of confidence that their votes would be counted.

Training Election Officers for the Florida General Elections 2002

With the 2000 presidential election experience fresh in their minds, the election authorities in Florida tried to raise the level of training for election officials. In some counties, polling officials received 24 hours or more of training, while other counties calculated the amount of training offered in aggregate of 'person hours', often reaching a level of 12, 000 'person hours'. Some counties felt the need to offer refresher training courses immediately before polling day. Many counties offered special courses to tackle the setting up and operation of the voting machines. The effort seemed to have worked reasonably well as many stakeholders reported improved performance by election officials during the 2002 elections over the presidential elections of 2000.

USA 2004 Presidential Elections

Electoral Officials

In the USA, the principal state and county election officials are either elected to their office or nominated by political parties. In the main, election officials in the USA perform their duties in a professional manner. As was revealed in Florida in 2000, sometimes election officers in the USA perform their duties in an incompetent manner. The method of appointment of election officials in the US would not be acceptable in some new and emerging democracies, but the political dimension of the appointments of those officials has not been a serious issue. Even though the potential for conflict of interest is real when a state or county election official runs for public office, or actively campaigns for a candidate, there seems to be little attempt on a national scale to legislate against such eventuality.

Votes Forwarded by Facsimile Transmission

Federal law in the USA established minimum standard for states to facilitate absentee voting for federal offices by out-of-country voting. Some states allow out-of-country voting by enabling marked ballots to be transmitted by facsimile method. That approach entailed sacrificing secrecy in order to ensure that the exercise of the franchise is done and the vote is counted.

Access to Polling Stations by Election Observers

There was no 'universal' access to polling stations in all states during the presidential elections of 2004. In some states, election observers reported limited or no access to polling stations in some counties. Access depended on state law which did not, except in the case of Missouri, provide for international observers (a concept that was not well understood in the USA) to be in polling places. Even where the state law was silent on the issue, access was often denied to international observers. There was no provision for non-partisan domestic election observers to enter polling stations. In several states in the USA election administrators had discretion whether or not to admit election observers into polling stations. To that extent, the voting process in many states in the USA in 2004 was not fully transparent and further reforms may be necessary.

Voting in Federal Elections in the USA

Voting in elections for federal office which include direct elections for the House of Representatives and the Senate and indirect elections for the President and Vice President is open to citizens of the United States who are also citizens of a state. The upshot is that citizens who are not of a state were not eligible to vote in federal legislative elections. This applies to citizens of Washington D.C., but with the exception that the citizens may vote in a presidential election. The District of Columbia and some US territories have been facilitated with a channel to the US Congress by the ability to each elect a non-voting delegate to the House of Representatives for two years by direct elections. Delegates elected by the non-state territories can participate in committee meetings, but cannot vote on issues that come for decisions to the full House. The apparent limitation of an important political right, that is, right of US citizens to vote in elections for the federal legislature, had attracted adverse comments by human rights activists and others for a long time, but the courts have not agreed with those critics.

Nature of Election Administration in the USA.

The electoral administration system in the USA was decentralized. There was no central administration body mandated to run elections throughout the USA. Two federal bodies had limited national mandates; these were the Federal Election Commission (FEC) and the Election Assistance Commission (EAC), both of which were appointed by the President and approved by the Senate. The FEC had responsibilities with respect to over viewing the campaign finance regulations and protection of the right to vote in federal elections. It was composed of six members (including the chairman), three Democrats and three Republicans. The members were all nominated by the President after consultations with congressional leaders. The EAC was an advisory body charged with the issuing of guidelines and recommendations with respect to the implementation of the 2002 electoral reform programme and the Help America Vote Act (HAVA). It had four members (including the chairman) two Republicans and two Democrats, who were nominated by the President after consultation with congressional leaders. These bodies strive to take decisions by consensus, but often fail. In most states, the election process was administered by or under the authority of the Secretary of State. Counties and other electoral jurisdictions had a high degree of autonomy in organizing and conducting elections in their areas.

Electoral Districts Delimitation-An Imperfect Formula

The formula for delimiting electoral districts for elections to the House of Representatives admits of the wishes of particular geographical groups of persons being taken into account. Some stakeholders believed that such flexibility had an effect on re-districting and could render some congressional contests uncompetitive.

Review of Available Election Technology

The widely publicized difficulties experienced in Florida in the 2000 presidential elections, ushered in national review of election technology in the USA, with a strong focus on voting machines. There were some five widely used voting technologies in the USA in 2000—lever machines, punch-card machines, paper ballots, optical scan, and direct-recording electronic (DRE) machines. Although the old technologies that performed so poorly in Florida in the 2000 presidential elections will inevitably be phased out, the states and their electoral sub-jurisdictions were not agreed on what was to replace them. The DRE machines were front runners in some states, but were subject to litigation in several states. It was reported that over 48 million voters used the DRE machines in the 2004 presidential elections. However, the DRE machines fall into three categories, namely, touch-screen voting systems with a paper trail, that allows verification by the voter before the vote is cast-(called voter-verified auditable paper trail (VVAPT)); touch-screen voting system without a voter verified paper trail; and push button devices. The machines used for voting had to be certified and there is a movement toward some form of standardization. In order to speed up that trend, the National Association of State Election Directors (NASED) established the Federal Voting Systems Standards (FVSS), but those standards were not legally binding.

Swiss Confederation Federal Election 2007

Particular Features of the Swiss Election Environment

The confederation of Switzerland had 26 cantons with varying degrees of autonomy. It is a parliamentary democracy which had four national languages, namely, German, French, Italian and Romansh. Among the special features of particular relevance to the Swiss electoral environment were the following:

- Members of the National Council were elected through a proportional system;
- Most members of the Council of States were elected through a majority system;
- The administration of elections in Switzerland was decentralized;
- Over 80 percent of Swiss voters voted by postal ballot;
- Swiss electorate had a high level of confidence in the electoral system and process and in the integrity and non-partisanship of the election administration;
- The legislative framework did not provide for non-partisan election observation, but some cantons did allow for election observers;
- Political parties did not receive funding from the Federal State for campaign activities and regulations for campaign financing or financial disclosures were lacking;
- There was no specific federal or cantonal regulation dealing with media coverage of election campaigns; and
- Women were only granted the franchise in federal elections in 1971 and remained under represented in parliament as there was no quota system to facilitate women's inclusion on election lists.

Legal Framework for the 2007 Elections

Federal elections in Switzerland are governed by the Federal Act on Political Rights of 17 December 1976 (as amended) which defined the general framework, and cantonal laws and decrees provided for the detailed rules and regulations for the conduct of elections. The election regulations dealing with matters such as election administration, election system, voting and counting procedures, or election observation, may vary from canton to canton. The cantons are required to publish election results promptly in the official gazette and not later than eight days after the election. That publication triggers the running of time for filing of complaints which must be done within three days of the publication of results.

Vote Splitting or 'Panachage'

One interesting feature of the Swiss voting process is vote splitting or 'panachage'. This happens when a voter change a pre-printed ballot paper by deleting one or more candidates, adding, or replacing candidates with names from other electoral lists from the same constituencies. However, a voter can vote by just using the pre-printed ballot paper without changing the list of candidates. A voter may also enter the name of one candidate twice, or may complete a blank ballot paper with candidates' names and party reference numbers.

High Level of Postal Voting

Over 80 percent of Swiss voters use postal voting, notwithstanding that there is the option of going in person to the polling station—in some areas more than 90 percent of voters voted by post. Postal voting can take place from the time the voting materials arrive until Election Day, as long as the materials reach the cantonal chancellery before the polls close. The cantonal chancellery usually arranged for a post-box delivery system for the ballots before polling day. The chancellery is responsible for the security of the ballots which were sorted according to polling station so that the ballots were counted together with those that were cast in person on polling day.

United Kingdom Devolved Election in Northern Ireland-26 November 2003

In the lead up to the devolved elections in Northern Ireland, the authorities took a number of measures to reduce the incidence of election irregularities which had occurred in past elections. Family registration, which had previously allowed, was abandoned and each person had to register individually. Photo identification requirements were introduced for registration and voting. The upshot was that the new voters' register was reduced by 10% or about 130,000 voters. However, some stakeholders were dissatisfied with the new requirements for registration on the grounds that they placed disadvantaged groups, such as the elderly and disabled voters, who had less access to the stipulated documents.

The EMB of Northern Ireland

The United Kingdom Electoral Commission was based in London with subsidiary offices in Northern Ireland, Wales and Scotland. It was an independent statutory body accountable to Parliament and had as its primary functions provision of advice and assistance to election officials, political parties and candidates. The Commission had the responsibility for the registration of political parties and the monitoring of national political party election campaign spending. Of particular relevance to Northern Ireland in the pre-election preparation in 2003 was the Commission's role in the conduct of voter outreach programmes in the light of the significant changes to the voter registration system. The Commission in conjunction with the Northern Ireland Electoral Office (EONI), published training manuals and handbooks for presiding officers, poll clerks, counting staff, and candidates and agents.

The Chief Electoral Officer (CEO), who is appointed by the Secretary of State for Northern Ireland, was responsible for compiling the voter register. The CEO was supported by officials of EONI based in Belfast and nine area electoral offices. The CEO was the returning officer of Northern Ireland, while the area election officers acted as deputy returning officers at the elections. The CEO was responsible for the recruitment, appointment and training of presiding officers and poll clerks for each polling station.

The Electoral Fraud Act 2002

The Electoral Fraud Act of 2002 set new standard for voter registration in Northern Ireland. As mentioned above, prospective voters were required to register individually and in doing so provide personal information, such as National Insurance Number. Four types of photo identification was acceptable for voting, namely, a current Northern Ireland or Great Britain driver's license, a UK or European Union passport, senior 'smart card' issued under the Northern Ireland Concessionary Fares Scheme, or a special electoral identity card issued by the Electoral Office. Each person was required to re-register annually. Registration was compulsory in Northern Ireland and eligible persons who failed to register were liable to pay a fine up to a 1, 000 pounds sterling.

Voting Procedures—Defects

The voting procedures in Northern Ireland came under close scrutiny for two reasons, namely, the electoral legislative scheme was very restrictive with respect to the admission of election observers at polling stations and the potential for the compromise of the secrecy of the ballot. The secrecy issue had come about because as each ballot was issued, the voter's number was written onto the counterfoil which was serially numbered. The same serial number was printed on the back of the ballot allowing each ballot to be traced to the person who cast it.

United Kingdom-General Elections 2005

Electoral Environment

Democratic elections had been conducted in Great Britain and Northern Ireland for a long time. In accordance with the established tradition, the May 2005 general elections were administered in a professional manner. The stakeholders had confidence in the electoral management. The voters were offered genuine choice in a competitive political environment. The election campaign was conducted in a fair and open manner in which the parties and candidates freely presented their platform to the electorate.

Although paid political broadcasting was not allowed, the self-regulating and free media gave broad coverage to the election campaign. The electoral legislative framework consisted of laws, regulations and court decisions, but needed further modernization to permit unrestricted access to polling stations during polling and counting of votes to domestic and international election observers. Many stakeholders expressed unease about the postal voting procedures and suggested that the protection against election fraud was inadequate.

Electoral System for Westminster Parliament

Members of the House of Commons are elected under the first past the post system in one round of voting and in single member constituencies. Candidates were sponsored by political parties or ran as independents. The candidate who received the highest number of votes in a constituency wins the seat. The average number of electors per constituency was 68, 390. A review and delimitation (where required) of constituency boundaries took place every ten years by independent boundary commissions. The delimitation process whenever it took place was considered to transparent and the local people may require an inquiry during the process.

Voter Registration System

The voter registration system for the Westminster Parliament had a number of features worth noting as follows:

- Voter registers are compiled by local government officials;
- The annual publication date for the voter registers was 1 December;
- Each householder was required to fill out a form listing all eligible voters in the household;
- Registration was not compulsory, except in Northern Ireland, but the registration form had to be returned, failing which sanctions would be incurred;
- Voluntary 'rolling registration' was introduced in 2000 to allow voters to amend their registration;

- There was no national register, as voter registration was decentralized and remained the responsibility of local government officials;
- There was no standardized format for voter registers;
- Voter registers were kept in two forms, namely, full registers, which contain names, addresses, and electoral numbers of voters, and 'edited' which could be purchased.

Postal Voting

Postal ballot was available on request in Great Britain for the 2005 general elections without the need to give reasons for the request. It was introduced to stimulate voter participation. A voter could apply in writing for a postal ballot up to six days prior to polling day. In order to be counted, a postal ballot must reach the presiding officer of a polling station or the electoral registration office by 22.00 hours on polling day in order to be counted. Postal voting procedures were established to facilitate voters who were unable or did not wish to go to in person to their assigned polling station. The volume of postal voting was on the increase to the extent that some election administrators had to contract out services to private companies in order to process the postal ballots in a timely manner. With that development, many stakeholders had become concerned that election materials were being processed by persons, other than election officials, some of whom might have been partisans who supported a particular party.

Ireland Parliamentary Elections May 2007

Electoral Environment

The elections of May 2007 to the Irish Parliament (Dáil Ėireann) were conducted in a stable and peaceful atmosphere reflecting the democratic tradition in Ireland. The stakeholders, in particular voters, political parties, and candidates indicated that they had confidence in the electoral administration and indeed in the process as a whole. The electoral legislative framework was good and capable of delivering free and fair elections; however, some stakeholders felt that the legislative scheme was somewhat inhibitive of the legitimate role of civil society organizations. The media provided extensive and balanced coverage of the election campaign. The public radio and television performed well and set up its own self-regulating mechanism to resolve complaints in an informal manner. The Department of Environment, Heritage and Local Government gave guidance to returning offices that were responsible for the elections to the Parliament. The legislative scheme did not provide for observers to enter polling and counting stations, but some international observers were granted access. There was no independent electoral management body in place.

Campaign Financing and Reporting

The election campaign period in Ireland during the 2007 parliamentary elections was regulated by law and donations received and expenditures incurred for the period commencing with the date on which the Parliament was dissolved and ending on election day had to be reported on to Standards in Public Office Commission. As in other democracies, the actual campaign spending started well before the official campaign period. Non-governmental organizations complained about certain provisions of the law (1997 Electoral Act) which limited their ability to advocate issues during the election campaign, because they were required to register as 'third parties' if they received donations which exceeded Euros126.97 for political purposes and disclose their donors. Donations for political purposes from the same donors in any year should not exceed Euros 6, 348.69.

High Cost of Challenges of Elections to the Dáil

The law (Electoral Act 1992) set the deposit fee for a challenge of an election to the Dáil at 5, 000 pounds sterling, but the court could set a lower fee. Some stakeholders felt that the high deposit could serve as a deterrence to legitimate aggrieved persons seeking legal redress.

Electoral System

The Dáil Ėireann (Parliament) had 166 members who were elected from 43 multi-member constituencies by a single transferable vote (STV) system. The system is proportional and each constituency returned three, four or five members, depending on the population size in the constituency. The STV system allowed a voter to indicate his/her preference for as many candidates as were included on the ballot paper and to rank them in numerical order of preference. This preferential system of voting allowed the voter to transfer his/her vote to another candidate if the candidate of first choice did not need the vote because he/she had already been elected (or cannot be elected).

Seats were allocated on the basis of candidates who received as many valid votes as the size of the quota, which was determined as one plus the ratio of the total of all valid votes divided by the number of seats allocated by a constituency plus one.

Electoral Administration

The electoral administration in Ireland during the 2007 elections was decentralised. There were 23 returning officers who were responsible for the election administration. They were selected from county registrars (except in the cases of Dublin City, Dublin County, Cork City and Cork County, where the sheriffs were appointed as returning officers). Some returning officers had responsibility for more than one constituency, in which case a deputy returning officer would be appointed by each such returning officer. The Franchise Section of the Environment, Heritage and Local Government performed an overseeing role with respect to election administration. The Section had a ten person team which provided policy and legislative advice, and provided guidance and to local authorities and returning officers during the parliamentary elections.

Features of the Voting Process-Ireland

There were about 6,000 polling stations or 'tables' run by presiding offices, assisted by poll clerks, both of whom were selected by returning officers. The training procedures entailed a briefing of presiding officers, although not all presiding offers attend briefings, as many seemed to settle for training materials only. Roving election officers are employed by returning officers to go from polling station to polling station to ensure that the guidelines and rules were being followed. Although there were no minimum numbers of voters assigned to each polling station, the numbers ranged from 400-700. Voters were notified of the polling stations where they should vote prior to polling day. There were a number of cases (involving some 3,000 voters) where special voting took place and the presiding officers, accompanied by police, took the ballot paper to the voter. There was posting for several categories of voters, such as civil servants abroad, defence forces abroad, police, certified disabled, students and prisoners. Stakeholders complained that there were instances of the official stamp not being used to stamp ballots rendering them invalid.

Voter Registration-Ireland

The voter registration process had been criticized by many stakeholders and the registers attracted even more complaints such as individuals receiving several poll cards in multiple counties as well as in the same county. The names of qualified persons were omitted from the register. The accuracy of the voter register in 2007 was an issue. The voter registration system in Ireland was locally based, although guidelines were issued by the central government. The register was compiled pursuant to the Electoral Act of 1992. The town and county council each year appointed the local registration authority in its respective area to undertake an intensive door to door canvass of each neighbourhood to compile the voter register. The register was used for local, national and European elections and was published by 1 November each year for public scrutiny.

Belize General Election-7 February 2008

An EMB Enmeshed in Bureaucracy

There were two election management bodies (EMBs), the Elections and Boundaries Commission and the Elections and Boundaries Department, in Belize. The Commission was responsible for the direction and supervision of registration of voters and the conduct of elections. The Elections and Boundaries Department in Belize was established in 1989 with functions of actually organizing and directing the registration of voters and the conduct of elections. However, the electoral staff matters, including those relating to the Chief Elections Officer, were dealt with by the Public Services Commission. The Department headed by the Chief Elections Officer fell under the oversight of the Office for Good Governance which in turn was under the Office of the Prime Minister. The Chief Elections Officer and staff were responsible for the day to day operations of the electoral process. Some stakeholders felt that the fact that one of the two election management bodies report to the Prime Minister's Office compromised the independence of election management structure. As if to complicate the already complex election management structure, the Director of the Office of Good Governance was the former Chief Elections Officer who was playing a hands-on and pro-active role on election matters during the election campaign.

No Cellular Phones with Cameras at Polling Stations

Stakeholders in the 2008 elections expressed strong concern about the proposed use of cellular phones with cameras in polling stations. Some civil society organizations were particularly disturbed with that development. The belief was that the cell phones would be used in polling booths to photograph how voters exercised their vote and be part of a vote-buying scheme. The Election and Boundaries Commission agreed to ban cell phones in polling stations, but the parties and the Commission could not agree on the administrative and legislative requirements to implement such a ban. Eventually, on the day before the elections, the Prime Minister signed a statutory instrument allowing cell phones into polling stations, but forbidding the taking of photos with them.

The Harmonized Elections of Zimbabwe in 2008

Electoral Environment

The environment was peaceful, although there were sporadic incidents of intimidation and political violence. The principal stakeholders played a constructive role in creating and maintaining calm and tranquillity during polling. Freedom of assembly, association, movement and of speech was exercised without due hindrance.

Dispersed Election Management Authority

The election management authority of Zimbabwe had always been dispersed and until the recent reforms prior to the 2008 elections there were four bodies, namely the Delimitation Commission, the Electoral Supervisory Commission, the Election Directorate and Registrar General of Voters, involved in organizing and conducting the electoral process. Despite the reforms carried out prior to the 2008 harmonized elections, when some of the foregoing bodies were either abolished or stripped of some of their responsibilities, their replacements were no less widely dispersed, prompting some observers to remark that the more things change in Zimbabwe, the more they stay the same. The upshot of the dispersed nature of the election management authority had been to reduce the authority of the Zimbabwe Electoral Commission (ZEC) to a mere supervisory entity. The management structure had been complicated by the legal ability of the Zimbabwe Electoral Commission to set up one or more sub-committees. In pursuance of the foregoing power, the ZEC established a National Logistics Committee and sub-committees to assist it in mobilizing resources for the 2008 elections. The members of the committee and its sub-committees were drawn from various government ministries, the security and other sector bodies.

Delimitation of Constituencies

The Zimbabwe Electoral Commission (ZEC) was responsible for the delimitation of constituencies, but according to stakeholders when the

ZEC carried out the delimitation exercise between 5 December 2007 and 10 January 2008, there was little or no consultation with stakeholders. Some observers felt that the delimitation process was insufficiently consultative and participative. Stakeholders expressed concern that the delimitation process distorted the constituency boundaries by linking urban areas with rural or sub-urban districts. They also pointed out that more new constituencies were created in rural than in urban areas where the opposition was believed to have had strong support.

Use of State Resources

Election stakeholders and observers reported that the incumbent President of Zimbabwe made various donations to communities and organizations throughout the country during the lead up to the elections of 2008. The donations included buses, television sets, food aid, and agricultural equipment.

Presidential Intervention in Polling Station Management-Zimbabwe 2008.

Contrary to good practice, the President, through Presidential Powers (Temporary Measures) (Amendment of Electoral Act) (No. 2) Regulation, departed from previous understandings by allowing the police to enter the polling stations and assist some voters in casting their ballots. That change was done without consultation with some principal stakeholders, apparently including the Electoral Commission.

Uzbekistan-Parliamentary Elections-December 26 2004

The Electoral Landscape

The electoral landscape in Uzbekistan displayed characteristics which were less than ideal to support free and fair multiparty elections. Stakeholders complained that the authorities implemented the legislative provisions in a manner which did not facilitate the organization of a pluralistic, competitive and transparent election. The mechanism for registering new political parties was restrictive and independent candidates were not encouraged. Fundamental freedoms, in particular, freedom of expression, association and assembly were restricted and what little existed was often not respected. The registration of candidates to contest the elections was anything but straightforward as there were difficulties with the verification of signatures and the perception was that those who criticized the incumbent administration would be rejected.

Election Administration

The election administrative structure that was in place for the 2004 Uzbekistan parliamentary elections consisted of the Central Election Commission (CEC), 120 District (Constituency) Election Committees (DECs) and 8,046 Polling Station Committees (PSCs). Stakeholders expressed dissatisfaction with the composition of DECs. The legislative scheme was not clear as how those bodies should be staffed, but members of any political party were excluded from all electoral committees.

Media Environment

Although the media environment in Uzbekistan displayed a measure of diversity in the period leading up to the 2004 elections, the free and independent media were not encouraged. Moreover, there was often strict state control on reporting on the government and presidential affairs. Some stakeholders believed that the environment was unfavourable, and even hostile, to independent journalists, who saw the use of the Internet as a way to escape some aspects of the restrictions. Many journalists and editors practised self-censorship to avoid the worst form of interference and control by to authorities. The registration of the broadcast media was complicated and involved multiple agencies and the licence had to be renewed annually.

The 2000 Parliamentary Elections in Zimbabwe

Delimitation of Constituencies

The Delimitation Commission was responsible for the delimitation of the 120 constituencies in Zimbabwe in 2000. The Constitution required the constituencies' boundaries to be reviewed every five years, but the review took place between April and May 2000, well after the review period had expired. The exercise was not conducted efficiently, as the preliminary report was submitted to the President without the usual accompanying maps on 12 May 2000. The final report, with maps, was submitted to the President on the 24 May 2000, five days before the registration of candidates (nomination day) to contest the elections, and the election dates had already been set for June 24-25 2000. Stakeholders expressed displeasure at the manner in which the delimitation review was carried out, and accused the Commission of constructing the constituencies' boundaries in unfair way which amounted to gerrymandering in favour of the incumbent party. They drew attention to the fact that in a number of cases parts of rural constituencies were incorporated into urban areas in a manner which appeared that the intention was to dilute the urban vote where the opposition parties were strong.

Multiple EMBs Led to Confusion

The multiplicity of election management bodies (EMB) in Zimbabwe at the time of the parliamentary elections in 2000 caused confusion at times. There were the Delimitation Commission, the Electoral Supervisory Commission (ESC), the Election Directorate, and the Registrar-General. The line of responsibility between each EMB was not always clear, and so when ESC was given the role of appointing election monitors but only after the monitors had been accredited by the Registrar General pursuant to the Electoral (Amendment) Regulations 2000, the ESC took the matter to the High Court unsuccessfully. The Registrar-General was responsible for the conduct of all aspects of the electoral process-the register of voters, appointment and training of polling staff, acquisition of election materials, accreditation of monitors, the counting of ballots and the announcement of results. The Electoral Law stated that the Registrar-General was not subject to the direction or control of any person or authority other than the Election Directorate, but shall have regard to any report or recommendation of the ESC. Yet the Office of Registrar-General falls under the portfolio of the Ministry of Home Affairs for the purposes of registration of voters and under the Ministry of Justice in the conduct of other aspects of the electoral process. Many stakeholders expressed concern about the independence of the Registrar-General. According to stakeholders, the Registrar-General fulfilled some of his duties for example, submitting timely reports on the registration of voters to the ESC grudgingly, or failed to do so at all.

Unbridled Violence

During the election campaign for the 2000 parliamentary elections in Zimbabwe, violence, intimidation and coercion occurred throughout the country, and mainly directed at the opposition. Stakeholders complained of rapes, murders, beatings and burning of houses of opposition supporters. Many hundreds were killed, thousands displaced and many thousands were injured. Attempts, often accompanied by violence, were made to're-educate' opposition supporters. Night time 'pungwe' sessions were held in some rural areas to persuade voters to support the ruling party. Some stakeholders reported the existence of 'no-go areas where opposition parties could not hold rallies. The war veterans were blamed for much of the violence and intimidation against the opposition.

Presidential Election of the Republic of Kazakhstan-December 2005

Electoral Landscape

The electoral landscape leading up to the Kazakhstan presidential elections of 2005 was characterized by restrictions and intimidation of opposition parties. There were restrictions on campaigning, harassment of campaign staff, outdoor political meetings were rarely allowed by the local authorities. Meetings of opposition candidates were often disrupted. Stakeholders reported that the ruling party put pressure on workers of state enterprises and private companies to support the ruling party.

Although state media honoured their obligation to grant free air time to all parties, there was distinct bias in favour of the incumbents. There were reports of several instances of the authorities confiscating entire editions of opposition newspapers. The representation of opposition parties on election commissions at all levels was low. Notwithstanding the many shortcomings, the Central Election Commission administered the election in a transparent manner, particularly in the preparatory stages.

Restrictions on Political Meetings

During the lead up to the presidential elections in 2005, the Law on Peaceful Assembles stipulated that local authorities had the authority to decide whether or not to grant permission for the holding of a meeting and the time and place there of. Ten days notice was required when requesting permission for a meeting. Some stakeholders consider such time period to be unreasonable. There were many vague grounds on which a local authority could substitute another time and venue for the ones applied for. The provisions of the Peaceful Assemblies Law applied to out door meetings as well.

Election Administration

The structure of the presidential elections in Kazakhstan consisted of a five-tiered system of election commissions of which the premiere body was the Central Election Commission (CEC). The other four levels of commissions were: the second level consisted of 16 commissioners; the third level had 14 Regional Election Commissions and the two city election commissions of Astana and Almaty (RECs); the fourth level consisted of 204 District Election Commissions (DECs); and the fifth level consisting of 9, 580 Precinct Election Commissions (PECs). The three lower tiers were convened during periods of election. Opposition representation on all the commissions remained low, although the lower-level commissions were composed of persons proposed by political parties. Stakeholders complained that the low representation of opposition parties on election commissions signified the flawed formula for selecting the members of election commissions.

Imperfect Voter Lists

Despite sustained efforts to improve the voter lists by the Central Elections Commission, stakeholders complained that there were inaccuracies in the lists. The CEC conceded that after the verification stage, more than 100, 000 eligible persons were added to the list. Furthermore, reports indicated that another 100,000 voters were added to the lists on polling day. A number of persons who applied to be included on the voter lists and who thought that their names had been entered there on discovered that their names were not on the lists either because they had not filed the proper papers or that the PECs did not properly process the papers.

Electronic Voting

Electronic voting was introduced in Kazakhstan in 2004 in the parliamentary elections on a pilot basis involving about 10% of the polling stations. Then in the 2005 presidential elections saw a modest expansion of e-voting using the 'Sailau' system, targeting 1451 polling stations. However, the CEC decided that voters at those polling stations would have a choice of using paper ballots or e-voting. The upgraded Sailau system used in 2005 displayed touch-screen voting terminals and was more voter friendly than the earlier models used in 2004. Not unknown in the earlier use of e-voting machines, the machines used in 2005 elections were unable to treat blank ballots properly, resulting in the blank e-ballots cast not being recorded in the results protocols and adversely affecting the possibility of proper audit trails being undertaken. The Precincts Elections Commissions did not know how and where to record the 'blank' votes. The system was so designed that actual votes were not stored individually, thus it could not countenance a recount.

Election Campaign-Absence of Level Playing Field

The presidential campaign for the 2005 Kazakhstan elections witnessed extensive use of billboards, banners and posters through the country. However, the incumbent President seemed to have acquired a near monopoly of large as well as small billboards at the start of the campaign.

Opposition candidates complained about the lack of advertising space after they were so told by the local administrators and private companies. The incumbent did not appear to have had similar experience. At the same time, there was extensive state advertising on billboards and banners portraying the incumbent in his official capacity as Head of State. That advertising remained throughout the campaign period, as election officials and local administrators took the view that 'official' advertising did not amount to campaigning.

Limitations on Freedom of the Media-Kazakhstan

Stakeholders reported severe limitations on the freedom of the media and difficulties in gaining access to information. There were seizures of editions of newspapers considered sympathetic to the opposition-the Svoboda Slova and Zhuma times just before polling day, and also immediately after. Cars transporting copies of the newspaper were stopped by the police after they left the printing house and the papers seized on the grounds that they contained materials infringement the honour and dignity of a candidate and president. The police stopped and searched without showing court orders. There were several similar incidents of seizures of individual editions of opposition supported newspapers. Several journalists were reported to be for reporting of the seizure of the newspaper *Svoboda Slova* on the 19 October 2005.

Kyrgyz Republic Parliamentary Elections-27 February & 13 March 2005

Electoral Landscape

The electoral landscape in Kyrgyzstan during the 2005 elections was characterized by:

- Competitive contests in many constituencies allowed voters a genuine choice;
- Active civil society contributed to the electoral process including domestic observers;

- Transparency measures, such as the use of ink to identify persons who had already voted, the use of transparent ballot boxes and the publication of the polling station results protocols on the Internet on the morning after the votes;
- Peace and order prevailed on both election days; however
- Widespread vote-buying existed in violation of the electoral law;
- De-registration of candidates on minor technical grounds;
- Administrative interference in the election process by officials;
- Flawed voter lists which adversely affected the confidence of stakeholders in the electoral process; and
- Fragmented complaints and appeals system reflected an imperfect legislative scheme for the resolution of final results.

The Electoral System

The Kyrgyzstan electoral system at the time of the 2005 elections consisted of a unicameral Parliament with 75 deputies elected in single-member constituencies for terms of five years. In order to be elected, a candidate must receive more than half of the votes cast at the election, failing which the two candidates who received the most votes, further contest a run-off election held two week after the first election, when the winning candidate would be the one who got the majority of the votes in the run-off poll.

The Right to Vote 'Against All'

The legislative scheme for the 2005 parliamentary elections of Kyrgyzstan allowed voters the option of voting against all the candidates in a given constituency. If the votes 'against all' were in the majority, the election was declared void and a repeat election would be called and the candidates who contested the previous election were excluded. Some stakeholders felt the scheme had loopholes in that it did not deal with a situation where the 'against all' vote was the second highest number of votes in a run-off election. It was possible to campaign on an 'against all' platform and two candidates who felt that they were wrongly de-registered in their respective constituencies campaigned for voters to vote 'against all' and were successful in both cases, where the elections were declared void.

Voter Lists

The accuracy of the voter lists for the 2005 parliamentary elections of Kyrgyzstan was questioned by stakeholders. The quality of the lists was not unknown to the Central Election Commission (CEC) as it encouraged the widespread use of additional voter list before and on Election Day. The CEC record showed that more than 10 per cent of the voters who voted in the first round, and slightly less than 10 percent in the run-off election, were from the additional voter lists. The preparation and delivery of voter lists was often behind schedule because of the outdated system in use. The transparency of the compilation and publication of the voter lists was compromised in part because the CEC considered voter lists contained confidential data which should be open to verification only by the voter and his/her family members, but that view was inconsistent with the interpretation of stakeholders of the applicable legal provisions. The complaints about the quality of the voter lists included the following:

- Not unusual, names of deceased and phantom persons on the lists;
- Multiple registrations; and
- Improperly recorded changes to the lists.

Candidate Registration—The Case of the Five Former Diplomats

During the preparation for the 2005 parliamentary elections in Kyrgyzstan, five former diplomats were refused registration on the grounds that they did not meet the residential qualification requirements—which were five years in-country residency prior to candidates' nomination. Stakeholders seemed to concede that the formal legal procedures might not have been met, but many felt that since the five diplomats were serving their country's interest abroad, their case should have been better provided for. Furthermore, in previous similar cases, former diplomats were able to register as candidates under the previous legislation. There was also the view held by some stakeholders that the former diplomats were refused registration on political grounds as some of them had expressed views opposed to the incumbent government.

Untidy Change of Power

The second round of the parliamentary election in Kyrgyzstan was held on13 March 2005 ended with many election results being disputed in court. Stakeholders complained of election irregularities and opposition protesters occupied local government buildings in the south of the country. The Supreme Court nullified a number of the election results upon challenges by opposition candidates. The Prime Minister soon resigned. The outgoing Parliament appointed an acting Prime Minister from the opposition, the President, Mr. Akaev had earlier left the country as the protests grew more intense. On March 26 the new Parliament was sworn in and the old Parliament was dissolved, although a number of constituencies were still to be resolved under the complaints and appeals procedures. President Akaev resigned on 11 April 2005.

Parliamentary Elections in Tajikistan-27 February and 13 March 2005

Electoral Environment

The Central Commission on Elections and Referenda (CCER) of Tajikistan in the period leading up to the 2005 elections met the election preparations deadline but apparently was not comfortable with briefing stakeholders regularly on the progress of the preparatory process along the way. In other respects, the CCER showed a willingness to adopt measures to improve transparency, such as transparent ballot boxes and better ballot security features. The election campaign was peaceful, if subdued in the view of some, and the six parties and a number of independent candidates offered considerable choice to voters. However, some stakeholders felt that some well-known political figures were prevented from contesting the elections by having court cases and criminal charges mounted against them. Polling day passed off without any significant incidents of violence and the polling procedures were largely followed. There were incidents of multiple voting and the tabulation process at the stage of the District Election Commissions because of evidence of tampering with many protocols of results at that level.

Electoral System

The electoral system in place for the 2005 parliamentary elections in Tajikistan consisted of a proportional and a majoritarian system. The proportional representation system attracted twenty-two of the 63 seats to be elected from a list system. The remaining 41 seats would be elected under a majoritarian to single-seats constituencies. To win a seat under the proportional system, political parties had to achieve a five percent threshold, while in majoritarian system a candidate had to win an absolute majority of the votes to be elected, failing which a second round of voting was held after two weeks between the two leading candidates. For any election to be valid there had to be at least 50% turn out, failing which a repeat election had to be held.

The Legislative Landscape

- The electoral legislative scheme of Tajikistan experienced some reform shortly before 2005 elections. Improvements included greater participation of the opposition parties, greater transparency by the CCER, greater access to for candidates and parties to State radio and television, and posting of election results of the count at the polling station. The electoral legal reform did not adequately deal with the following: inclusive and pluralistic composition of election commissions;
- Resolution of complaints;
- Domestic non-partisan observers;
- Registration of voters;
- Voting procedures; and
- Counting and tabulation procedures.

Voter Registration

The voter registration exercise in Tajikistan in the pre-election period of 2005 was carried out in a post-conflict environment. There was internal displacement of large numbers of citizens and large scale migration to Russia. There was no central voter register. Polling Station Commissions

(PSCs), assisted by local authorities, are responsible for compiling and updating voter lists for their precincts. The system of compiling the voter register did not have adequate safeguard against multiple registration—there was no reliable way of checking if a voter was registered in more than one precinct. Voters could be included in the voter lists up to and on polling day on the presentation of suitable identification.

Candidate Registration

Citizens of Tajikistan of 25 years and over could apply for registration to contest the 2005 elections, provided they met certain other conditions the most onerous of which were:

- All candidates had to post up $800.00 from their own funds; in case of single mandates, the deposit would be returned only to the winning candidate. In the case of party lists, the deposit would be forfeited unless the nominating party achieved the 5 per cent threshold in country-wide constituency. Many stakeholders considered that the deposit was too high and had the effect of excluded many promising individuals from contesting the elections.
- Prospective candidates should have higher education;
- All candidates had to provide income and property statements;
- Candidates in single seat constituencies had to submit at least 500 signatures of eligible votes from the constituency.

Polling Irregularities

Stakeholders in the Tajikistan 2005 elections complained of numerous polling irregularities including the following:

- Voting materials delivered to polling stations were not properly recorded in many cases;
- The record of persons who voted was not properly kept;
- Voters who were not properly identified were allowed to vote;
- Multiple voting; and

- Some polling stations were inadequate and compromised the secrecy of the ballot.

Albania Parliamentary Elections 24 June-19 August 2001

Electoral Environment

The principal electoral management body, the Central Election Commission (CEC) performed in relative independent environment with a considerable measure of transparency. Except for isolated pockets of incidents, the election campaign was mainly calm. The media offered good and balanced information to the electorate, and the public media afforded equitable access to the main contestants in the elections. Polling was generally orderly, and overall there was an absence of interference by the governmental authorities in the process.

A Fragmented Electoral Process

A notable feature of the 2001 Albania election process was the peculiarly fragmented nature of the process. It took five rounds of voting, which took place on 24 June, 8 July, 22 July, 29 July and 19 August 2001, to complete the polling process. As if to add complications to the process, in many zones where polling was conducted, repeat elections were held in some polling stations, in some cases, repeat polling was held more than once. The multiple voting exercises threw up a great variety of electoral shortcomings, including ballot box stuffing, pre-marked ballot papers, and errors in the vote tabulation process. The protracted multiple voting rounds, coupled with mounting errors in each round, had an adverse effect on stakeholders, and attracted low rating by independent observers.

Pseudo Independent Candidates

The concept of 'pseudo independent' candidates was an important issue in the 2001 elections in Albania. The pseudo independent proposition has been encountered in other mixed electoral systems where parties wished to circumvent the compensative element or just wanted to introduce confusion into the electoral process. In Albania in 2001, Article 66 of the Electoral Code contained a provision aimed at distributing 40 mandates in a manner that would allow compensation for parties which had secured a share of the national vote, but did not win enough single-member constituencies commensurate with their electoral support. However, some parties and candidates decided to manipulate the process by allowing a candidate of a party to register also as an independent candidate. When a voter voted for the candidate as an independent, and then cast his/her second ballot for the party of which the candidate is a member, the independent candidate's mandate is not considered to have been won by the political party who supported the 'independent' candidate. That was the way in which the political parties were able to improperly increase their share of the 40 national mandates. The allocation of mandates and the use of the pseudo 'independent' candidate concept became a contentious issue in the campaign. When the larger parties resorted to the use of the 'pseudo independent' candidates during the registration of candidates, the smaller political parties complained to the Central Election Commission (CEC), asking it to classify those candidates as party candidates and when the CEC responded in the negative, the parties appealed to the Constitutional Court which found against them.

Albania—Local Government Elections 2004

Local Elections Environment in 2004

The local government elections landscape in Albania in 2004 was endowed with a new and improved Electoral Code which provided a reasonable framework for democratic elections. It had a large measure of multiparty contribution in a parliamentary committee that achieved consensus on the provisions of the Code. The Code permitted a structure of a number of commissions to be established. The head of the administrative structure was the Central Election Commission (CEC) which operated in a professional manner with considerable transparency and even-handedness. The lower-ranked commissions also operated in a transparency manner, although the larger political parties used their representations on the commissions to pursue their political line. Voter registration did not proceed as smoothly as it could have, as the process became politicised with some parties attempted to exclude qualified persons on political grounds. The election campaign was conducted in a calm atmosphere in which the main political parties treated each other as legitimate opponents. However, election officers did not perform well in some cases as there were errors in the counting procedures and in distinguishing between valid and invalid ballots. There were many complaints by stakeholders that the logistics did not enable voters to locate their polling centres readily.

Ballot Paper Confusion

The ballot paper design for the local government elections of October 2003 and January 2004 in Albania threw up a particular difficulty. The ballot paper consisted of two separate sections and a voter had a vote for each ballot section. The was no clear rules on how to separately count the votes on each ballot paper and that led to inevitable problems during the counting of the votes. Some Voting Centre Commissions (VCC) did not know how to deal with ballots on which a vote was on one ballot section but not on the other. There was also a measure of confusion about the voting procedure in so far as a provision of the Election Code allowed unsigned ballot paper by the chairman of vice chairman of a VCC to go through and not delay the voting process, but another provision stated that a ballot was considered 'irregular' if any required signatures were missing.

Uneven Distribution of Public Funds

Public funds for the local government elections campaign in 2003-4 were released in a haphazard manner. The assistance was given to registered political parties but some parties did not receive any funding until the third week of the campaign. Others complained that they received no funding at all. The delay was reportedly caused by failure of the government to determine and approve the funds for allocation by the Central Elections Commission on a timely basis. Many stakeholders complained that delay in distributing the funds was deliberate and restricted their ability to campaign. They also claimed that the manner of handling the public funding placed the incumbent parties in an advantageous position.

Fair Media Access

The Electoral Code placed all television broadcasters, public and private, under an obligation to provide equal and balanced airtime for all political parties on the basis of their parliamentary size. Television coverage of any activity of government potentially relevant to the campaign was counted as being included in the proportion of airtime given to the incumbent party. Those stringent stipulations did not find favour with the broadcasters. The Central Election Commissions (CEC) established a Media Monitoring Board (MMB) composed of seven members, six of whom were nominated by the political parties and the chairperson was appointed by the People's Advocate. The MMB was mandated to advise the CEC on all electronic media-related issues and was required to undertake monitoring of campaign coverage in order to identify violations and advise upon appropriate sanctions. The CEC preferred the MMB to adopt a low profile as against a pro-active posture, but the composition of the MMB and partisanship approach of some members compromised the standing of the body.

Local Elections of the Republic of Albania 18 February 2007

The Local Government Elections Environment in Albania in 2007

The Local Government Elections environment consisted of political parties that did not always play a helpful role in advancing democratic elections. The behaviour of the parties was said to be responsible for the election date being deferred for a month from the date of 20 January 2007. The deadlock between parties was settled with outside diplomatic intervention. The electoral system was characterised by direct elections—mayors were elected in a first past the post contest and the councillors were elected by a proportional system. Under the latter system, the order of candidates on the proportion list could be changed after the Election Day. The voter register was improved in so far as multiple registrations were significantly reduced. The use of birth certificate as a form of identification was controversial. The campaign was bedevilled by allegations of widespread abuse of public administrative resources, stakeholders were not able verify such allegations. Observers and stakeholders gave the performance of election officials of Election Day high marks for professional performance.

The Legal Landscape

Since the local government elections in Albania in 2003/04, a number of improvements were made to the legislative scheme. The general legal framework was considered adequate to deliver free and fair democratic elections. The Electoral Code gave political parties the right to nominate members of election commissions at all levels. The membership of the Central Elections Commission was increased from seven to nine. Some improvements were made to the counting procedures however some stakeholders expressed concern about the ability of political parties to change the order of candidates on the list after the election results were known and the continuing confused state of the use of birth certificate as identification for the purposes of voting. The administrative structure consisted of a three-tiered commission system, namely, the Central Election Commission (CEC), 384 Local Government Election Commissions (LGECs) and over 4, 700 Voting Centre Commissions (VCCs), and up to 15 counting teams.

Voting and Counting Procedures

In general, the voting and counting procedures were largely followed but some irregularities were encountered by stakeholders including the following:

- Some voting centres opened late and some did not open at all;
- In a number of instances, the index book for birth certificate was not provided to voting centres commissions;

- A large number of voters were turned way from voting centres because their names were not on the voter list;
- There were complaints that the indelible ink used to stain the hand of voters was easily removed;
- Unauthorized persons were seen in polling centres and in some cases they interfered with the process;
- Multiple voting was reported, largely through the use of the proxy voting procedure; and
- In some voting centres confusion developed at the close of the poll and some voters who were in the queue were unable to vote.

Vote Count in the Albanian Local Elections-18 February 2007

Although the counting of the votes was well organized, the training commissioners were insufficient because of late appointments. The materials for counting centres were delivered in good time. In some counting centres, there were a larger number of party agents than anticipated, and some interfered with the process. Some counting centres experienced tension so much so that in centre fistfight broke out between supporters of the two main political parties. In a few centres, counting was interrupted as commissioners representing different political interests walked out. In a number of centres unauthorized persons were present and some of them sought to interfere and to influence the counting teams. In a few instances inspectors were sent in to resolve differences at the counting centres in order to complete the exercise in a timely manner. In one area criminal charges were filed against members of the Local Government Election Commission after they failed to follow a decision of the Central Election Commission.

Post-Election Election Environment in 1997 in Guyana

The Herdmanton Accord

The 15 December1997 elections in Guyana triggered widespread unrest as a result of the opposition and other stakeholders rejected the election results on the grounds of irregularities. The private-sector leaders proposed that an international election audit should be undertaken, and was accepted by the Government, but the main opposition party was opposed to that proposal and suggested that fresh elections be held. The continued protests caused the Government to declare a one-month ban on public assemblies and demonstrations in Georgetown, but the protests continued in defiance of the ban. In January 1998, the President and the Leader of the Opposition signed the Herdmanston which ended the political impasse. The Herdmanston Accord brought about an agreement between the ruling PPV/Civic and the Opposition and set out certain reforms to the electoral law, and stipulated that new elections should be held within 36 months, on 17 January 2001. The Accord provided for an independent audit of the December 1997 elections to be carried out under CARICOM's auspices after consultation with the political parties that participated in the elections.

An Election Audit

Pursuant to the Herdmanston Accord, which the brought an end to the protests triggered by the disputed Guyana elections of 1997, provided for an audit of the 1997 elections results. The ruling PPP-Civic party and the Opposition, People's National Congress/Reform (PNC/R) agreed to a CARICOM audit of the election results which took place between 19 March 1998 and the end of May 1998. The CARICOM Commission's report was released in June and it upheld the published results of the December poll and found that there were only minor procedural irregularities.

A Court Decision that Nullified a General Elections

An elections petition was brought in 1998 by a supporter of the opposition PNC/R challenging the legality of the 1997 Regional and General elections and the legality of the results of those elections. The petition asked that the 1997 elections declared null and void on grounds that there were many irregularities that materially affected the results, and that the requirement that the presentation of a voter identification card was a prerequisite for voting in the 1997. The ground of election irregularities was found not to rise to the level of nullifying the elections, however, on the ground of requirement of voter identification card, the Court found that the Elections Law (Amendment) Act No. 22 of 1997 (which required the voter identification card) was ultra vires Articles 59 and 159 of the Guyana Constitution, thus making the Act null and void. On that basis Justice Claudette Singh declared the 1997 election unlawful and consequently null and void. The effect of the judgment was far reaching. Following her ruling, Justice Singh delivered 'Consequential Orders' which indicated that the Government should remain in Office until March 19 2001. During the period subsequent to the Court ruling and the date of the elections no legislation could be introduced in Parliament except those required for the proper and timely holding of fresh national and regional elections and or in compliance with the Herdmanston Accord.

Parliamentary Elections in Albania 3 July 2005

Electoral Environment

In general, there was a competitive political environment in which a multiplicity of political parties offered themselves to the electorate. The election campaign was rigorous and the media was surprisingly balanced in their coverage of the campaign, although the major parties appeared to have gotten a greater share of coverage than smaller parties. The elections were held under a new Election Code was more conducive for the conduct of democratic elections than the previous Code. The Central Election Commission (CEC) performed well and displayed effectiveness, transparency and impartiality in the organization and conduct of the elections. There was improvement in the voter registration process and there was no complaint by stakeholders of deliberate attempts to disenfranchise voters. The process of counting the votes was not well managed and little attention was paid to the procedures laid down, particularly with respect to multiple voting and the secrecy of the vote. There were reports of election officials deliberately erroneously counting the votes in a dishonest manner.

Election Organization

The administration of the 2005 Albanian parliamentary elections showed signs of poor planning. An example of this was the appointment of zones election commissions (ZECs) which should have been appointed 3 March 2005, but by that date the election zone boundaries had not been approved. A new deadline was set by the CEC for the appointment of ZECs on 16 May, but the full complement could not be appointed on that date because the two major political parties did not complete their nominations by the new deadline. Indeed, some members of the ZECs were not appointed until after training had been completed. As if to compound the difficulties of the CEC, some local government authorities failed to meet legal deadlines for submitting the final numbers of registered voters and the location of voting centres, forcing the CEC to issue fines on some local government authorities.

Registration of Candidates and Party Lists—Albania

The registration of candidates and party lists proved cumbersome. The Electoral Code drew a distinction between parliamentary and non-parliamentary parties. Non-parliamentary parties were required to submit the signatures of at least 7,000 registered voters and coalition of non-parliamentary parties had to submit at least10,000 signatures. Parties represented in the out-going parliament were required to submit a signed declaration by at least one sitting MP verifying that he or she was a member of the party concerned. The Central Election Commission (CEC) had some flexibility in that where errors existed in the registration documents, parties were allowed two days to make corrections. The process of verifying signatures was unsatisfactory. The Election Code was silent on the issue and the CEC did not issue guidelines to deal with the matter. The registration of candidates in single seat zones was more straightforward; candidates of parliamentary parties and sitting MPs elected as independents were not required to submit support signatures. Candidates of non-parliamentary parties and independent candidates were required to submit 300 signatures of registered voters in the zone where they stood.

New Approach to Voter Registration-Albania

The new approach to voter registration adopted for the 2005 parliamentary elections entailed a transfer of the responsibilities for voter registration from the Central Election Commission (CEC) to local government units. The change meant an overhauling of the civil registers kept and maintained by local government units and the compilation of temporary resident registers with the civil registry offices. A door-to-door verification and identification process was undertaken between November 2004 and February 2005. Upon verification and identification citizens were given a number based on digital locality maps. This was followed by computerised voters lists based on the civil registries. The Ministry of Local Government and Decentralisation (MLDG) was given the task of checking the computerised lists for multiple entries. The MLDG created a country-wide voter database from the preliminary voter lists submitted by local government units. Whenever the MLDG identified multiple entries, it instructed the local government units to resolve them, and so the responsibility to compile and maintain voter registers remained with local government. The MLDG identified some 203,034 potential multiple entries in the preliminary lists involving about 100,000 registered voters.

Mayor Fined for Failure to Register Students

During the lead up to the 2005 parliamentary elections, the Mayor of a borough in Tirana failed to register as voters 1,422 university students and thus prevented the students from exercising their right to vote. The University staff in the area scheduled exams on Election Day and the students could not return to their place of permanent residence and were in effect disenfranchised. Some of the students brought a court action against the Mayor's decision, but disappointingly the Court cancelled the Mayor's decision against only those students who brought the action. Unfortunately, even those students who succeeded in the court action were not able to register as the final voter lists had already been printed. The Central Election Commission fined the Mayor the equivalent of about 670 Euros for his infringement of the electoral rules.

Nigeria: The End of Military Regime 1998-99[32]

The sudden death of the military dictator of Nigeria, General Abacha, in mid 1998 ushered in a period in which the incoming military Head of State promised swift return to civilian rule and set about creating the electoral environment to accommodate such change. There was dismantling of the existing political parties and the transitional bodies created under the previous regime, including the National Electoral Commission. Political detainees were released and various prison terms and death sentences imposed on political foes of the past regime commuted or granted pardon. A new independent electoral body was created with the responsibility to conduct elections, register political parties, and prepare new voter register. International election observers from the UN, Commonwealth and the African Union would be invited to observe the elections. General Abubaker, the new Head of State named a date when elections would be held and the new civilian Government would take office. The new electoral administrative structure was constituted on August 6 1998 and consisted of 14 members of the Independent National Electoral Commission under the Chairmanship of a former Justice of the Supreme Court, Justice Akpata. The Head of State also appointed Resident Electoral Commissioners for each of the 36 states and the Federal Capital Territory, Abuja.

Voter Registration under Tight Time Constraint

The transitional election time table set forth by General Abubakar in Nigeria was very tight, but so great was the appetite for return to civilian rule that doubts were muted. The voter registration of the estimated 60 million voters took place from 5-19 October 1998. Only two days were allowed for scrutiny of the lists before they were closed. The registration exercise was huge being conducted at some 110,000 registration centres, with 500 eligible persons registered at each centre which became the voting station for those persons who were registered there. Some stakeholders

---

32 The author assisted the Independent National Electoral Commission (INEC) with various aspects of preparations for those elections.

were dissatisfied with the voter registration process. They complained, among other things, about the distribution of registration cards, voicing the view that the cards were not distributed on an equitable geographic basis and that a quantity of cards had gotten into the hands of those who sought to manipulate the process. The Independent National Electoral Commission (INEC) took note of those concerns and introduced measures to mitigate their effects. Thus the accreditation procedure prior to voting was introduced to reduce the likely attempts at multiple voting on polling day. Similarly, the introduction of the use of indelible ink to stain voter's finger after voting was aimed at reducing the incidence of multiple voting.

The Voting Accreditation Process

The accreditation process entailed prospective voters between 8.00 a.m. and 11.00 a. m. joining the queue at their polling station to present their voter's card and be checked against the register at their polling station. The back of the voter's card would then be stamped, signed and dated by the presiding officer to indicate that every thing was in order. The elector was then required to remain at the station until voting began to prevent the accreditation of that voter at more than one station. Subsequent to accreditation, the accredited voters were required to join a queue between 11.00 a.m. and 11.30 a.m. to be told by the presiding officer about the voting procedure. Only those in the queue at 11.30 were allowed to vote. An official was required to stand at the end of the queue at 11.30 a.m. to prevent anyone joining thereafter. Voting took place from 11.30 a.m. to 2.30 p.m. The rationale for accreditation was quickly called into question by stakeholders when it was realized that many accredited persons simply left the polling station compound which was usually exposed to the hot sun, and did not return until later in the day. Indeed, many persons did not return to vote, particularly women with children.

Open Secret Ballot System

In the 1998-99 elections, Nigeria used what they called the 'open secret ballot system'. It entailed each voter presenting his/her stamped and signed voter's card to be checked against the register, which would be marked accordingly. The voter was then issued with the ballot paper. The ballot paper was then stamped and signed by the residing officer and indelible ink applied to the voter's thumb (left in the National Assembly elections and right in the presidential election). The ballot paper bore the names of the political parties and not those of the candidates. The voter marked the ballot paper in secret with a thumb print and then deposited the folded paper in a transparent ballot box situated in full public view. (The concept of 'open secret ballot' was in contrast with a previous procedure in Nigeria where the voting was done in secret and the ballot was deposited in the ballot box also in secret. That procedure attracted criticism that it encouraged vote buying and ballot stuffing.)

Elections' Shortcomings

The series of transitional elections, Local Government, State, Gubernatorial, Federal, Legislative and Senate, and Presidential, held between December 1998 and February 1999, not surprisingly, threw up a great variety of shortcomings and irregularities. Some of the more glaring ones were the following:

- The accreditation procedure did not work as was intended;
- Indelible ink was not always applied to the correct digit or at all;
- Some polling stations were short of materials;
- Many polling stations were short of the complement of staff;
- Some election staff displayed lack of adequate training;
- There was under-age voting;
- Attempted vote-buying incidents;
- Inflated voting figures by election officials;
- Preparation of pre-marked ballot papers; and
- Ballot box stuffing.

Fiji Islands General Elections 2001-5 August to 5 September.

The political and electoral environment prior to the 2001 general elections in Fiji Islands was characterized by a number of military coups beginning with a coup in May 14 1987 led by Lt Col Sitiveni Rabuka. Although a government of national unity was formed in September1987, Lt. Col Rambuka staged a second coup on 25 September of that year. A period of relative calm followed during which elections were held and Rambuka twice became Prime Minister. A constitutional Commission was established in 1995 and in 1996 the Commission reported proposing a multi-ethnic representation based on the Westminster system. A constitutional amendment was passed in1997 incorporating much of the Constitutional Commission's report. The general elections of 1999 resulted in the first non-indigenous Prime Minister in Mr Mahendra Chaudhry. On May 19 2000, one George Speight and his supporters took the Prime Minister and his Cabinet hostage and held them for 56 days until 3 July. The President, Ratu Kamisese Mara dismiss the Prime Minister and the Cabinet and prorogue Parliament for six months, but the President soon resigned and turned the reigns of power over to the Commander of the Military Forces of Fiji, Commodore J. V. Bainimarama who abolished the 1997 Constitution and began ruling by decree. An Interim Government headed by the former head of Fiji Development Bank, Mr. Laisenia Quarase, was set up on 3 July 2000 and the hostages were released. The Interim Government was declared illegal by the High Court and the decision was upheld by the Fijian Court of Appeal. The Court held that the 1997 Constitution was still in place. Although the Prime Minister of the Interim Government resigned upon the findings of the Court, he re-emerged as the Acting Prime Minister under the restored Constitution. The Acting Prime Minister then called general elections for 25 August to 7 September 2001.

A Peculiar Postal Voting System

In the postal voting system in the Fiji Islands in the 2001 general election, voters could deliver their postal ballots by hand, send them by registered post or take their postal ballot application form to a special centre where they were issued with a ballot paper, if they were registered. The voters marked their ballot papers in the normal way, in secrecy, and deposited their papers in the postal vote ballot box for their constituency. The postal ballots were taken to the appropriate counting centre where, after verification, they were included in the ordinary votes. Postal ballot teams were sent to persons entitled to vote but could not attend postal ballot stations in person, such as hospital patients and some categories of prisoners, including the coup plotters of May 2000-George Speight and his co-prisoners. To avoid double voting, each night the Districts Officers were supplied with the details of any voter who had cast a postal vote, so that their names could be marked off on the appropriate polling station register. There were an unusually high number of postal voters at the 2001 elections in the Suva area due to the fact that a number of meetings were being held in that area, in particular the Methodist Church and the Assemblies of God conferences, as well as major netball and rugby tournaments. The postal ballot boxes should have been checked on Sunday 2 September but the verification process held back the checking and counting processes, the verification continued up to Wednesday.

Political Party Voting 'Sheds'—Fiji

The political parties set up 'sheds' where voters checked their registration details before entering the polling station. The sheds usually consisted of a corrugated iron roof supported by corner poles and with matted floors. A desk with copies of the registers was used by party staff to assist voters. Some sheds were placed too near to the polling stations and had to be moved to meet the legal requirements of more than 50 metres away from the station. The sheds often had a good supply of 'kava', a narcotic drink made from the root of the yaqona plant, and voters were supplied with the drink. Some sheds supplied slips to the voter with their details from the register, and sometimes contain instructions on the voting procedure.

Flawed Ballot Paper Design-Fiji

Some voters found the voting system complicated. The problem was marking the ballot paper which voters were confused whether to mark above or below the line. The system required that voters should mark above the line and place the number below the line, however, a number of voters ticked below the line, thus rendering the ballot spoiled. The complication of the procedure was aggravated by some of the political parties which posted advertisements and banners showing a tick next to their name and symbol below the line. Under the rules then, even where the intention of the voter was clear the counting officers had no discretion but to treat the ballot with ticks below the line as invalid.

The Parliamentary Elections in Sri Lanka-10 October 2000

Electoral Environment

The Parliamentary elections were conducted on a system of proportional representation. The Delimitation Commission divided Sri Lanka into 22 multi-member electoral districts which returned 225 members to the Parliament. One hundred and ninety-six members were elected on a proportional basis in each of the electoral districts—160 seats were allocated on the basis of the proportion of the number of registered voters in each district and 36 seats on a provincial or territorial basis with the electoral districts forming the provinces returning four members each. The remaining 29 seats were allocated to the political parties and independent groups in proportion to the national total of votes received by each of them. Votes were cast for a political party or independent group or for candidates representing various interests in order of preference under the system of proportional representation. The voting procedure entailed that votes were cast on the same ballot paper and the voter is given a choice of marking his/her preferences for not more than three candidates identified by numbers allocated to them on the list of candidates submitted by the parties or independent groups contesting the elections.

Postal Voting

In the 2000 parliamentary elections in Sri Lanka, certain categories of voters were allowed to apply to the returning officer of the relevant district to be treated as postal voters. Those categories included public and other officers—members of the Sri Lankan Army, Navy and Air Force, Department of Police Force, Prisons, Telecommunications, other servants in the public or Local Government service. The reason for postal voting was that those persons were unable or unlikely to be able to go in person at the polling station allotted to them because of their employment. (Proxy voting was not allowed under the legislative scheme.)

Positive Evidence of Good Election Organization-Sri Lanka 2000

Many stakeholders gave the Commissioner of Elections and his staff high marks for their organizations of the elections. Polling staff performed competently, signifying that they were well trained. The polling procedures were adhered to and applied in a calm atmosphere. Polling stations were well organized and displayed a good signage system. Voter's fingers were correctly marked with the indelible ink to prevent multiple voting. Women voted in large numbers and there was no evidence of gender bias. Muslim women were allowed to vote separately, in accordance with their cultural tradition. Where it was practicable, separate polling stations or queues were afforded women. Voting and counting processes were transparent and thorough.

Organized Thugs to Disrupt Elections-Sri Lanka 2000

Stakeholders reported the intervention of well-organized thugs who disrupted and unlawfully interfered with the affairs of many polling activities. The thugs took over polling stations and stuffed or destroyed ballot boxes. The gangs operated in groups of 20-30 persons who were not afraid of the police—often they entered the polling stations intimidating voters and polling staff and overwhelming the police. The gangs had the ability to move quickly wreaking havoc and moved away before police reinforcements moved in.

Malawi-Presidential and Parliamentary Elections 15 June 1999

Difficulties for Alliances

The Malawi Congress Party (MCP) and the AFORD announced that they formed a co-operative agreement for the 1999 elections, including a joint ticket for the Presidency. The alliance chose the MCP leader, Mr. Gwanda Chakuamba, as its presidential candidate and AFORD leader, Mr. Chakufwa Chihana, as his running mate. The alliance was not acceptable to the Electoral Commission. Their ruling was challenged by the MCP and AFORD in the High Court. The Court held that there was nothing in the Constitution to prevent an alliance formation between two parties and that a presidential candidate was free to choose his running mate from any party, group or independents. The Court upheld the alliance. The Commission appealed against the Court's decision, but a new Electoral Commission was constituted and it withdrew its appeal.

Court Injected Flexibility

It was left to the High Court of Malawi to inject some flexibility into the registration of the procedure for registering candidates to contest the 1999 parliamentary elections. Each prospective parliamentary candidate was required to registered within their constituency and present the signatures of ten registered voters within that constituency. Each presidential candidate had to present ten signatures from each of the 26 electoral districts. There was failure to open all the registration centres and an action was brought before the Court to have the position clarified. The Court ruled that in view of the failure to open all registration centres candidates could be nominated by eligible voters who had not as yet been registered. As if taking its cue from the Court, the Electoral Commission gave a flexible interpretation to the nomination rules and accepted applications after the closing date.

Shades of Good Practices in Elections Organization

The 1999 presidential and parliamentary elections displayed shades of good practices. The arrangements at polling stations were described by some stakeholders as models of good practice—they were generally well laid out, well organized and had a good system of signage. The secrecy of the ballot was protected. The staff, eight per station, with several women, plus two security guards, was well trained and competent. The election rules and procedures were followed and carefully applied. The voter registration card system worked and most voters seemed to have understood the electoral process. Women voted in large numbers and there was no evidence of discrimination. The security was light but effective. The parties and candidates conducted themselves well. The fear of widespread shortage of electoral materials did not materialize.

General Elections-Trinidad & Tobago, 11 December 2000[33]

Vote Padding

The process of registration became a contentious issue in Trinidad & Tobago for the first time when a number of voters had applied for transfers across marginal constituencies based on false statements as to their place of residence. The reason for that development was to strengthen the party of the voters concerned in the marginal constituencies in which they were seeking to transfer their votes. In Trinidad the practice was called vote padding. The Election and Boundaries Commission ordered an inquiry into the allegations and subsequently rejected 252 applications for transfers into marginal constituencies and provided information on those cases to the police. The police subsequently made several arrests and laid charges against individuals. The relevant provisions of the Representation of the People required a person registered in the constituency in he/she

[33] The author was head of the Commonwealth Support Team to the Commonwealth Observers of these elections.

resided and that he/she should reside for a period of two months in the constituency in which registration was being sought. It was a known practice in Trinidad and Tobago for people to retain their original registration at a place (usually at the address of the ancestral home) other than where they currently resided. However, while the well-known common practice had been followed with good intention, the transfers of votes attempted in the lead up to the 2000 elections was aimed at doing something that was less than consistent with the long-standing 'ancestral vote' situation.

Effect of Dual Nationality

The Constitution of Trinidad and Tobago and the election rules precluded a person with dual nationality from registering to contest national elections. The issue became the focus of attention in the 2000 elections when two candidates with dual citizenship were nominated to contest the parliamentary elections. The two candidates contested the elections and were successful. The opposition party publicly declared that it would legally challenge the legitimacy of the election of the two candidates.

Multiplicity of Challenges

The 'vote padding' incidents triggered the fear of extensive challenges to voters by opposition party agents at the polling stations on ground of residence. It was believed that such challenges would lengthen the voting process. The challenges would be that the voters in question did not meet the residential qualification, that is to say, did not live in the constituency for the required period. Upon a challenge being made, the procedure required the voter in question to take the appropriate oath and vote. Subsequently action could be taken against the voter if it was found that he/she did not meet the residential qualification. The multiplicity of challenges did not materialize partly because the opposition realized that the practice of using the 'ancestral-home' address was used by prominent and decent citizens from all parties without intent to manipulate the electoral process.

The 29 October 2000 Zanzibar, Tanzania, Elections34

The Shehas' Role

The shehas were officers appointed by the Government under the provisions of section of the Regional Administration Authority Act of 1998 and charged with certain responsibilities with respect to registration of voters and the voting process. The amendments of August 2000 to the Electoral Act of 1984 gave the shehas considerable administrative powers during the 2000 Zanzibar elections. The role played by the shehas in the voter registration process during August 2000 caused the opposition parties serious concern. Their role was to verify the identity of each applicant for registration. Many persons were refused registration because the shehas declared that they did not know the applicants. There was particular concern that persons who might not have qualified to vote for the Zanzibar constituency concerned, but was qualified to vote for the Union elections and the election for the President of Zanzibar were deprived of their franchise through the actions of the shehas. Stakeholders reported that shehas often exceeded their authority and purported to over-rule or ignore decisions taken by the Zanzibar Electoral Commission and or the central police authorities. The shehas were known to be in collusion with local district commanding officers to encourage people to deny the opposition, especially the Civic United Front (CUF) access to open spaces, although the shehas were not invested with any such powers. The shehas were also present at polling stations to advise the election officials on voters' identity. Many stakeholders were of the view that government-appointed local officials should not fulfil the role assigned to the shehas.

---

[34] The author was the leader of the Support Team to the Commonwealth Observer Mission to these elections in Zanzibar in 2000.

Lack of a Level Playing Field

The 2000 Zanzibar elections were characterized by the absence of a level playing field. That shortcoming drew persistent complaints by the opposition parties and candidates. They complained about the ruling party's preferred position with respect to the state-owned media and its use of public funds and vehicles during the election campaign. The small political parties reported that they did not receive government subsidies and were thus hampered in their campaign efforts. Some stakeholders complained that campaign rules were not evenly enforced, as opposition rallies were ended promptly at 18.00 hrs, while those of the ruling party were allowed to go beyond that hour. There were regular complaints by opposition parties against police who were seen behaving in a partisan manner. The police often mounted roadblocks on roads leading to opposition rallies and subjected opposition supporters to car and body searches. Such actions resulted in discouraging opposition supporters from going to rallies, or to go very early to avoid the harassment by the police. Opposition rallies were often disrupted by unidentified youths believed to be connected to the ruling party.

Deviations from Procedures

Observers and stakeholders noted a number of significant deviations for procedures during the 2000 Zanzibar elections, in particular the following:

- Failure to deliver ballot papers to polling stations on time or at all;
- Fingers were not checked for indelible ink before voters were given ballot paper;
- In many polling stations ballot boxes were not sealed or locked;
- Voter's registration certificate number was written on the ballot paper counter-foil and on the ballot paper itself;
- Ballot paper was not stamped twice as required by the rules;
- Many persons who were not disabled sought and received assistance in the polling booth to mark their ballot.

Massive Organisational Failure

There was massive organizational failure at the 2000 Zanzibar elections. That was the conclusion of stakeholders and election observers alike. There were no ballot papers at many polling stations in the afternoon on polling day. At others where ballot papers had arrived, they quickly ran out as there was short supply. Often, it was found that some polling stations in a polling centre received ballot papers, while other stations in the same centre received none. At 21.30 hrs, there were still many voters at polling stations waiting to vote in the hope that ballot papers would turn up, but that never happened. Indeed, people waited until midnight and ballot papers failed to turn up. At 11.30 p.m. Mr. Abdul Jumbe, the Chairman of the Zanzibar Electoral Commission announced that due to shortage of ballot paper voting had stopped in 16 of the 50 constituencies in Uuguja, Zanzibar. He later admitted to gross inefficiency and offered an apology to the voters. Ultimately, elections in 16 constituencies were cancelled and election operations were suspended in 34 other constituencies.

Electoral Environment of Bosnia and Herzegovina—1998 September 12-13

At the time of the 1998 elections, Bosnia and Herzegovina was experiencing conflict resolution process; nevertheless the atmosphere was relatively free from violence and intimidation. However, at the outset of the elections serious problems were encountered when large numbers of final voters registers from all over the country were found to be incomplete and inaccurate, or had not been delivered. Then on polling morning many polling stations opened late and more than 50 failed to open on the first day. The election campaign was conducted in a competitive manner and media coverage was relatively balanced. The large numbers of refugees and displaced persons impacted negatively on the campaign in the rural areas. Moreover, the conflict atmosphere which still prevailed then allowed unusual measures to be introduced in the election organization process, such as striking candidates off party lists for reasons which did not relate to them personally, and involved the electoral authorities in the political process in ways that created the perception that they were behaving in a partisanship way.

Multiple Tiers and Several Electoral Systems

Certain institutions in the 1998 elections of Bosnia and Herzegovina such as the presidency of Bosnia and Herzegovina, and the President and Vice President of the Republic of Srpska were elected by a majority system. The Bosniac and Croat members were elected by a single direct ballot by the voters registered to vote in the Federation and those candidates who received the highest number of votes were elected. The Serb members were elected by a single direct ballot of voters registered to vote in the Republic Srpska and those who received the highest number of votes were elected. Institutions such as the House of Representatives of Bosnia and Herzegovina, House of Representatives of the Federation, National Assembly of Republika Srpska, Canton Assemblies of the Federation, and Municipal Councils, were elected by a system of proportional representation on political party lists or coalition lists and independent candidates. The proportional representation in use was based on the Saint-Lague method which distributed seats won using the total valid votes cast for each electoral entity by dividing by 1,3,5,7, etc sequentially until the number of divisors used was equal to the number of mandates for the particular legislative body. The resultant numbers from the division were arranged in order from the highest number to the lowest. Mandates were then distributed in order, from the highest to the lowest until all mandates for that institution had been distributes.

Gender Issues and Candidate Lists

The Electoral Law of Bosnia and Herzegovina provided that every list of candidates was to contain a number of persons from the minority gender. The proportion was in the region of one third up to a maximum of three, so that if the candidate list contained nine candidates, three should be of the minority gender. The provision initially stated that in cases where a political party did not meet the requirements and received three mandates, one seat would remain vacant, if between four and eight mandates, two seats would remain vacant, while nine or more mandates would result in three seats remaining vacant. The provision was later revised as a number of parties and coalitions failed to meet the requirements. Political parties were then allowed to move candidates of the minority gender up their list. Subsequently, further changes allowed minority gender persons to be added to the list of candidates up to Election Day in order to meet the requirement. The concept of seats remaining vacant did not go over well with stakeholders and attempts were made to overcome the vacant seat position by awarding the vacant seats to the party, coalition or voting alliance with the next highest resulting number, but that proposal was not accepted by the Provisional Election Commission.

Harsh Sanctions

In the ongoing conflict environment in Bosnia and Herzegovina at the time of the 1998 elections harsh sanctions against political parties and candidates were the order of the times. Under the election rules and regulations political parties and coalitions were responsible for the actions of their members and supporters. Thus where the Election Appeals Sub-Commission (EASC) found that a party member or supporter violated the rules and regulations it had power to impose penalties and fines against the offending party. The EASC had power to prohibit a political party or coalition from contesting an election; decertify a political party or coalition that was already listed on the ballot; and remove a candidate from a candidates list or an independent candidate from the ballot. Stakeholders reported that between August and the end of September 1998 some 42 candidates from six parties were removed from party lists for a variety of reasons. Those sanctions of striking off candidates from party lists prior to an election amounted to irregular activities which were hardly consistent with democratic elections.

Extensive Use of Tendered Ballot

There was extensive use of tendered ballots in the 1998 elections of Bosnia and Herzegovina-some 188, 675 persons voted by tendered ballots of which 75, 829 were rejected largely because their names were not on the final voter register (FVR), or because they voted more than once, or that their particulars were incomplete and could not be verified. The reasons for the large number of tendered ballots were, among other things, many refugees had returned after the registration period and were not included in the FVR and voters went to the wrong polling station. The large numbers of tendered ballots created an air of suspicion about the voting process and created problems for the polling and counting officers. Some polling officers dealt effectively with the influx of persons seeking to vote by tendered ballot by allowing them to vote by tendered ballot, but other polling officers sent them away to find their correct polling stations. The verification of tendered ballots in such large numbers added another dimension to the counting process. Some stakeholders expressed concern about the lack of transparency in the sorting, heckling and verification of the tendered ballots.

Concern about the Voters' Lists

In Antigua and Barbuda complaints were lodged in a particular constituency, St. John's Rural East, which was the Prime Minister's constituency. The complaints were lodged by the candidate of the main opposition party in the constituency before the Revising Magistrate. The complaints against most of the registered persons were dismissed. In another constituency, St. John's City West, a number of objections were also dismissed, and the objector appealed to the Court of Appeal against the ruling of the Revising Magistrate, but the Court of Appeal dismissed the appeals on the grounds that the objector had not discharged the burden of proof that rested on him.

Registration of Candidates to Contest the General Election 1999

The eligibility of three candidates to contest the 1999 elections was challenged on the grounds that they held dual nationality at the time of their nominations contrary to section 39(1) (a) of the Constitution of Antigua and Barbuda, which stated that 'no person shall be qualified to be elected as a member of the House who is by virtue of his own act, under any acknowledgement of allegiance, obedience or adherence to a foreign power or state'. The Antigua Labour Party (ALP) indicated that the persons concerned had renounced their second citizenships before the

High Court and were therefore eligible to stand at the election. The Court ruled in favour of the candidates shortly before the polls.

Recommendation of the Creation of an Independent Electoral Commission[35]

The Commonwealth Election Observation Mission to the 1999 general election recommended that an independent election management body should be established in Antigua and Barbuda. That view was broadly supported by many stakeholders in Antigua and Barbuda. In recommending the creation of an independent electoral commission in Antigua and Barbuda, the Commonwealth Observer Mission noted that the trend in the Commonwealth was towards the creation of independent electoral management bodies which in their constitution and functions were seen as to be wholly independent of government and party influence.

Lesotho National Assembly Elections—23 May 1998

Abuse of Incumbency Status

Stakeholders in the National Assembly elections in Lesotho in 1998 complained of the open abuse of their incumbency status by the ruling party. The Lesotho Congress for Democracy (LCD) was accused of using official vehicles and other public resources for party campaign purposes. When, in early May the Government announced new pay and grading structures for all public servants, including civil servants, teachers, and health service personnel, members of the security forces, chiefs and other categories, immediately many stakeholders charged that the ruling party was using its incumbency status to influence voters. The criticisms intensified and

---

35 The author was subsequently engaged under the Commonwealth's Technical Assistance Programme to assist Antigua and Barbuda in establishing an independent electoral commission and implement other recommendations of the Observer Mission to the 1999 general election

were elevated to the level of vote buying when the Government further announced extra subsidies for farmers a few weeks before polling day.

Independent Electoral Commission's Competence Questioned

During the lead up to the 1998 National Assembly elections, stakeholders levelled numerous complaints against the Independent Electoral Commission (IEC) and questioning the competence of that election management body. They pointed to a quantity of lost registration forms found in a river in April 1998, although the IEC acknowledged the loss of the forms and explained that the loss occurred when a vehicle was stolen. Several political parties complained that they had not been given copies of the provisional voters' register, even though they were entitled to be given a hard copy by the IEC. Some stakeholders accused the IEC of shortening the period of public display of the provisional register in the constituencies and thus not allowing sufficient time for voters to examine it. Others pointed out that the register was flawed in that it contained many 'phantom voters', while at the same time omitted many Basotho miners who worked in South Africa. Further, there were complaints that many voters had the same birthday and that that was evidence of serious irregularities in the preparation of the register.[36]

Trouble with Journalists

The Independent Electoral Commission (IEC) issued a set of media guidelines for Election Day for the1998 National Assembly elections in Lesotho. Those media guidelines upset journalists from the privately-owned media who objected to the guidelines on the grounds

---

[36] The improbable coincident of many voters having the same birthday was explained by the IEC that because voters did not often know their exact birth dates at the time of registration, they were allocated a nominal date such as 1 March.

that they were denied the automatic right to visit any polling station they wanted. The journalists secured the services of an advocate to argue their case with the IEC and argued that the IEC had no power to restrict their constitutional rights. The issue was settled by an arrangement whereby the IEC would allow journalists to apply in writing to be accredited to visit specified polling stations (without restriction). Thus in effect the journalists succeeded in being able to visit whichever polling stations they wanted. Photographers were not allowed to take pictures inside polling stations for fear of infringing voters' right to secrecy.

Kenya General Election 27 December 2002

The Electoral Landscape

There were considerable improvements in the electoral legal landscape prior to the 2002 general election in Kenya. Those included the following:

- Continuous registration of voters, (except between the dissolution of Parliament and the date of the election);
- The replacement of lost, destroyed or unserviceable electors' card, up to the day before polling;
- Much greater flexibility was introduced into the voting method, allowing any marking of any kind on the ballot paper clearly indicating the voter's choice—the cross was no longer the only acceptable mark by which voting was done;
- An illiterate or incapacitated voter was allowed to be accompanied by an escort to assist the voter; and
- Votes were counted at the polling stations.

Electoral Code of Conduct with Teeth

In order to improve the relationship with the political parties, the Electoral Commission of Kenya (ECK) encouraged the formation of a Political Party Advisory Committee consisting of the representatives of the parties. Against that background, the ECK devised a Code of Conduct governing the conduct of political parties and their candidates during the campaign period. The Code gave the ECK the power to issue penalties on political parties, their officials, members and supporters, or candidates who violated its provisions. The penalties which could be imposed included formal warnings, imposition of fines, and exclusion from use of the state media, prohibiting a party from holding public meetings or demonstrating, barring a party from entering a specified area or undertaking any form of campaigning. In the case of serious breaches, the matter could be referred to the High Court which had power to disqualify a party or a candidate. The ECK recorded many cases in which fines were levied against political parties and candidates for breaches of the provisions of the Code.

Limits of Incumbency?

Many stakeholders believe that a clear distinction should be made between the role of politicians of the governing party as ministers of government and as representatives of the party organization. The issue came to the fore in the election campaign in Kenya in 2002 when the incumbents of the ruling party were accused of extensive use of state resources including state personnel, offices, vehicles and aircraft. Many stakeholders advocated that regulations should be introduced to reduce the use and abuse of state resources for party campaign purpose by the ruling party.

Resort to the 'Black Book'

In the lead up to the 2002 elections, there was a measure of confusion as to who was eligible to vote in the elections. The Chairman of the ECK at first said that those voters who were not on the register would be able to vote, if they had the prescribed documents, and their names could be found in any register compiled since 1997 or in the 'black book' kept by the presiding officer. The 'black book' was the handwritten compilation of the voter register from which the 2002 computerised database was compiled. Then the Chairman of the ECK later changed the rule, announcing that only those on the 2002 register and with the correct identity documentation would be allowed to vote. Wide publicity was given to the later ruling and although many voters were confused, the election officials enforced the later ruling of the Commission.

Election Organization Shortcomings Identified

Stakeholders in the 2002 Kenyan general election identified some crucial shortcomings as follows:

- The counting process was very slow and complicated;
- The use of many forms coupled with the need to produce multiple copies of handwritten for party agents at the end of the count proved to be onerous;
- There was frequent confusion about some aspects of the process, for example, the difference between a spoiled ballot paper and a rejected ballot;
- Ballot papers which were placed in the wrong ballot box were sometimes treated as rejected ballots and in some cases they were transferred to the correct box and counted as valid;
- In some cases, the results of the count were posted up outside the building, and in other cases they were not; and
- Failure to make proper arrangements for food and transport for election officials.

Spain, Ninth Parliamentary Elections-14 March 2004

Electoral Landscape

The 2004 parliamentary elections were the ninth since democratic elections were introduced in 1977. In this relatively short period of time, the Spanish electorate has shown a remarkable degree of trust in the electoral system. Stakeholders have also displayed confidence in the electoral administration. The electoral landscape exhibited a strong electoral legislative scheme and a well-organized electoral administrative structure. Interestingly, the electoral processes displayed a number of unusual features which worked smoothly, such as selecting polling station officials by drawing lots among all persons on the voter lists. In the same vein, ballots and ballot envelopes were not controlled but allowed to circulate freely until they were put in the ballot box. The legislative scheme provided for secrecy, but in practice open voting was widely practised. Just three days before polling there was a devastating terrorist bombing in the capital city of Spain which killed many people and plunged they country into mourning. It was believed by many stakeholders that the bombings not only influenced the turn out on polling day but may have impacted on the outcome of the election results. The election environment in the Basque region was influenced by the separatist movement and that was aggravated by the then still fresh banning of the Batasuna, the Basque-based political party in 2003 pursuant to a new Political Parties Law, on the grounds that it supported terrorism.

Ballot Papers Produced by Political Parties

The Spanish electoral legislative scheme allows political parties contesting the elections to produce and distribute their own ballot papers according to the approved model. The cost of ballot printing by political parties was covered by the government. Political parties were allowed to mail ballots to voters at their homes and may hand them out freely on the streets or elsewhere. Ballots and ballot envelopes were not numbered or controlled in any way before they are dropped into the ballot boxes. The procedure proved acceptable to stakeholders, despite obvious weaknesses such as high cost to political parties to produce and distribute ballot papers and envelopes, potential waste in printing excess ballot papers, and the potential to attract influence and intimidation of voters.

Immediate Destruction of Ballots

In Spain the electoral law allows for the immediate destruction of voted ballots after the count. The destruction of the ballots was carried out by the polling station commissions in the presence of the representatives of the political parties at the polling station. The invalid ballots and ballots subject to any claim were not destroyed. The system has worked for Spain, but the procedure rendered it impossible to recount ballots at a later stage if a dispute arose.

Selection of Polling Officials by Lots

Polling Station Commissions (PSCs) 2004 parliamentary elections in Spain were created by the city councils under the supervision of higher level election commissions. All members of the PSCs were selected by lot from among all the names on the voter list for each polling station. The president of the commission was required to have a university or other degree. Each PSC member had a substitute who was also selected by lot. Once selected, a person had to serve, and if unable a request had to be made to be relieved of the responsibility, and such a request was rarely granted. The randomness of the lot procedure aided impartiality, but was also capable of throwing up inexperienced persons to serve.

Role of the Ministry of Interior

The Spanish Ministry of the Interior plays a prominent role in administering elections under the supervision of the Central Election Commission (CEC) and lower level election commissions. The Ministry was responsible for the procurement, logistics and distribution of all election materials, such s ballots, ballot boxes and voting booths. It also arranged voter education programmes to be carried y the media. The Ministry also organized a system for electronic tabulation of the preliminary results of the elections which were announced on election night by the Minister of the Interior instead of the CEC. The Ministry operated largely by contracting out through public tenders to private companies. The Ministry also assigned representatives to each polling station to assist polling officials, where necessary.

Moldova, Local Elections 3 & 17 June 2007

Electoral Environment

Stakeholders reported that the local elections of Moldova were relatively well organized, but problems arose with the registration of candidates who wished to contest the elections. The procedure to determine the order of candidates and party lists on the ballot paper. It was felt that a number of

District Electoral Commissions did not handle the matter in a transparent manner that benefited the incumbent party. Further, there were credible reports by stakeholders that a number of opposition candidates were intimidated and pressured by the authorities into withdrawing their candidature. The Central Election Commission (CEC) issued regulations which provided for allocation of municipal billboard space, but were often not followed. There were complaints by opposition parties that their campaign staff were harassed by the police while they were conducting lawful campaign activities. There were complaints that campaign finance regulations, including reporting requirements were not enforced.

Limited Effectiveness of the Central Election Commission (CEC)

The CEC of Moldova was criticised by stakeholders for not ensuring that its instructions and directives were followed and implemented by the fourth tier, the Precinct Electoral Bureaus (PEBs), of the electoral administration. In 2006 by an amendment to the Electoral Code, the power of the CEC to issue warnings and impose fines in cases of violation of the Electoral Code were removed, leaving the CEC powerless to deal effectively with non-compliance with the election rules and its decisions.

Candidate Registration

Although a large number of candidates were registered-a total of 4,766 candidates for contested 899 mayoral positions, and 60,000 competed for 11, 967 seats in districts, municipal, town, commune and village councils, there were complaints that the registration process was flawed. Stakeholders pointed to problems with the sequence of registration which determined the order in which electoral contestants appeared on the ballot. They reported that a number of District Election Commissions (DECs) did not act in a transparent, consistent and impartial manner. Some DECs allegedly registered candidates from the ruling party before the official date for submission of application. In other cases DECs were accused of arbitrarily determined the rankings, while in yet other circumstances, the DECs were said to conduct lots in an irregular manner to determine the order of the contestants in cases of simultaneous submissions. In further cases, the chairpersons of DECs were said to have made decisions without consulting the other members of the commission. Many of the complaints were ultimately dismissed due to insufficient evidence.

Compiling Voters' Register

In Moldova, for the local election of 2007 the Electoral Code stipulated that the Central Election Commission (CEC) shall exercise control over drawing up and verification of voter lists in cooperation with local and central public administrative bodies. The actual compilation of the list was done by mayoral offices and verified by door-to-door checks in the first two months of each year with a further second verification no later than 20 days before Election Day. For the 2007 elections, the first verification was carried out up to March 1 2007, the CEC put the number of voters at 2, 447,715. A second verification was done and the number of voters was reported at 2, 328, 522. Following the 3 June poll the number of eligible voters was given as 2, 226, 096. Stakeholders attributed the variation of the number of voters eligible to a number of factors, including lack of uniformity in the preparation, verification and handling of voter lists. Further, the CEC did not issue any guidance on the matter. According to stakeholders and observers, the shortcomings in the preparation of the voter lists included: lists posted late and outside legal deadline; posted up in the wrong places, that is, in mayoral buildings instead of at polling stations; in some cases lists were not posted up and were available only on request for individual scrutiny; and lists did not include all the information required in the Code such as type and number of identity documents.

Finance Campaign Accountability

Candidates contesting the local elections in 2007 in Moldova were required to open a special bank account for use with respect to all campaign-related financial transactions. Natural and legal persons could contribute to a candidate's campaign funds. Candidates could get loans from the State and be repaid in proportion to the number of votes received. Foreign funding was prohibited. The Central Election Commission (CEC) had power to request the Court of Accounts or the Fiscal Inspector of the Ministry of Finance to audit the electoral accounts. Political parties were required to publicly declare and report all financial and non-financial support received for their campaign. Bi-weekly reports setting out the sources of income and electoral expenditure had to be sent to relevant electoral bodies. The electoral bodies issued weekly reports on sources of income and electoral expenditures for all candidates registered with them. According to the report released by the CEC just prior to the first round elections, four of twenty-one parties and electoral blocks participating in the elections did not file complete reports and one did not open an electoral account.

Complaints and Appeals

The complaints and appeals process that was in place for the 2007 Moldova local elections was flawed. There was a relatively low utilization rate of these bodies attributed largely to the lack of trust in their impartiality by stakeholders. Furthermore, there was overlapping jurisdiction of the electoral bodies and the courts and that led to confusion, duplication of efforts, delays and conflicting rulings. Some times a complaint was heard simultaneously in court and before electoral bodies. For example, a complaint was submitted at the same time to the CEC and to the Chişinau Court of Appeal resulting in conflicting decisions on whether the ruling Party of Communists of the Republic of Moldova (PCRM) or the Christian Democratic People's Party. (PPCD) would have permission to hold a rally on the capital's main square. The complaints submitted to electoral bodies and the courts included matters relating to the composition of electoral bodies; candidate registration; suspension of public duties; misuse of public administrative resources; unauthorized campaigning; intimidation of candidates; accuracy of voter lists; and financial disclosure.

Croatia's Parliamentary Elections, 25 November 2007

Electoral Environment

The electoral environment in Croatia in November 2007 was competitive and pluralistic and administered transparently and in a professional manner. There was an active media service which provided voters with adequate information about the contestants and their campaign activities. There were 251 candidates' lists involving 3,586 candidates, which represented a wide range of political parties, coalitions and groups of independent candidates. The legal framework was conducive to the holding of democratic elections. The electoral administration was headed by the State Election Commission (SEC), but which was not operating as a permanent body. The SEC and subordinate election management bodies enjoyed considerable general public support and their performance was rated satisfactory and professional. The membership of the lower level commissions consisted in part of political party appointments, but the vagueness of the procedures governing the appointments attracted adverse criticisms. There was an Ethics Commission, set up under the auspices of the Constitutional Court, to ensure compliance with an Election Code of Ethics.

Annulment of Polling Station Results

The 1999 Law on Election of Representatives to the Croatian Parliament (LERCP) provided that if the number of ballots in a ballot box exceeded the number of voters recorded as having received them, the count at that polling station had to stop and the Municipal or City Election Commission had to annul the voting and conduct repeat election there. During the November 2007 elections, a number of polling stations showed votes exceeding the number of ballot issued and, in accordance with the rule, re-runs were conducted on the 9 December, as a result the announcement of the final national results was delayed for about two weeks. Those re-runs showed a rather low turn out, probably because it was known that the results of the re-runs would not have any impact on the preliminary results previously reported.

'Reminders'—Croatian elections 2007

'Reminders' were instructions issued by the State Election Commission (SEC) to voting committees. They were not considered to be mandatory instructions or of any particular legal basis. The reminders manuals often contained important material which some stakeholders felt that the reminders were at variance with the law. They pointed to the SEC reminder on voting procedures indicated that citizens voting in the Serb national minority elections should be instructed to vote for 1-3 candidates, but the election law stated that a voting slip in which the voter cast his/her vote for two or more lists or candidates was invalid. The 2007 reminder specified that minority voters may choose to cast a regular constituency ballot, but voters who were not on a minority list could not obtain a minority ballot. This was considered as an important rule that was not adopted in mandatory form.

Inadequate Time for Preparation-Croatia

The election of 25 November 2007 was called on 15 October 2007, allowing only 41 days between the announcement and the elections. Voters were required to apply for a change in polling station through pre-registration or temporary registration (where required) by 10 November. That deadline was set before the deadline for the establishment of polling stations, and meant that the voters could not be told where they would be voting on Election Day. The printing of ballot papers also had to be done before the official number of registered voters was finalized. The upshot was that the ballot papers had to be ordered by the constituency election commission (CEC) on the basis of estimates rather than the numbers actually required. The voter list commissions who were appointed to review and verify the voter lists for their municipalities and cities had inadequate time for an in-depth review of the completion of their work.

Extended Members

The Croatian election law in 2007 allowed the majority parliamentary parties, and the opposition parliamentary parties, by agreement among them, to have their representatives in the extended membership of all constituency, municipality and city election commissions, as well as in the voting committees who serve at polling stations. The aim of this procedure was to offer enhanced transparency to the voting procedure. However, some stakeholders felt that the short timeframe for the election preparation and the lack of clarity in the legal provisions on how the extended members were to be appointed. The legal deadline for the submission of proposed party representatives was 8 days prior to the election, and the actual appointment of those members had to be done no later than 5 days prior to the election. The extended members had little or no time to attend training sessions and thus impacting adversely on their understanding of the polling and counting procedures. The law provides that if agreement cannot be achieved, the extended members are to be chosen by lot. The agreements among the opposition parties were struck late and that meant that extended members joined the work of the Commission shortly before the elections and after the preparatory work was almost completed. Some parties did not avail themselves of the opportunity to submit nominees to serve on election commissions or voting committees.

Presidential Election, Armenia 19 February 2008

Electoral Environment

The electoral environment of the presidential election 2008 in Armenia was characterized by little confidence in the election process by the general public. Many well-placed stakeholders, including the President, Mr. Kocharian, were aware of the general lack of confidence in the electoral process and tried to reassure voters that the conduct of the elections would meet international standards. At the same time, the Prosecutor General reminded the public that penalties existed for election offences, and the Central Election Commission (CEC), through its Chairman, reassured voters of the secrecy of the vote. In the same vein, the Ombudsman criticized the practice of vote buying and vote selling. The election law prohibited candidates or their agents from giving or promising to give money, goods, or services to citizens during pre-elections campaign. The existence of vote buying-schemes in certain villages was confirmed by stakeholders.

The Police Compiled Voters' Register

Pursuant to the Electoral Code, the police were responsible for maintaining the centralized computerized National Register f Voters. The voter register was compiled on the basis of citizens' registered addresses and was updated continuously. Separate voter lists were compiled by heads of detention facilities and commanders of military units. In the run up to the elections, the police conducted door-to-door verification of the voter register in many communities. The voter lists were made available on the Central Election Commission website and at polling places. Citizens could also check their registration through a telephone hotline and voter information was provided through media announcements. If voters failed to find their names on the voter list, they could apply to a court or to the police for a certificate to facilitate their registration. The Election Code required that a person voted at his/her place of 'actual' residence, rather than their legally registered residence. Some persons had to be reregistered in order to vote at their actual residence.

Prime Minister's Status

The Electoral Code of Armenia, in 2008, permitted civil servants, high state officials, and persons in political or discretionary positions, to register as candidates. The question arose as whether the serving Prime Minister, Mr. Sargsyan could continue in office while being a presidential candidate. The Central Election Commission (CEC) sort to clarify the position by stating that candidates who were state servants had to take leave from their duties, while those holding political and discretionary positions, were not state servants and consequently could retain their posts. Some stakeholders felt that the CEC might have exceeded its competence in purporting to decide that matter.

Abuse of Incumbency

The Election Code of Armenia provided that candidates holding political and discretionary positions were prohibited from campaigning while performing official duties, from abusing their official position to gain electoral advantage. It prohibited the media from covering the activity of such candidates, subject to a few exceptions. Candidates who held discretionary positions should conduct their campaigns on general grounds without special privileges, except retaining protection and security arrangements. The Code was not very clear under what conditions those persons could legitimately campaign on behalf of a candidate, that is say, whether they should take leave of absence and forego the use of all state-owned resources enjoyed in their official capacity. Whatever was the scope of the rule, it was not uniformly applied during the presidential elections in 2008, for while the Prime Minister's campaign manager, the Minister of Territorial Administration took leave of absence during the campaign and so apparently did some regional governors belonging to the ruling party, many local government officials actively campaigned for the Prime Minister without taking leave. Stakeholders also complained of mayors and governors accompanied the Prime Minister on campaign events on several occasions. Stakeholders reported numerous cases of state employees and local government officials showing 'partiality' towards the Prime Minister Sarsyan. Uniformed police were seen handing out ruling party flags at a campaign event Public sector and local government employees, including school teachers, attended the Prime Minister's rallies in large numbers, some times even during working hours.

Parliamentary Elections, Turkey 3 November 2002

Electoral Environment

The electoral legislative framework offered ample scope for a number of political parties to campaign freely throughout the country. However, the legislative scheme at the same time set drastic limits on scope of political debate during the campaign. Some political parties were in danger of being closed down during the election campaign. Some candidates were banned from contesting the elections due to past convictions for political actions which violated the strict rules on political speeches. The restrictions on free speech and the frequent practice of dissolving political parties and the banning of candidates from contesting the elections imposed severe limits on democratic elections in Turkey. Other interesting features of the Turkish electoral environment included the high threshold of 10% of the vote cast which parties had to achieve in order to enter the Turkish Grand National Assembly (TGNA). Only two of the eighteen contestant parties achieved the threshold resulting in 45% of the votes cast went to parties that were not eligible for seats in the TGNA. Despite the apparently harsh electoral environment, the Turkish electorate showed a high level of confidence in the integrity of the electoral process. One reason for the high public confidence was because the election administration included political parties at polling stations, county and provincial levels. Also the system is generally open and transparent and contained strong checks and balances in the voting and counting procedure. The media was bound by the same tight restrictions on freedom of expression as parties and candidates. All media houses were required to provide fair and equitable election coverage breach of which obligation led to suspension of broadcasting for up to six days.

Turkish Electoral System

The Turkish Grand National Assembly (TGNA) had 550 deputies elected from 85 electoral districts, based on the provinces. Each province had at least one deputy, and the remaining deputies were distributed according to the size of the population. Provinces which had 1-18 deputies were single election district, provinces with 19-35 deputies formed two districts, and provinces, like Istanbul, with more than 35 deputies formed 3 districts. The deputies to the TGNA were elected by a proportional system, using the d'Hondt method to calculate seats won. In order to be registered and contest election successfully, a party had to be organized in at least half of the provinces in the country and one third of the districts within each of those provinces. In addition, a party had to obtain at least 10% of the votes cast nationally. Independent candidates were permitted to contest the elections and were awarded seats if they obtained sufficient number of votes under the d'Hondt method of seat allocation in the district in which they ran. Voting was compulsory and failure to vote attracted a small fine.

Registration of Parties and Candidates to Contest the Elections.

An infelicitous aspect of the rules related to the registration of parties and candidates to contest the Turkish parliamentary elections of 2002 were the various restrictions on eligibility to become a deputy. In particular, under Article 76 of the Constitution and Article 11 of the Parliamentary Election Law, conviction for a number of vague offences, such as 'involvement in ideological or anarchistic activities' or 'provoking enmity among the people on the basis of social class' prevented a person from registering as a deputy to contest the elections. Among the prospective candidates, who were prevented from contesting the elections in 2002, was a former mayor of Istanbul and leader of the Justice and Development Party (AK), Mr. Recep Erdoğan, who was convicted in 1998 for inciting hatred on religious differences by reciting a poem at a political rally. Many other prominent politicians were banned and many other persons were refused registration (some 60 of them) and thus prevented from contesting the elections on grounds of failure to meet the legal requirements. The Chief Public Prosecutor initiated legal proceedings to dissolve many political parties, including the AK Party, which won the elections.

The 10% Threshold

Under the Turkish electoral system, a political party had to achieve 10% of the national vote to enter the Turkish Grand National Assembly (TGNA). The system was designed to prevent the fragmentation of Parliament and to promote political stability. At previous Turkish elections, many parties had achieved a threshold of 10% or more, but fragmentation often set in after parties entered the TGNA, as was the case after the 1999 elections when five parties entered the TGNA and by the time election was called in 2002 there were eleven parties. The upshot of the high threshold of 10% was that a very high percentage of the electorate cast their votes for parties that were not represented in Parliament. Some stakeholders criticized the high threshold on the ground that it led to high 'wastage' of votes and distorted the purpose of the proportional system. The system allowed the victorious party to gain almost two-thirds of the seats in the National Assembly with only 35% of the votes. The system also worked against regional or minority parties gaining seats in the TGNA.

Restrictions on Freedom of Expression

The Turkish legal landscape is riddled with restrictions on freedom of expression. The Penal Code provided for possible imprisonment for 'insult to the State and to State institutions and threats to the indivisible unity of the Turkish Republic'. Prospective candidates may be barred for incitement of religious hatred. Separatist propaganda is banned. Under the elections law dealing with voter registration (Article 58), it is forbidden to use language other than Turkish in campaigning, but law reform amendments in 2002 changed the position in part allowing broadcasting and education in languages other than Turkish. However, the restrictions on the use of the Kurdish Language, during election campaign, were of great concern to many of the parties and severely restricted the scope of allowable legal debate.

Uneven Treatment of Independent Candidates

Independent candidates were treated differently from political parties during the 2002 elections in so far as the ballot design was concerned. All political parties were listed on a single, long ballot, showing the name of the party and its leader, and the symbol of the party. Each independent candidate had his/her separate, small ballot paper, listing the name of the candidate, but with no symbol. Voters who voted for an independent candidate stamped the small ballot paper with 'yes' stamp, place it in the envelope, discard the larger ballot. Stakeholders believed that the procedure compromised the secrecy of the ballot, as the ballot selected, because of the difference in size and type was revealed by the bulk of the envelope.

Turkey, Parliamentary Elections 22 July 2007

Electoral Environment

The electoral environment for the July parliamentary elections was conducive to the holding of democratic elections. The primary election management body, the Supreme Board of Elections, (SBE) was composed of senior judges and was held in high esteem and generated widespread public confidence. The general confidence in the electoral administration was strengthened by the transparency, professionalism and competence of the SBE. However, restrictions on freedom of expression and their adverse impact on the election campaign created inhibitions on parties and candidates during the campaign period. Some stakeholders regarded the restrictions on campaigning as a breach of the respect for fundamental civil and political rights. The requirement of 10% threshold for political parties to gain allocation of seats in the Turkish Grand National Assembly was considered to be a constraint on democratic elections. The elections were called against a background of political tension caused by the failure of Parliament to elect a new President; however, the major election processes, such as registration of political parties and independent candidates, voting and counting, took place in a calm and orderly manner.

Curbs on Freedom to Campaign

Freedom of expression, and consequently political campaigning, during the 2007 election campaign was constrained by the legislative scheme and characterized by the insertion of many vague phrases which were open to broad interpretation and application. Among such legal provisions were those dealing with imprisonment for insulting Turkishness, the republic, and state bodies and institutions-Penal Code Article 301; the criminalization of inciting enmity or hatred among the population—Penal Code, Article 216; prohibition of political parties from promoting the concept of the existence of national minorities and the use of languages other than Turkish in their campaign-Political Parties' Law (LPP) Article 81; prohibition of prohibition of a terrorist organization-Article 7 of Law No. 3713 on Anti-Terrorism; prohibition of violation of the existence and independence of the Turkish Republic, the territorial and national integrity of the State, the reforms and principles of Atatürk-Law No.298 On Basic Provisions on Elections and Voter Registration (LBPEVR), Article 4; prohibition on insulting the memory of Atatürk, the founder of the Turkish Republic—Law No. 5651 On the Prevention of Crimes in the Computer Domain.

Voter Registration

Law No. 298—On Basic Provisions on Election and Voter Registration (LBPEVR) regulates voter registration in Turkey. The voter registration process was based on identity and residence, but also required information of a personal nature such as voter registration number, name, family name, mother's and father's name, place and date of birth, district, street name and house number. There was a nationwide system for registration of personal identity based on an 11-digit unique personal identity number assigned to each citizen at birth. Citizens were required to register their residence address with the head of the district who report registrations to the district offices of the Ministry of Interior. When there was a change of residence, citizens were required to report the change to the district head at the previous address. The muchtar (district head) provided the citizen with a document that certified departure, which the citizen presented to the muchtar of new residence confirming the new address. The preliminary voter list of particular ballot box areas is published by the muchtar for 13 days to facilitate public scrutiny and updating by individual voters. Changes to the voter lists are not allowed after the expiry of the period of public scrutiny, except for administrative errors. Persons were not eligible to vote if their names were not on the ballot box voter lists. The personal identity number of a person was essential for entry on the ballot box voter list in order to safeguard against multiple voting.

Treatment of Minorities

Turkey was not known for its warmth towards minorities in political terms. The Constitution of Turkey made no mention of minorities. In the lead up to the 2007 elections, the basic legal position was unchanged. Turkey recognized and granted the status of minority only to the non-Mulim population which was construed as including Orthodox Christians, Greeks and Armenians, and Jews. Turkish citizens of Kurdish origin and other ethnic, linguistic or cultural minorities were not recognized as minorities under Turkish law. The Turkish official population census did not deal with questions on ethnicity or language and so information on minorities was not available. The law prohibited the use of languages other than Turkish in election campaign. The Political Parties Law (Article 81) prohibited the use of any language other than Turkish in written material and publications, in statutes and programmes, at party conferences and meetings in the public or in their campaign. The use of flags, posters, records, sound and movie tracks, leaflets and announcements in minority languages were prohibited. Those restrictions were enforced during the 2007 election campaign. Some independent candidates and other stakeholders complained that the prohibition on the use of languages other than the Turkish language resulted in an unfair campaign conditions. There was no national voter education programmes carried out in Kurdish or other minority languages.

Bulgarian Parliamentary Elections 19 April 1997

Registration of Voters

The list of voters was prepared by the Ministry of Regional Development and Construction for the Bulgarian parliamentary election of 1997. The preliminary list had about 6, 747 054 persons and was sent to the Section Electoral Commissions to be posted for public scrutiny for one month. At the end of that period of scrutiny more than 100,000 voters were added to the lists. At the time of polling, the number of voters on the roll was estimated to be about 77% of the population, an unusually high percentage by general international standard. Many stakeholders complained that the voters list contained a substantial number of 'phantom' voters. The voters list lacked credibility in the view of many stakeholders.

Registration of Additional and Certified Electors

The voter registration procedure for the 1997 Bulgarian parliamentary elections allowed citizens who were not on the original voters list submitted to the Section Electoral Commission *(SEC)* by the municipality to vote if they produced their passport with proof of residence. Their names were added below the line drawn under the original list of voters submitted to the SEC by the municipality. Those voters were known as 'additional voters' or 'below the line voters'. Person working on elections or observing elections could secure a 'certificate to vote elsewhere' which they could take to any other polling station. Some stakeholders complained that the number of additional voters who registered on polling day was more than 450, 000 and was improbably high and was mainly in the urban districts. However, the Central Electoral Commission attributed the high number of 'additional voters' as being due to human error in that some 507 SECs added the of additional voters to the number of people registered on the original list rather than just writing in the number of additional voters in line 2 of the protocol, thereby inflating the number of registered voters by 350-400,000. Impartial independent election observers who took sample checks of the figures in a number of SECs tended to corroborate the explanation put forward by the CEC, but to damage had already been done and many stakeholders were left with the perception that the 'additional voters' were used to inflated the election results in some areas.

Multiple Coloured Ballot Papers

Each political party contesting the 1997 Bulgarian parliamentary elections was allocated a coloured ballot paper by the Central Electoral Commission (CEC). Parties that had contested the National Assembly elections of 1990 were allowed to claim the same ballot paper colour allocation as in 1990. The other parties were allocated ballot papers on a first come first served basis, and were allocated multi-coloured and multi-striped ballot papers by the CEC. Non-party candidates were allocated plain white ballot papers. That process was intended to differentiate one political party from another, but it generated considerable dissatisfaction amongst parties. The parties which were allocated multi-coloured ballot papers complained that it was confusing and placed them in a less advantageous position than parties which were allocated full coloured ballot papers. Many stakeholders were unhappy with the unusually high cost of printing more than 200 million multi-coloured ballot papers.

Parliamentary Elections of Croatia 2-3 January 2000

Frequent Changes of Electoral System

Between 1990 and 2000, there were several changes to the electoral system of Croatia. At first, there was a mixed system with 60 members elected from single mandate constituencies and 60 members elected by proportional representation from country-wide constituency. Thirteen seats were reserved for ethnic-Serb voters and a small number of were reserved for other smaller national minorities. That system was amended in 1995 when the reduction of the number of members elected from single mandate constituencies to 28 and the number of members elected through proportional representation increased to 80. The amendments included the introduction of a fixed number of 12 seats for out-of country voters. The number of seats reserved for ethnic-Serb population was reduced from 13 to 3. The amendments of 1999 dispensed with the single mandate constituencies. Ten territorial constituencies were established, each with14 members on the basis of candidates lists. Each of the ten in country constituencies should not vary by more than + or-5%. In those 1-10 constituencies mandates are allocated to the party lists proportional to valid votes cast for each party using the D'Hondt method. In participate in the distribution of mandates, a party or coalition had to achieve 5% or more than of the valid votes cast in that constituency. The amended 1999 law also created a special constituency-No.11 for Croatian citizens without permanent residence in Croatia which may return up to 14 members on similar weight as in country mandates. Seats for constituency No.11 are allocated by the D'Hondt method. The 1999 law created a separate constituency for ethnic minorities, constituency No.12, who elect a total of five members. Members of ethnic minorities could vote for either a candidate or party contesting the specific minority election or vote for a list in the constituency of their permanent residence. Seats for national minority representatives were allocated according to the first past the post system.

National Minorities and Elections in Croatia

The minorities place in the parliamentary elections of 2000 was defined by the1999 amendment to the electoral law which reserved five seats for members of the national minorities, creating special rules to ensure that they were represented in a way which might otherwise not be possible in a society polarised along ethnic lines. Although that arrangement gave minorities an important window in the national legislature, many stakeholders were concerned about the reduction of seats for ethnic Serb citizens. Others were concerned that the existing treatment of minorities' issues might perpetuate the identification of citizens by their ethnicity; and that the number of seats allocated did not provide sufficient and effective representation. Many stakeholders complained that the creation of reserved seats for national minorities in the election law and the provisions of the Law on Electoral Registers have been used to justify the inclusion of 'nationality', or ethnic identification, on voter registers. They also expressed concern about the inclusion of ethnicity on the notification of entry in voter registers that were sent to all voters.

Election Administration during the 2000 Parliamentary Elections

The election administration comprised a four-tier structure the State Election Commission, 11 Constituency Commissions; 543 Municipal Election Commissions (MECs) or City Election Commissions (CiECs) and more than 6,500 Voting Committees (VCs). The 1999 amendment to the electoral law allowed partial party representation on election commissions at all levels, which served as a confidence-building measure. Each election commission had a standing core membership that was supported by additional members nominated by political parties and coalitions and appointed after approval of candidate lists. Political parties nominated members of voting committees in large numbers and enhanced the transparency of the process. The members nominated by political parties and coalitions had to be proposed by consensus, failing which membership was determined by lottery.

Registration of Out-of-Country Voters

Two categories of voters voted abroad-those who had permanent residence in Croatia and could have their names added to the registers on Election Day if they produced proof of citizenship and the right to vote. The State Election Commission extended the above category to include voters without permanent residence in Croatia provided that they could adduce evidence as to Croatian citizenship and an identification document with a photograph. Those persons could also register on polling day. The registers for voters without permanent residence in Croatia were not publicly posted and could only be verified by contact with the administrative office in Zagreb. There were some 350,000 voters who registered as voters without permanent residence in Croatia. Observers and stakeholder reported that the incidence of inaccurate registers with large numbers of voters who were registered on polling day was widespread. They complained that the procedure which allowed persons to produce a Croatian passport, which did not prove residence, facilitated multiple voting.

Special Polling Stations

During the Croatian parliamentary elections of 2000, there were many different polling stations for various categories of voters. There were polling stations for 'expelled' persons; 'displaced persons'; for persons without permanent residence in Croatia, but were temporarily in Croatia; persons with permanent residence in Bosnia and Herzegovina and temporary residence in Croatia; those temporarily away from the constituency of their permanent residence; military, prisoners and those serving on ships; and those without permanent residence in Croatia, permanently residing abroad. Some polling stations handled 16 different types of ballot papers and 16 different result protocols and minutes and multiple ballot boxes. 'Expelled' persons voted close to their place of temporary residence. The reports suggested that too few polling stations were set up for 'displaced' persons resulting in displaced persons having to travel long distances to vote. The registers were inaccurate and many persons had to get certificate to vote.

Presidential Elections in Bulgaria 22 and 29 October 2006

Electoral Environment

The electoral environment in Bulgaria in 2006 was competitive and the electoral process was credible, although there were areas of weaknesses which needed strengthening. The election campaign was low-key and calm with limited activities due to financial constraints. Voter turn out was low. Multi-party election commissions at all levels, including the Central Election Commission (CEC), were characteristic of the attempt to introduce transparency and accountability into the electoral process. That development led to considerable enhancement of stakeholders' confidence in the process. The CEC was a temporary body which lasted only for the preparation and conduct of the presidential election. Stakeholders argued that there was need for the CEC to be made permanent in order to ensure continuity and to build institutional capacity. The media coverage was balanced, but limited as candidates had to pay for appearances in all election-related programmes on the public media, including candidates' debates. This limited the amount of information that reached the electorate. Stakeholders pronounced the election to be well organized and administered, but the counting of the votes in some precinct election commissions had difficulties distinguishing between valid, invalid and spoiled ballots. The use of transparent ballot boxes and the elimination of the use of ballot envelopes compromised the secrecy in some cases as the ballot papers unfolded when deposited in the ballot box.

Reformed Polling Procedures—Bulgaria

Two months before the presidential elections of 2006, a new law came into force aimed at harmonizing the polling procedures of the presidential elections with those of the parliamentary elections. The changes included the use of white ballot containing the names of all candidates, rather than separate ballots used in the past. Also, ballot envelopes were discarded. A double-stamping procedure was introduced whereby one stamp was applied to the reverse side of the ballot before handing it over to a voter and a second one before the voter deposits the ballot in the ballot box. Transparent ballot boxes were introduced for use in the elections. The introduction of the transparent ballot boxes and the simultaneous elimination of the ballot envelopes drew complaints from stakeholders that the new procedure had the potential to compromise the secrecy of the ballot.

Disadvantaged Voters

The Parliamentary Election Law of Bulgaria provided that disabled and blind voters could request assistance during voting by a person of their choice, who could not be a member of Precinct Election Commission (PECs). No person could assist more than two persons. When a person was assisted, the fact of assistance and details of the person assisting was noted in the comment column of the voter list. The law required polling stations to be available on the ground floor in order to facilitate the participation of disabled and infirm voters. Where polling stations were located in buildings with stairs leading to the ground floor, ramps were provided, although that was not always the case. Where disabled voters were registered at a station on the same building, the disabled were allowed to vote at a station designated for disabled voters on that building and their names were struck off the list in their regular polling station and added to the supplementary in the polling station designated for disabled voters. A form was required in two copies, one for each of the PECs involved. A PEC member from the designated polling station had to go to the other polling station to complete the process. There was no provision to assist illiterate voters.

Electoral Reform in a City

Vancouver's City Government

The City of Vancouver was governed under the Vancouver Charter which set out how the powers of the City were exercised. The governing body of the city was composed of the City Council of 10 Councillors and the Mayor who were elected from the city at large. The Mayor and Councils served for three years and pass resolutions and by-laws for the City. The

Mayor was the Chairman of the Council. The election of Mayor and Councillors was carried out at large, that were to say, city wide and not according to wards or zones. The reform was considered in the context of moving from the at large to a ward or partial ward system.[37] Under the at large system, each citizen has 10 votes, not one. Supporters of the 'at large system' pointed to the advantage of voters having had the right of choice of candidates from different parties and to split their votes. It allowed voters to have a city-wide representation and perspective over local and parochial interests. The main criticism of the 'at large system' was that of poor geographic representation.

The Ballot under 'the At Large System'

Under the 'at large system', each citizen was entitled to vote 10 candidates on the ballot, and at times there were more than 50 candidates to choose from, plus the voters under the at large system had to vote for nine school trustees and seven park commissioners. The recent past elections at large in Vancouver produced a total number of candidates as follows in 1996, 94; in 1999, 94; and in 2002, it was 118, which led one voter to describe the ballot paper as looking like a telephone book. Stakeholders readily admitted that the ballot paper caused many voters trouble and was not user-friendly. A concern of many voters about the ballot size pointed beyond the size issue and to the complaint that the candidates were for the most part unknown to the voters, denying the voters the right to make informed decisions when voting.

Campaign Financing Reform in Vancouver

There had been concern by many stakeholders about the influence of money on the vote in the at-large system. The Berger Commission Report suggested that it could no longer be seriously contended that the sheer

---

[37] See Report of the 2004 Vancouver Electoral Reform Commission (Thomas R. Berger, O.C.,Q.C., Commissioner)

amount of money spent on election campaigns was not a crucial factor in determining the outcome. The Report cited with approval the decision of the Supreme Court of Canada in *Harper v. Canada* where Justice Bastarache said of the purpose of controls on electoral finance:

"62 The Court's conception of electoral fairness . . . is consistent with the egalitarian model of elections adopted by Parliament as an essential component of our democratic society. This model . . . promotes an electoral process that requires the wealthy to be prevented from controlling the electoral process to the detriment of others with less economic power. The state can equalize participation in the electoral process in two ways. First, the State can provide a voice to those who might otherwise not be heard . . . Second, the State can restrict the voices which dominate the political discourse so that others may be head as well. In Canada, electoral regulation has focussed on the latter by regulating electoral spending through comprehensive election finance provisions. These provisions seek to create a level playing field for those who wish to engage in the electoral discourse. This, in turn, enables voters to be better informed; no one voice is overwhelmed by another."[38]

The Vancouver Charter did not impose any limits on campaign contribution, but required disclosure of contributions made to candidates and electoral organizations for election campaign expenses.

Randomized Ballot Paper?

The ballot paper in Vancouver listed candidates' names in alphabetical order, but some stakeholders complained that under that system, the candidates at the top of the alphabet were favoured by the voters. The Vancouver Charter provided that ballot should be alphabetical unless the Council decided that the order of candidates should be determined by lot. Critics of the lot system pointed out that under a lot system once lots were drawn the order of the names was fixed similar to the alphabetical order,

---

[38] Harper v. Canada 2004 SCC 33.

in so far as the names at the top of the list may still be favoured. Some stakeholders advocated that the Charter should be amended to permit random ballots, if the at-large elections were retained. In a randomized ballot system, batches of ballot would be prepared with several different orders of candidates on them. Candidate A might be first on the list in one print run, and 10th in another. In that way, it was argued by supporters of the randomized ballot system, the 'donkey votes' favouring those early on the list would be randomly distributed among all candidates and cancel one anther out.

Bhutan 2008 National Assembly Elections 24 March

Electoral Environment for the Transition from Absolute Monarchy to Constitutional Monarchy.

The electoral process of 24 March 2008 was in line with international standards for democratic elections, but there were limitations on the right to stand as candidates and with respect to freedom of expression. The voting and counting of votes went smoothly and the use of electronic voting machines (EVMs) facilitated the voting process. Candidates were required to hold a bachelor degree and persons married to non-citizens were excluded from standing as candidates. The legal framework provided a good basis for the conduct of democratic elections. The Constitution afforded many fundamental freedoms and Election Bill provided for a level playing field among candidates with respect to campaign activities, campaign finance and media time. The Electoral Commission of Bhutan (ECB), which was in charge of the election administration, carried out its duties with impartiality, transparency, professionalism and implementing procedures on a timely basis. Stakeholders expressed confidence in voters register. However, the ECB imposed strict rules on the election campaign, which permitted campaign materials could be printed only in Dzongkha and English, although campaign meetings could be held in other languages. Candidates had to limit their speeches to the party's manifesto and party workers were not allowed to campaign on their behalf. Candidates were not permitted to extol their past achievements as senior civil servants, or to discuss citizenship and security.

The New Electoral System

The electoral system in place for the March election in Bhutan in 2008 provided for a two-tier chamber Parliament consisting of the National Council (upper house) and National Assembly (lower house). The lower house consisted of 47 members elected on a first past the post (FPTP) basis from single-member constituencies. Elections to the National Assembly were held in two rounds. The two parties that received the highest number of votes contested the second round, but because there were only two registered parties contesting the elections, no primary round were needed. Independent candidates were not allowed. The choice of the FPTP system was arrived at through national consultation process. In the first democratic elections, the FPTP system disappointed some stakeholders by producing uneven distribution of seats that were not proportionate to the votes gained. The People's Democratic Party (PDP) received 33% of the votes, but it received only two seats, while the Druk Phuensum Tshogpa (Party of Blissful Harmony, DPT) received 67% of the votes and won 45 seats.

Election Administration in Bhutan

The Election Commission of Bhutan (ECB) was an independent body with overall responsibility for the conduct of elections. It was composed of a Chairman and two Election Commissioners. The ECB members and the Secretariat staff were civil servants. The Election Bill[39]conferred broad powers on the ECB, including issuing of election rules, delimitation of electoral boundaries, compile voters register, registration of political parties, voter education, oversight of party and campaign finance, and adjudication of election-related complaints. The Commissioners were supported by the Secretariat headed by a Director. In each of the 20 districts, the governor was designated as the Chief Election Coordinator

---

39 The Election Bill was to be enacted when the new Constitution came into force; in the meanwhile it was in part enacted by Decree by the King in order to govern the election of 2008.

during the election period. The ECB also had a permanent representative in each of the 20 districts, and appointed civil servants as returning officers in each constituency for the election period. The returning officers appoint a presiding officer and three polling officers for each of the 865 polling stations. The ECB co-opted civil servants for the election period to report independently on the conduct of election officials, political parties and voters at the local level. There were 52 National Observers, at least one in each constituency appointed by ECB, but their role was not uniform and not very clear-it varied from supervising election officials, including returning officials, to following candidates in the campaign around. Election observers reported that some of the National Observers played a positive role as an extension of the ECB in the field, particularly in rural areas. Some observers felt that the role of national observers was closer to that of supervisors than observers.

Registration of Candidates

In order to contest the National Assembly Elections of Bhutan in 2008, candidates had to be citizens of Bhutan, between the ages of 25 and 65, members of the political party for which they were running and registered to vote in the constituency where they contested the elections. However, there were restrictions on the persons who did not have a first degree and that requirement meant that only just about 15,000 Bhutanese were eligible. Some election observers considered this requirement unreasonable. It appeared that not even a distance learning course degree was good enough, as the High Court had so ruled in a case that came before with respect to a potential National Council candidate. The Election Bill disqualified persons who married non-citizens from contesting as a candidate. Civil servants were required to resign in order to run for office and were not permitted to rejoin the civil service following an election bid, as they were regarded as partisan.

Political Party Registration

Political party registration was regulated by the draft Political Parties Rules. Political parties must demonstrate that they met the constituencies criteria for political party registration, including: broad based and cross-national membership, commitment to national cohesion and stability, no illegal or foreign donations and that membership was not based on region, gender, language, religion or other status. Regional parties were not allowed or parties that represent a certain segment of the population. The People's Democratic Party (PDP) and the Druk Phuensum Tshogpa (DPT) were registered in September and October 2007 respectively. A third party was refused registration by the Election Commission of Bhutan (ECB) in November 2007 on the grounds that it had insufficient membership and lacked credible leadership. The ECB said that the party did not have members in all districts, which was an objective criterion that could be verified, but was not mentioned in the Election Bill. The criterion of 'credible leadership' was subjective and it was difficult to say on what basis to measure 'credible leadership'.

Banning Civil Society

Civil society organizations in Bhutan during the 2008 National Assembly Elections were forbidden by law from engaging in activities directly related to elections. The restriction on the possibility of civil society groups to observe the election process was contrary to international best practices, which recognized the role of independent domestic observers in safeguarding the election integrity locally. The national observers appointed by the Election Commission of Bhutan (ECB) did not adequately replace independent observers as they were not independent of the election administration.

Electronic Voting Machines that Worked.

The use of advanced electronic voting machines (EVMs) made the voting process and procedures more user-friendly and significantly reduced a large potential area of human error. Portable battery-operated electronic voting machines were used. The polling officials were well trained in the operational use of EVMs and voters were educated in the application of their use. The EVMs consisted of two pieces—a ballot unit that displays choices for the voter and a control unit that records the votes. Each unit was self-contained and independent of any network. The ballot unit included the names of the candidates, party symbols and photos of candidates. The device had a digital counter and does not produce any paper record. At the end of polling, the EVM tallied the votes for each candidate, which was then entered by the Counting Supervisor in a results sheet. There was transparency in so far as each candidate or political party had the possibility to be present during the polling and counting the control unit was sealed by the counting officials and party representatives at the end of the count to prevent any tampering with the result. The counting process did not throw up any significant issues and was given high marks by observers and stakeholders.

Egypt Presidential Election, September 7 2005

Electoral Environment

The 2005 presidential election in Egypt was the first direct election which multiple candidates contested. Voters had an opportunity to choose from among several candidates running for the position of president and open campaigning was allowed for candidates representing opposition political parties. The voting took place in a calm and non—violent atmosphere. However, the competitive nature of the contest was limited by restrictions on the persons who could be registered as candidates to contest the election. Transparency was also limited as the accreditation of international observers was not permitted. The election was held during a period when a state of emergency existed in the country. The enforcement of the state of emergency impacted adversely on the proper development of political parties, and hindered proper election campaigning. Body which enforced the Political Parties Law was the Political Parties Affairs Committee (PPAC) which applied a strict interpretation to the law. The law was construed in such a way that new political parties would only be formed if they 'added something new' to existing parties, as a consequence, the PPAC approved only three new parties over a period of 30 years.

Election Administration

The 2005 presidential election of Egypt was organized and conducted under the supervision of the Presidential Election Committee (PEC). Stakeholders felt that the establishment of an election management body separate from the Ministry of the Interior was a positive development, although some had doubts about the some members of the Committee who were believed to be former high-ranking members of the incumbent party. The decisions of the PEC were final and not subject to appeal. The procedure for registering candidates to contesting the election was such that independent persons were unable to obtain registration. The PEC was reluctant to meet regularly with parties and candidates, or to issue regular briefings, and sometimes issued conflicting statements. The PEC guarded the perception of its independence so much that it explained its reluctance to meet with domestic or international in that context.

Poor Voters Register and Low Turnout

The voter turnout at the Egyptian presidential election in 2005 was put at 18 per cent by independent observers and at 23 per cent by government. The low turnout was blamed on apathy and by voters register that lacked credibility, but also on the failure by the electoral authorities to re-open the voter registration process which had been closed for 2005 before the announcement of multi-candidates for the 2005 election was made. The voters' lists were reported to contain the names of deceased persons, and many names of opposition supporters were missing. The compilation of the voters' lists lacked transparency which undermined their credibility. Stakeholders complained that it was very difficult for opposition candidates to get hold of the voters' lists, despite that the law required that each party putting up a candidate could get a copy of the lists for a small fee. According to stakeholders, the incumbent candidate had not difficulty getting copies of the voters' list.

Judges' Club

The Judges' Club, the primary association of all judges in Egypt, made a strong effort to ensure the transparency of the electoral process during the presidential election of 2005. The Judges' Club interpreted its supervisory role as one that enabled the Judges to exercise supervision over the electoral process and apply international standards that would assist the achievement of a fair and credible election. In a public bid to expand their supervisory role of the electoral processes, the Judges threatened to withdraw their services from the supervisory role, if the government failed to guarantee them full oversight of the process. The judges were no more than about 8,000 strong and could not service the 54,000 polling stations. The Judges Club conducted lengthy negotiations with the Ministry of Justice and with the Presidential Election Committee (PEC) to find a solution to the Judges' concerns. The position was not helped when the PEC removed some 1500 of the more activist Judges from the roster of Judges to serve. Eventually, a compromise was found and formulated as follows:

- Judges would permit members of civil society groups to enter polling stations and observe the vote;
- Judges would give copies of voting results to candidates' proxies; and
- Those Judges who had been excluded from monitoring would form their own fact-finding commissions and monitor the vote by visiting polling stations throughout polling day.

Although the compromise worked, the barring of the activists judges did have an adverse effect on the Judges' supervisory role.

Maldives Parliamentary Elections 22 January 2005

Constitutional & Electoral Landscape

The Citizens' Special Majlis was set up in 1980 to amend the Constitution and reported in 1998. Among the provisions in the proposed Constitution were a formal multi-candidate contest was allowed for the legislature's nomination of the presidential candidate; the President was allowed to serve an unlimited number of terms; and the post of Commissioner of Elections was elevated to a constitutional body. In August 2004, political unrest resulted in the declaration of a state of emergency and detention of political activities. The European Parliament passed a resolution calling for immediate cessation of all non-humanitarian aid and imposition of immediate travel ban on members of the Government and officials from entering the EU. On the 26 December 2004, a tsunami made some 12,000 people homeless and significant internal displacement took place. Nevertheless, the elections were set for 22 January 2005.

Influence of Public Sector

The public sector in Maldives had extensive influence over the community. The Government's influence extended to curbs on fundamental freedoms of speech, assembly, association, and the press, as well as control of employment. The perception of stakeholders with respect to the proposed constitutional reforms was somewhat negative, particularly the separation of powers and the introduction of a multi-party system.

Commissioner of Elections

The Constitution of Maldives provided for a Commissioner of Elections who was appointed and could be dismissed by the President. The Commissioner of Elections was responsible for the conduct of elections and the preparation there for, including the voters register. The Commissioner was not required to conduct research, to advise the Majlis, to educate the electorate or to run public campaign. However he may make subordinate legislation. There was an advisory body to the Commissioner, the Committee on Elections. Some stakeholders felt the Committee on Elections was not needed.

Centralized Counting of Votes

Many stakeholders advocated that the counting of the votes in the January 22 2005 Maldives' parliamentary elections should be done in situ at polling stations and not in the capital at Malé. They feared that transporting the ballot boxes would render them vulnerable to tampering. However, election observers who accompanied the boxes reported that the centralized exercise was done in a manner that was efficient and effective. Every thing was done to ensure that the process was carried out satisfactorily. The audit trail was reported to be good.

Uganda-Presidential and Parliamentary Elections—23 February 2006

Constitutional & Electoral Landscape

The stage for the restoration of multiparty democracy in Uganda after the Constitutional Court ruled in 2003 that political parties could operate, and in the following year, the Court went further and declared the provisions of the Political Parties and Organizations Act (PPOA) which restricted political meetings and the registration of political parties unconstitutional. In 2005, by referendum, Ugandan voted in favour of restoring multiparty elections, and in that same year, Parliament voted in favour of removing the two-term limit on the presidency. Several political parties quickly emerged. At the same time, many independent candidates contested the 2006 elections.

Women Representatives

During the years of the Movement system in Uganda, much attention was paid to women's participation in politics. A dedicated seat was created in each district for one woman MP. That development led to women holding leadership positions in many spheres of community activities, including politics. Stakeholders expressed satisfaction with the high level of female participation in politics at local and national levels.

Election Administration

There is an independent electoral commission created under the Constitution (Article 60) with a Chairman, Deputy Chairman and five members appointed by the President upon approval of the Parliament. The term of appointment was for seven years and could be renewed for another term, a situation which had the potential to compromise the independence of the members of the Commissioners. The Commission's responsibilities included organizing, conducting and supervising elections in accordance with the Constitution. The Commission displayed courage and independence when during the preparation for the 2006 elections of Uganda when it accepted the nomination of a presidential candidate who was at that time under arrest and against the advice of the Attorney General. The Commission stood by its decision even after the Attorney General took the matter to the Constitutional Court.

The 2006 Uganda Elections Campaign

The 2006 Ugandan election campaign was not conducted on a level playing field. The ruling party, National Resistance Movement-Organization (NRM-O), was reported as unfairly exploiting its position as the governing party. Extreme difficulties were put on the presidential candidate of the Forum for Democratic Change (FDC), who was constrained to attend 27 hearings in the High Court and the General Court Martial, to answer charges during the election campaign period. The Commission restricted campaign hours to between the hours of 7 a.m. and 6 p.m., but the restrictions were often enforced selectively against the opposition FDC and less so against the NRM-O.

National Elections in Papua New Guinea, June-August 2007

The Voting System

The electorate of Papua New Guinea (PNG) had experienced swings from electoral systems to electoral systems. Legislative elections before independence were conducted on an optional preferential system. Upon independence, the electoral system was changed to the first past the post poll which was believed to more suitable to PNG needs because of its simplicity and its user-friendly perception. In 2007, the voting system was changed to a limited preferential vote (LPV) system in order the better reflect amount of votes gained to the number of seats awarded to the parties and to increase amount of votes that it took to win a seat. It was believed that preferential voting required candidates to seek the support (in the form of preferences) outside of their clans and communities. Although the LPV system did not prove as difficult for the voters as was feared by some stakeholders, nevertheless, there seemed to have been a high level of voters, especially in rural areas, who required assistance to vote. Stakeholders also reported that the LPV system a more representative system and a stronger mandate to the winning candidate.

A New Ballot Paper Design

At the time of the new LPV electoral system was introduced in Papua New Guinea (PNG), a new ballot paper design which had not been used before in that country. The new ballot paper required voters to write the names and/or the allocated numbers of their preferred candidates on the ballot paper with the photographic posters provided in the polling booths for voters' reference. The design was developed to ensure a workable preferential vote, while avoiding the use of too large ballot papers which would otherwise be required. Doubt was expressed as to the ability of the voters to use the ballot paper correctly. Some stakeholders believed that the use of the new ballot papers was open to election fraud as it required that if there was inconsistency between the number and the name filled in for any preference on the paper, the written name would be counted as the preference. The belief was that, if a number was filled in and the name space left blank, then later a different name could be written into the blank name space.

The Voters Register

A new voters' register was compiled between 2005 and 2007 for the 2007 Papua New Guinea (PNG) elections. The previous register which was compiled in 2002 was discarded as being inflated with 'ghost' names. The new register contained 3, 938,839 a decrease of over 1.4 million voters from the 2002 register. Each ward had its separate printed roll and not one roll for the whole electorate. That made the roll more user-friendly for the election officials. Some stakeholders complained that names were missing from the new register due in part to the compilation being rushed and in part to corruption. They pointed out that in certain areas, for example in the East New Britain Province, public servants were used to visit all the wards to register voters, but they visited during day when people were out, the registration exercise was left incomplete. In some cases data which were sent to the Commission in Port Moresby seemed to have disappeared. The register contained errors which stakeholders felt should have been corrected.

Errors in the Electoral Process

Observers saw errors in the Enga Province as follows:

- Failure to use the electoral roll properly or at all;
- Underage boys voting;
- Polling places without indelible ink, which facilitated multiple voting;
- The secrecy of the vote was compromised by open voting;
- Voters' identity was not routinely established before voting;
- Vote-buying was seen in the vicinity of a polling station; and
- Omission to lock or seal the ballot box at one polling station.

Solomon Islands General Election, 5 April 2006

Flawed Composition of Electoral Commission

The Electoral Commission of Solomon Islands for the 2006 general election was composed of the Speaker of the National Parliament as the Chair, and two other members appointed by the Governor General acting on the advice of the Judicial and Legal Service Commission. Problem arose because during the 2006 election, the Chairman of the Commission, in addition to being the Speaker of Parliament, was also president of a political party. Stakeholders complained that there was clear conflict of interest on the part of the Chairman. The Commission had responsibility for the supervision of registration of voters and conduct of elections for the members of parliament. The Chairman serves for a four-year term which coincided with the life of Parliament. The other two members served a period that was specified in the instrument of appointment. That arrangement meant that the Electoral Commission came on stream towards the end of a particular parliament to conduct the election of the subsequent parliament.

Registration of Voters

The Electoral Commission of Solomon Islands was responsible for voter registration. Some stakeholders were critical of the system whereby the incoming Electoral Commission was responsible for the compiling of the register which was overseen by the outgoing Commission members. The register was reported to have been inflated and not purged of deceased persons and persons who had changed address. The number of the registered voter population of 342,199 in 2006 out of the national population of 470, 681 (in 2005) is improbably high by international standards. Some local stakeholders estimated that the number of qualified persons was more in the region of 250, 000. The basic rule governing registration required that a person be ordinarily resident in the constituency in which registration was sought. However, there was a practice of persons registering in their traditional village or province and also in the urban constituency where they were ordinarily resident, although the law prohibited double or multiple registrations. It was believed that it was that practice that led to the inflation of the register. There was no provision for transfer of vote or registration, and so people who registered at one location and subsequently moved to a new location tended to register at the new location, without necessarily ensuring that the previous registration was deleted. Further, stakeholders attributed the inflated register to the practice in rural parts of heads of families usually register the whole family whether or not all the members of the family were of voting age or resident in the village. Individual members of such families usually register at their new addresses.

New Voting System

A new voting system of voting was introduced for the 2006 elections. Previously, a separate ballot box was provided for each candidate and voters were not required to mark ballot papers but merely put his or her ballot into the ballot box of the candidate of choice. The old system was considered to be vulnerable to abuse and corruption. The new system involved single ballot box and the necessity for voters to make a mark on the ballot paper beside the candidate of choice before inserting it in the box. The single ballot box also reduces the material to be handled by the polling officers.

The Dark Room

The Commonwealth Election Observers' report tells of the dark voting room which they saw in a rural area. The room was in a separate building from that of the presiding officer's room. The separate building was so dark that voters had to use a flashlight to cast their ballot, but even then a polling assistant had to assist some voters to use the ballot papers properly. Some voters were shy of the dark room and sought to cast their ballot where they could vote in some light. That resulted in the police office in the dark room or the election officer had to follow the voter around while he/she search for a suitable place to mark the ballot paper. Yet, the Observers reported that there was enough light and space in the room occupied by the presiding officer.

Elections in the Democratic Republic of the Congo Presidential, Parliamentary and Provincial, 30 July 2006 and 29 October 2006

Setting the Stage for Democratic Elections

The 32 years of the Mobutu dictatorship in the country then called Zaire came to an end in May 1997, when Laurent Kabila, backed by neighbouring Rwanda and Uganda, took power. Kabila became President and re-named the country 'Democratic Republic of the Congo'. Laurent Kabila's administration came to an end when he was assassinated in January 2001 and his son, Joseph Kabila became President. In 2002, an accord was signed in Pretoria, South Africa, by the warring parties and politicians of the Congo to end the fighting and form a government of national unity. In June 2003 a transitional government was installed and given a two-year period to hold democratic elections. The transitional government consisted of President Kabila and four Vice Presidents, supported by a transitional parliament, with a National Assembly of 500 members and a Senate with 120 members. The transitional arrangements were to end in June 2005, but were extended at the request of the Independent Electoral Commission to end June 2006 when elections could be held. A constitutional referendum was set for February 2005, but was deferred until 18-19 December 2005. The referendum went off relatively smoothly and a large majority of Congolese voters endorsed the post-transitional constitution which was promulgated on 18 February 2006.

The New Constitution of DR Congo

The new Constitution established a unitary state with a considerable measure of decentralization. Executive power is split between the President and the Prime Minister. The President is elected by direct suffrage with absolute majority for five years and may be re-elected once. The Prime Minister was appointed by the President from the largest party or coalition represented in the Parliament. The bicameral parliament enjoyed a five—year term. The Constitution increased the number of autonomous provinces and the capital city, Kinshasa 26, taking account of cultural and ethnic considerations.

The New Electoral Environment in the DR Congo

A number of legal measures relating to the 2006 elections in the Democratic Republic of the Congo (DRC) were enacted between 2004 and March 2006. Those measures included guidelines on how elections were to be prepared and conducted; dispute resolution procedures; procedures dealing with the implementation of the Electoral Law; as well as related matters such as citizenship and political parties. The election of members to the National Assembly and to provincial assemblies was done on a constituency basis with open list system. Voters could select their candidate from a party's list or an independent candidate. A total of 500 members were elected from 169 electoral districts. The 108 senators were be elected indirectly by the provincial assemblies. Each of the 25 assemblies elected 4 senators from within or outside the provincial assembly. The Kinshasa provincial assembly elected 8 senators. The new provincial assemblies would take three years to be operational and the composition of the senator and the provincial assemblies would until then be constituted on the existing territorial arrangement of 11 provinces, including Kinshasa.

Voter Registration for 2006 DR Congo Elections

There was no reliable population data in the Democratic Republic of the Congo (DRC). The last population census was taken in 1981 and the frequent civil disturbance had resulted in shifts in population, as well as internal displacements and significant refugee problem. The Independent Electoral Commission decided to undertake a registration exercise based on the exclusive identification and registration of prospective voters. The registration process was confined to registration of Congolese citizens residing in the country, of age 18 and over, and eligible to vote. The holders of dual nationality were not eligible. Registration was compulsory. Members of the military and police forces were not eligible. The registration process started on June 20 2005 and continued until February 2006. The process was computerised and recorded the total of 25,712,552 voters out of estimated eligible persons of 28 million. The purged register eventually came to 24,440,410, but that figure was achieved despite a boycott by the Union pourla Démocratie et le Progrès Social (UDPS) party.

The Campaign for the 2006 DR Congo Elections

The election campaign for the three tiers of elections in 2006 in the DR Congo was relatively peaceful. The official campaign period was to last 60 days before polling days and end 24 hours before polling commenced. The political parties and candidates subscribed to a Code of Conduct. Controversy developed over the number of excess ballot paper that was printed for the elections. Some presidential candidates argued that more than 5 million extra ballot papers than the 26 million voters on the register was excessive. They called for the extra ballots to be destroyed and for the campaign to be suspended. The Electoral Commission explained the perceived excess ballot paper in terms of the breakdown of the required number of ballot papers to be sent to each station taking account of voting by party agents or local observers who were allowed to vote legally outside their registered constituencies. It gave the breakdown of 33 million ballot papers received for 26 million voters distributed to approximately 50,000 polling stations received an average of 660 each.

Uneven Media Access

During the 2006 elections campaign of the DR Congo, the Media High Authority (HAM) had not faired well in ensuring the observation of the Code of Conduct by the media houses. The stakeholders complained that the incumbent President got much greater exposure than the other candidates. A journalist who was not always friendly towards the transitional government was killed during the campaign. In another incident, a French radio correspondent was deported after being accused of being biased against President Kabila. There was hostile campaigning by both the Bemba side and the Kabila camp. The state-owned electronic media was favourable to the incumbent President Kabila and his political allies and hostile to the main opposition, Bemba. However, Bemba had his own TV stations which were wholly supportive of the Bemba ticket and hostile to Kabila and his allies. The Code was not effective in ensuring a level playing field between candidates. Bemba's TV stations in Lubumbashi in October 2006 and Kinshasa in September 2006 were destroyed by fire.

Flashes of Intimidation & Violence.

Although on the whole the election organization was relatively smooth and peaceful, there was serious sporadic intimidation and violence. The campaign for the first round of elections experienced isolated violence, including the destruction of the headquarters of the Media High Authority. The supporters of parties opposed to the electoral process were often prevented from demonstrating. Persons alleged to be plotting the overthrow of President Kabila were arrested. Some candidates who opposed the President had their campaign materials seized. During the run-off elections, clashes between Kabila's and Bemba's supporters caused the death of several persons. The intense competitive rivalry between Kabila and Bemba stirred up ethnic tension which brought great strain on the Code of Conduct govern parties' conduct.

Madagascar National Assembly Elections, 23 September 2007

The Electoral Environment

The election environment was informed by the presidential elections the previous December which was largely peaceful. The participation in the December 2006 elections was over 61 percent of the registered voters. The incumbent President Ravalomanana was re-elected for a second term. A constitutional referendum was held in Madagascar on 4 April 2007. The proposed changes were believed to be intended to consolidate the power of the President. Opposition parties campaigned against the changes proposed in the referendum. The President however maintained that the changes were necessary to speed up the development of the country through decentralization. The referendum was approved by over 75% of the voters. The new Constitution entered into force on 27 April 2007.

The Madagascar Election Administration

The election administration of Madagascar was carried out by three bodies, namely, the Ministry of the Interior and Administrative Reform (Mira), the National Electoral Council (CNE) and the High Constitutional Court (HCC). The Mira was responsible for the overall organization of elections. The CNE had supervisory and oversight role of the electoral process; and the HCC was responsible for final verification and announcement of results. The CNE had seven members appointed by different entities of the society. The Government authorities were closely involved with the organization and conduct of elections and stakeholders felt that the election authorities were not impartial or independent. In particular, they complained that the Mira was subject to undue political influence. Some stakeholders also expressed concern about the appointment procedure for appointing the members of the CNE and further of the apparent overlapping mandates of the election bodies.

Voter registration for the 2007 Elections in Madagascar

The Ministry of the Interior and Administrative Reform (Mira) was responsible for voter registration and compiling the national voters' roll. Registration is voluntary and is open to all Malagasy citizens of 18 years and over. The possession of a valid identity card was a precondition to be able to register. The voters' lists had been computerised since 2006. The lists were reviewed in 2007 for the referendum on the Constitution, and updated further in 2007 for the parliamentary elections. According to the figures released by Mira the register stood at 7 466 164 voters, an increase of 1.49% on the April 2007 figures for the constitutional referendum.

Constructing Constituencies in Madagascar for the 2007 Elections

The country was divided into 119 constituencies for the National Assembly elections returning a total of 127 members. The distribution of seats was two seats for six constituencies in Antananarivo and one seat each for the other constituencies through the country. Opposition parties complained that the distribution was unfair and constructed to give advantage to the incumbent. In support of their complaint, they cited the Antananarivo II and III, which were given two seats each for a population of respectively 136 001 and 191 506, while some single-member constituencies such as

Vohibato and Mananjary with population estimated at 527 144 and 707 256 respectively, were given one seat. They pointed out that the population criterion was often overlooked in the delimitation exercise.

The Election Campaign for the Madagascar Elections in 2007

The official campaign period was short, running from 8 September to 22 September 2007. The campaign consisted of rallies, marches, door-to-door canvassing, motorcades, and concerts. The campaign was relatively peaceful. However, many voters from all levels of society reported that they were pressured to vote for the ruling party candidates. There were complaints that the candidates of the ruling party had more resources than opposition ones. There was no public funding of political parties or independent candidates in Madagascar. Stakeholders suggested that there was need to control the use of public resources by the incumbent party and to introduce a disclosure regime with respect to contributions to parties and candidates, as well as disclosure of expenditures.

Ballot Papers Produced and Paid for by Candidates in Madagascar

Madagascar used multiple ballot papers, which allows a different ballot paper for each candidate. The Electoral Code determined the design of the ballot paper and the number of ballot papers to be provided for the election by political parties or independent candidates. Candidates were responsible for the cost of the printing and delivery of their own ballot papers, to be supplied to a special commission established by the Ministry of the Interior and Administrative Reform (Mira) between 14 and 29 August 2007 at central, regional or district levels. The ballot paper used in the National Assembly elections were 105mm x 80mm and contained the particulars of the candidate, name, photo and party emblem or symbol. Many candidates were unable to submit their ballot papers on time and were disqualified; other candidates had insufficient number of ballot papers resulting in a shortage of ballot papers for some candidates in some polling stations. Ballot papers for the different candidates were of different quality. This system whereby candidates are responsible to print and distribute their ballot paper posed severe financial burden on candidates and political parties. Candidates with limited financial resources were discriminated against. The electoral authorities should be responsible for the printing and distribution of all ballot papers in order to create a level playing field and produce standardised quality ballot paper.

Namibia's Presidential and National Assembly Elections 15-16 November 2004

Electoral Environment

In 1998, the Constitution of Namibia was amended to allow the incumbent President Sam Nujoma to contest the presidency for a third time. He contested the election and was successful. Otherwise the president serves for a term of five years and may contest for a second term. A candidate for the presidency was elected by direct suffrage with more than 50% of votes cast. Namibia had a bicameral legislative scheme namely the National Assembly and the National Council. The National Assembly consisted of 72 members elected by proportional representation and seats distributed by a quota system. The Second Chamber consist of two members from each of the 13 regions in Namibia elected for a term of six years and may be re-elected. Regional councillors were elected in their respective constituencies under the first past the post system. The electoral administration was managed by the electoral commission supported by a directorate of electorate.

Namibia's Electoral System

The National Assembly and local authority elections were conducted under the proportional representation system. Political parties which intended to contest an election had to submit a list of candidates equal to the number of seats to be filled in the National Assembly, or to the seats available in the given local authority council. The quota for allocating seats in the National Assembly was done by dividing the number of valid ballots by 72, and each party received the number of seats in accordance with the number of votes divided by the quota. Remaining seats were distributed to the parties with the largest fractional remainder after the first round allocation.

Political Party Funding in Namibia

Namibia allows public funding of political parties in order to promote and sustain multiparty democracy, but funding is limited to parties represented in the National Assembly. Further, the funding was calculated on the basis of the votes received at the most recent election. In the circumstances of Namibia where the ruling party is overwhelmingly popular and based on ethnicity, stakeholders complained that the formula for calculating public funding was flawed with respect to creating a level playing field. Foreign funding of political parties was allowed, provided that such funding was disclosed within a stipulated period of time. Namibia did not have a comprehensive campaign finance regulatory scheme, although parties had to disclose donations above $500.00.

Namibian Women in Politics

The Southern African Development Community (SADC) required a target of 30% representation of women in Parliament pursuant to the 1997 SADC Declaration on Gender and Development. In terms of the voters in Namibia, the register for the 2004 elections showed that women outnumbered men by almost 45,000. Namibia had been making progress in the area of women's involvement in politics. There was over 26% women's representation in the outgoing Parliament. The political parties professed their commitment to meet SADC's target for women's representation of 30%, but close examination revealed that women were always placed low down on the party lists so that the 30% nomination may be achieved but is not often reflected in the allocation of seats.

Tendered Ballots in Namibia

In Namibia, voters may cast a tendered ballot at any polling station outside the constituency where the voter was registered. The tendered vote was placed in an envelope marked with his/her constituency. The Namibian tendered ballot system was criticized for slowing up the voting process and exposing it to potential abuse. The counting of the votes in the 2004 elections was marred by delays which were blamed on the large numbers of tendered ballots that were involved. Stakeholders complained that the proportion of tendered ballots to ordinary ballots was much too high and recommended that counting of ballots take place at the polling stations and change the procedure for dealing with tendered ballots.

Mauritius—National Assembly Elections 3 July 2005

Electoral Environment

At a seminar on 'Elections and Peace and Security in Africa' one speaker put forward the view that there was no country in the African Union that had adopted the culture of holding democratic elections. Another speaker quickly rose on a point of correction and named Cape Verde Islands and Mauritius as the only two members of the AU about whom it could be said fell outside that category. Whether or not any of the two speakers at the seminar was correct, Mauritius had been given good marks for producing an environment conducive to the organization and conduct of democratic elections. Although Mauritius had multiple election management bodies, namely, the Electoral Commissioner, the Electoral Supervisory Commission (ESC), and the Electoral Boundaries Commission (ECB), they work in harmony and their roles were clearly defined. Stakeholders felt that the Constitution and the electoral laws offered sufficient guarantees of freedoms and human rights, including political rights, to ensure the peaceful elections.

The Electoral System in Place for the 2005 Elections

In 2005, Mauritius had in place for the National Assembly Elections a constituency-based block vote system which was a variation of the first pass the post system. The constituencies were often multi-member constituencies and each voter could cast as many votes as seats in the constituency and the candidates with the most votes were allocated seats. There were 20 three-member constituencies on the main island and one two-member constituency on Rodriques, making a total of 62 elected, and there were 8 seats to be filled by allocation of seats to 'best losers' from parties and communities. The block vote system does not achieve proportional results with respect to relating the amount of votes received to the number of seats gained. The inadequacies and unfairness in seats distribution were revealed in a previous election in 1995, when the successful coalition was allocated all 60 seats after gaining 66.22% of the votes. There were many attempts to reform the system—a commission was set up to study the block system and recommendations for changes. The Sachs Commission, as it was called, recommended a mixed proportional representation system and the first past the post system. A joint committee of the main parties examined the Commission's recommendations and adopted its main recommendations, but some stakeholders did not agree and at the time of the 2005 elections, the block vote system remained in place.

Voters' Registration for the 2005 Mauritian Elections

The electoral register was updated by means of house-to-house enquiry in January each year. Additions could be made over a period of two months at particular centres in constituencies across the country. The final computerised register had to be published by 14 August and come into force on August 16. These rules operated in such a way as to render existing 2004 register to be the one governing the 2005 elections. Although the rule was correctly applied, some stakeholders complained that by setting the election date in July 2005, thus rendering the 2005 register which was due on 16 August 2005 ineligible for use in 2005 elections, an estimated 5,000 to 7,000 prospective voters who had become of voting age were effectively disenfranchised. While the legal merits of this complaint might have been questionable, it highlighted the need to improve the registration process through rolling or continuous registration.

Party and Candidates Registration

Persons who wanted to contest elections had to submit nomination papers on nomination day between 9.00 hours and 15.00 hours. A prospective candidate had to be supported by eight registered electors of the constituency and must declare the membership of ethnic communities of Mauritius he/she belonged to. One political party challenged the stipulation requiring prospective candidates to specify their ethnic affiliation on the grounds that it is discriminatory. Prospective candidates from that party refused to declare that information in their nomination papers. The nomination papers of those prospective candidates were rejected as invalid because of the absence of declaration as to ethnicity. Consequently, the party took the Electoral Commissioner, the Electoral Supervisory Commission and staff in their respective constituencies to court The Supreme Court of Mauritius ruled in favour of the complainants and ordered their inclusion in the list candidates for the 2005 elections.

The Election Campaign in the 2005 Elections

There was no official campaign period in Mauritius and no formal code of conduct with respect to the behaviour of political parties during the campaign. Notwithstanding the foregoing, the campaign environment was peaceful and calm. Candidates, parties and coalitions showed due respect for each other. The campaign consisted of mainly house-to-house visits, rallies, motorcades and entertainments. There was no formal end of the campaign activities. Apart from sporadic incidence of violence, the main stakeholders joined to keep the incidence of campaign violence and intimidation at bay. However, some stakeholders accused the ruling alliance of abusing their incumbent position by using state funds for advertising on billboards and in press.

Pakistan National and Provincial Assembly Elections 18 February 2008.

The Electoral Environment in Pakistan in 2008.

The environment was hostile to the holding of democratic elections in so far as there was a state of emergency was in place throughout the country and the Constitution was suspended along with fundamental rights. Thousands of people, including judges and journalists, were detained. The emergency rule was dismantled only one day before the beginning of the campaign period. The tension in the country was increased when prior to formal election campaigning, Ms Bhutto, the leader of the Pakistan People's Party (PPP), one of the major political parties, was assassinated in late December 2007 and the riots that followed claimed many lives. In addition, stakeholders in the elections did not have confidence in the Election Commission of Pakistan (ECP) which was perceived as not independent. The ECP was considered not to operate in a transparent manner and was reluctant to deal with political parties and other stakeholders.

The Security Environment

Pakistan's border areas with Afghanistan were major sources of instability through 2007 causing military conflicts with militants and insurgents. In July 2007, the Government stormed the Red Mosque in Islamabad and that triggered incidents in the North West Frontier Province from where many of the students killed in the Red Mosque came. Further, there had been ongoing incidents of violence in Baluchistan between the Pakistan and Balochi insurgents. An aborted address by the deposed Chief Justice at the Sindh High Court in Karachi in May 2007 triggered violence in which more than 40 people were killed. An attack on Bhutto's rally in October 2007 led to the death of more than 140 people. On 27 December 2007, Benazir Bhutto, leader of Pakistan People's Party, was assassinated at a rally in Rawalpindi. The election date was deferred from 8 January 2008 to 18 February 2008. There was widespread rioting and some electoral buildings and materials were destroyed. The violence continued between

December 2007 and March 2008 during which some 413 people were killed and many more injured.

Electoral Legal Environment

In 2008, the electoral legal environment was not adequate to support democratic elections. There was poor safeguard for independence and transparency in the legislative scheme. The President was given considerable influence over the operations of the Election Commission. The President had the right to approve the rules issued by the Chief Election Commissioner (CEC) and to approve the appointment of members of the tribunals that decided on the nomination of candidates. The President had a general power to intervene to remove difficulties. The extent of this latter power was not well understood by stakeholders. The removal of the Chief Justice and other senior Judges by the President under the emergency rule undermined the general legal environment. Stakeholders lost confidence in the Electoral Commission as the President was responsible for the appointment of the Chief Election Commissioner. The other four members of the Commission were High Court Judges, one from each province, appointed by the President after consultation with the Chief Justice of the Province High Court and the CEC. However, the system of appointments to the Commission broke down as the re-constituted judiciary by the executive order in November 2007 meant that the President was consulting with those that were in his camp. The stakeholders further contended that the dismissal of the Chief Justice and other senior Judges adversely affected the elections in so far as the judiciary played leading roles in the electoral administration (as members of the CEC and the Election Commission of Pakistan (ECP)). Also returning officers (ROs) and district returning officers (DROs) who were appointed by the ECP were predominantly from the session court judges. They were assigned the task of deciding issues with political implications, such as the eligibility of candidates (ROs) and the location of polling stations (the DROs).

Election Administration in 2008 in Pakistan

The Elections Commission of Pakistan (ECP) consisted of five members, the Chief Elections Commissioner (CEC) appointed by the President, and four other members appointed by the President in consultation with the Chief Justice of the respective Provincial High Court and the CEC. The President role in appointment of the members of ECP had eroded the confidence of the principal stakeholders to operate independently. They pointed to ECP's acceptance of General Musharraf's presidential nomination in September 2007 contrary to the legal and public opinion as proof of lack of independence. The ECP had consisted of three members until January 5 2008 when President Musharraf appointed two members of the enlarged Commission, although there was no consultation with opposition parties. The extensive influence of the judiciary at all levels of election organization was considered weakened by the dismissal of the Chief Justice and senior Judges and the general loss of confidence in the independence of the Judiciary. The stakeholders complained about the lack of transparency on the part of the ECP. The smooth organization of the elections was interrupted by the assassination of Benazir Bhutto and the disturbance that followed. Some electoral buildings and materials were destroyed. The date fixed for the elections was deferred from 8 January to18 February 2008. The ECP had issued a Code of Conduct for political parties and candidates. Opposition parties were not consulted by ECP when developing the Code of Conduct. The Code did not have inbuilt sanctions and the ECP did not investigate complaints on a timely basis and did enforce the Code.

Voter Registration for 2008 Pakistan Elections

The Elections Commission of Pakistan (ECP) created a new voters' list for the 2008 elections. The resultant roll was thought to be accurate, but was found to have omitted some 25 million eligible persons and so entries from the 2002 list were included although that list was pronounced inadequate by the ECP and stakeholders. The problem came about because the enumeration exercise of 2007 yielded only 55.7 million voters as compared to the 2002 register which had 72.1 million entries and the estimate of the voters in 2007 was about 80 million. The Pakistan

People's Party took the matter to the Supreme Court and subsequent to the Court's ruling the ECP included names from the 2002 electoral database and announced a new total of over 80 million. The Supreme Court ruling allowed eligible people to register without a national identity card (NIC), or a computerised national identity card (CNIC), which was a requirement for the 2006/07 registration process. Although the waiver of the national identity card applied to registration, it apparently did not extend to voting, because all registrants were required to show a C/NIC as a condition to receiving a ballot paper.

Registration of Candidates to Contest the Elections in Pakistan in 2008.

Among the requirements to contest the elections in 2008 was possession of a bachelor degree or an equivalent educational qualification issued by a religious school (madrassa). This condition was considered to be unfair as the majority of the electorate could not meet the qualification. Another qualification which attracted criticism was that the potential candidate should be sagacious, righteous, non-profligate, honest and of good character. They should not be known to commonly violate Islamic injunctions and to have adequate knowledge of Islamic teachings, and to abstain from major sins. These vague and ambiguous criteria afforded the returning officers to arbitrarily reject prospective candidates. There was also a requirement that a prospective candidate could be rejected for outstanding or unlawfully written off debts or un-paid utility bills. A candidate could be registered to contest the elections in more than one constituency.

Participation of Women in the 2008 Elections in Pakistan

Women were under-represented at all levels in the electoral process. There were restrictions on the exercise of women's political rights, although Pakistan was a Party to the Convention on Political Rights of Women (CPRW) and the Convention on the Elimination of All Forms of Discrimination against Women (CEDAW). Women constituted

44% of the voters roll. Custom and tradition had confined women to the background in the household and the male head often omitted to enlist them during enumeration of electorate. During the 2006-07 enumeration exercise the Election Commission of Pakistan did not use female enumerators. A disproportionate percentage of women did not have national identification card. The ID cards of some women did not carry photographs which were considered culturally inappropriate. That modification of the ID card rendered it susceptible to election fraud. Further, the enumeration process did not have proper procedure to cope with name changes through marriage and divorce and that led to divergence of the names on ID card and names on the roll. Women were often inhibited by security concerns from voting in the 2008 elections. Stakeholders complained that the lack of confidence in female voters was due to lower levels literacy. Stakeholders reported that in some areas of the North West Frontier Province, and also in certain other rural areas, local leaders, sometimes with the knowledge of local party representatives, entered into agreements with tribal agencies to ban women from voting. That issue reached the Peshawar High Court which in 2004 ruled against the practice of restraining women from voting, but the record of the ECP in dealing with the matter had been patchy. Men and women voted mainly in separate queue and in separate booth. The female polling booth was often staffed by females.

Swaziland National Elections of 2003

Electoral Environment

In 2003, the electoral environment was very much overshadowed by the Swazi King in whom executive authority vested. The 1992 Swaziland Order which established Parliament stated that the executive authority of Swaziland vested in the King. The Prime Minister was appointed on the bass of having the confidence of the King and not of Parliament. The King had veto powers over legislation that the Parliament approved. The two main bodies that advised the King, Council of Ministers and the Swazi National Council wielded more influence than the Government or the Parliament. In 2001, the King increased his absolute power by Decree No. 2 which restricted freedom of speech and freedom of the press, as well as introduced a 'non-bailable' offence. Under public pressure, Decree No.2 was withdrawn, but Decree No. 3 was issued and it contained some of the provisions, including the 'non-bailable' clause. The Court of Appeal ruled against that clause. The Government announced that it would not be bound by the Court's ruling. The Government's refusal to follow the Court's ruling triggered the resignation of the Judges of the Appeal Court. That incident raised the question of the rule of law in Swaziland. Coupled with the questionable status of the rule of law, there was a ban on political parties and a denial of the right of freedom of association Attempts by fledgling democratic activists to enforce the right of association was often met with police action against any such meetings.

Election Administration in Swaziland

The framework for electoral management and administration was under-developed at the time of the 2003 October elections. There was a Chief Electoral Officer and a Deputy Electoral Officer, both of whom were appointed by the King. The foregoing officers were supported by a Secretariat of three staff members. During the election period, the Secretariat was assisted by officials drawn from the Regional Administration.

Election Campaign in the 2003 Swaziland Elections

The election campaign period started on 22 September and closed on 17 October 2003, but due to the various restrictions the campaign was low key. There was an absence of the usual rallies or motorcades, and bill boards, banners or posters were hardly seen. Instead of leaflets and manifestos there were A4 sized sheets with the name and photograph of the candidate. But indeed there was a more discreet type of campaigning used by some candidates such as purchasing beer and food for villagers, organizing parties, donating kits for local football teams, or even assisting with funerals for members of the community who could not afford burials. Some candidates assisted communities in building bridges. In practice, the chiefdom customs made it difficult for candidates to campaign in some areas and so the returning officers took candidates to some chiefdom to facilitate meeting with communities.

Montenegro Parliamentary Elections 10 September 2006

Election Environment

The general electoral environment leading up to the 2006 parliamentary elections in Montenegro was calm and peaceful. The voters were provided with a choice of five political parties, six coalitions and a group of citizens all of whom submitted their lists in good time. The legal framework, although it had some deficiencies, as allowing persons in the electoral administration to run as candidates and imposing some restrictions on freedom of speech, permitted the holding of democratic elections. The media facilitated a level playing field by providing voters with adequate information to make informed choices. Some stakeholders did complain that the ruling parties got disproportionate coverage from the public broadcaster and other broadcast media. The voter register was generally accurate and acceptable to stakeholders. The voting process was considered to be reasonably well conducted.

The Election System of Montenegro for the 2006 Elections

Montenegro had proportional representation system utilizing closed nation-wide lists of candidate. Its Parliament was unicameral and enjoyed a four-year term. The quota was a member for every 6,000 voters and that formula yielded 81 members for the 2006 elections. Lists of candidates were submitted by registered political parties, coalitions and group of citizens. Each voter had one vote. Seat allocations were done using the d'Hondt formula. The threshold for a political party to receive any allocation was three percent of all the votes cast in all the polling stations-apparently not only the valid votes cast. Only half of the seats won by a party or coalition were required to be allocated in the order of candidates on the electoral list. The party or coalition was free to allocate the remaining seats to names anywhere on the list. This feature of the legislative scheme had been criticized by observers and other stakeholders as restricting transparency of the system.

Voter Registration in Montenegro for the 2006 Elections

Montenegrin citizens who achieved age 18 and over on polling day were eligible provided that they had resided in Montenegro for the least 24 months and were not deemed incapacitated by court order. The registration process entailed that the eligible voters were included in the voter register based on the information provided by the Ministry of the Interior and municipal registrar offices. A period was allowed for exhibition (or public scrutiny) of the voters list and subsequently changes were permitted up to 10 days before the elections. The total size of the register was given as 484 430 voters. The accuracy of the register won praise from observers and stakeholders, but certain shortcomings were listed as including difficulty in proving eligibility and purging the register of deceased persons, as well as recording changes of addresses and of names through marriage or otherwise.

Minorities and Elections in Montenegro in 2006

In the census of 2003 in Montenegro listed the various minorities as 32 per cent Serbs and 12 percent Bosniaks and Muslims, 5 per cent Albania, and 1 per cent Croats, and 7 per cent others. The main parties were interested in equitable representation for their communities in institutions, such as the Parliament. There was very little campaign discussion on the issue of minorities. The Government tried unsuccessful attempt to legislate on the issue but the Constitutional Court declared that the legislation was unconstitutional. The Albanian community was the only group which enjoyed special provisions in the election process through the election of MPs based on votes cast in specially designed polling stations. The privilege enjoyed by the Albanian community did not extend to any other group in Montenegro.

Presidential Elections in Cameroon 11 October 2004

Electoral Environment in Cameroon 2006

Multiparty elections were re-introduced to Cameroon in 1990 and the first multiparty elections were held in 1992 and when the results went in favour of the ruling party, the opposition parties protested vigorously. The traditional chiefs in Cameroon played a prominent role in the lower-level tiers of government and for their services they are paid by the state. They were responsible for mobilizing eligible persons for registration, handing out voters' cards and identifying polling stations sites. Cameroon was noted for political harassment and detention against opposition parties and activists aimed at preventing them from holding public or private meetings. In 2003 the United Nations Committee against Torture named the Cameroon police in using systematic torture against suspects. In 2004 Amnesty International expressed concern over human rights abuses in Cameroon, including extrajudicial executions and torture and other forms of inhuman or degrading treatment.

Administrative Structure for Elections in Cameroon in 2004

The Ministry of Territorial Administration and Decentralization (MINATD) had overall responsibility for organizing elections in the Cameroon. It is assisted by Divisional and Sub-Divisional Commissions and representatives of the local administration. There were a number of commissions with responsibility for different aspects of the electoral process—commission for the revision of the register of electors, commission for supervising the establishment and distribution of registration cards, local polling commission, divisional supervisory joint commissions, and the National Commission for the Final Counting of Votes. Those commissions were chaired by a representative of the Administration appointed by the Senior Divisional Officer, and a representative of each of the legally authorized political party. The multiplicity of commissions gave rise to overlapping mandates.

The National Elections Observatory (NEO) was an independent body charged with supervisory and control roles respecting elections and referendums. It had 11 members and was required to monitor electoral processes, report and ensure compliance with the electoral law.

Impartiality of the Electoral Administration Questioned

The impartiality of the election administration was doubted by stakeholders largely because of the feeling that many of the Administration officials were sympathizers of the ruling party. Some had the ruling party posters on their building. During the registration of voters often took place on the premises of the traditional leaders who exerted considerable authority and they belonged to one of the political parties. The placing of registration centres on premises of traditional leaders was not considered an ideal location as many eligible persons were inhibited from registering because of that fact.

Voter Registration Requirements in Cameroon

The 2004 registration exercise in Cameroon was not well organized. The process was dominated by the ruling party, as the opposition parties lacked the resources to play their full role on the commissions. Stakeholders reported that in some places the Administration officials took over the role of the commissions and in other places the traditional rulers were the main operators of the exercise. There were no uniform procedures in place for most of the period; the officials relied on the electoral law which was interpreted and applied differently in various places. Although the National Identification Card (NIC) was not a condition precedent to registration, in many parts of the country, the NIC was the only form of identification acceptable and consequently many persons who did have the NIC did not bother to turn up at the registration centre. The practice of requiring a qualified person to show the NIC before registration was ruled as not proper by the Minister for Territorial Administration and Decentralization, but that ruling was only towards the end of the registration exercise. The manual compilation of the register was believed to be one reason for the lack of high level of confidence in the register.

The registered voter was not given a receipt when registered so that if his/her name did not appear on the register, there was no evidence to support a claim to be put on the register.

Convening of the Electorate in Cameroon

After election was called in the Cameroon, the convening of the electorate took place whereby the Voters' Registration Card Commissions were established to compile and distribute the cards. Despite the attribution of that activity to the commissions, it was reported that the Administration actually controlled the production and distribution of the voters' registration cards. The cards were to be distributed within a period of 15 days before polling day, but many were not distributed before polling day were made available at the polling stations. It did not appear that any extensive awareness programme was mounted to let voters know that they could pick up their voter's card at the polling station.

Incumbency and Code of Conduct for Political Parties

There was no code of conduct for political parties or candidates in the Cameroon in 2004. The incumbency rules were often informed by the code of conduct for parties, but of course there was no such code in Cameroon. The governing party had always benefited from incumbency and the use of public resources by the ruling party. There were civil servants campaigning for the ruling party and there was use of Government vehicles and other public resources. The ruling party's posters were placed on public buildings and government officials wore the ruling party T-shirts and scarves. Good practice requires that the profile of Government should be lowered at election time so that the playing field should level. Government ministers should not combine official visits around the country with electioneering, and public resources should not be used for party purposes.

Sierra Leone, Presidential and Parliamentary Elections 2007

Structure of the Electoral Management Body of Sierra Leone

The National Electoral Commission (NEC) consisted of the Chairperson and four members appointed by the President, after consultation with all registered parties, and on approval of the Parliament. There was security of tenure by the Chairperson and members of the NEC. There was also a provision in the Constitution guaranteeing the independence of the NEC. However, there were requirements for accountability in the form of submitting an annual report to the President which shall be laid before Parliament. The functions of the NEC were to conduct registration of voters and determine the number of constituencies and their boundaries. Election observers and stakeholders gave the NEC high performance marks.

Construction of Constituencies in Sierra Leone

After the conflict in Sierra Leone the displacement of the population made it inappropriate to delimit constituencies into single-member constituencies as existed before the conflict. Instead, a list proportional representation system was introduced for the parliamentary elections of 1996 and 2002. In 2006 the National Electoral Commission (NEC) decided that the country would be divided into single-member constituencies. Parliament decided that there would be 112 constituencies as previously. The NEC decided that population would be the sole basis for the delimitation. The country's population of 4.9 million yielded a quota of 44, 336 persons per constituency in a Parliament of 112 single-member constituencies. The Parliament approved the 112 divisions in January 2007.

The Polling Environment

The polling preparation was well organized for the 2007 elections. Voting materials, in particular the ballot boxes, voters' lists, ballot papers, voting screens, indelible ink, and seals, were delivered to polling stations in a timely manner in the main. The ballot papers for the presidential and parliamentary elections were of different colours, and the ballot boxes for the two elections were marked clearly. At the opening of the polls, some stations were late in opening, but in most places the polling staff, party agents, and security personnel were in place. There was confusion over the allocation of voters to polling stations. The electoral authorities were unable to achieve good queue control and voters had difficulty locating their polling stations. The polling officers followed the stipulated procedures and showed an attitude to master the details of electoral conduct. Disadvantaged voters, such as the disabled, mothers with babies, pregnant women were paced at the front of the queue at polling stations.

Sierra Leone, Human Rights and the Electoral Process

The experience of the people of Sierra Leone during the conflict brought human rights to the forefront of the electoral process in 2007. It had been appreciated that democracy would not flourish unless the fundamental rights were freedoms of all citizens were protected by the state and its organs. Competitive politics could not survive and flourish if there was no freedom of expression and debate. The Constitution of Sierra Leone protected the freedom of expression. The stakeholders noted with satisfaction that there was no attempt to restrict or violate the fundamental rights and freedoms during the 2007 election campaign. The incumbent Government had established a Human Rights Commission, but the formula for appointment of the Commissioners, which allowed the President to appoint the five members with the approval by Parliament, was criticized by stakeholders for not independent of the Government.

Zimbabwe Run-Off Election 27 June 2008.

Election Environment

The election environment for the Zimbabwe run-off presidential election in June 2008 was held in an atmosphere that was mired in controversy. The run-off election was scheduled under the law to be held within 21 days after the announcement of the results of the first round, but the

Zimbabwe Electoral Commission applied its regulatory powers under the electoral law to extend the period beyond the 21 days set out in the law. Reports of election observers and stakeholders in the election reported widespread intimidation and violence against opposition supporters. Many were murdered and many more were beaten up and hospitalized and many thousands were displaced as a result of the political violence. Permit applications to hold rallies by the opposition presidential candidate were often refused and when appeals to the court were upheld, thugs said to be ruling party supporters, disrupted the rallies or occupied the designated venue. The police often failed to protect opposition rally sites and were reported to display open partisanship in favour of the ruling party. The intensity of the violence and the failure by the police authorities to offer protection, forced some local observer groups to abandon observation efforts. The high level of violence, intimidation and lack of security protection forced the opposition candidate, Mr. Morgan Tsvangirai of the Movement for Democratic Change (Tsvangirai faction), to abandon his candidacy, leaving the incumbent and ruling party (Zimbabwe African National Union-Patriotic Front, (ZANU-PF)) candidate, Mr Robert Mugabe, as the lone candidate.

Un-level playing Field & Lack of Security

The run-off election in Zimbabwe in June 2008 not only an extremely poor environment which was not conducive to the holding of credible elections, but the deterioration of the security situation in the country, so far as opposition supporters were concerned, was so bad that many fled their homes in fear of their lives. The publicly owned media displayed a high level of open partisanship in favour of ruling party (ZANU-PF). Mention was seldom made of the Movement for Democratic Change (Tsvangirai faction) (MDC-T) and mainly in a negative light. The senior ranks of the security forces made statements revealing their support for the ruling party. The Zimbabwe Electoral Commission (ZEC) did not behave as a competent and impartial body, as it drastically reduced the number of domestic election observers that it accredited to the run-off election which was much below the number accredited for the first round. Further, some stakeholders put the blame for not ensuring a more level playing field with respect to the publicly owned media on the ZEC.

Implications for Democracy in the African Union

The run-off elections in Zimbabwe, like the Kenyan general elections a few months before attracted international attention. Mr. Mugabe, eventually the sole contestant after Mr Morgan Tsvangirai withdrew his candidature due to intimidation and violence instigated by the ruling party, was declared the winner of the presidential runoff election. The opposition parties declared the election a farce and refused to accept the results of the run-off election. Many governments of the African Union (AU) express their concern about the violence and intimidation that surrounded the run-off election. Regional organizations such as the Southern African Development Community (SADC), the Pan-African Parliament, the African Union Commission, as well as the United Nations expressed doubts about the credibility of the run-off elections. Many stakeholders in elections in Zimbabwe and the African Union looked to the latter to take steps to prevent similar election-related problems to those that occurred in Kenya and Zimbabwe arising in the future. The AU established a Democracy and Electoral Assistance Unit[40] in the Political Affairs Department during 2008 to improve standards of electoral organization and conduct and to raise the level of its election observation missions.

Gambia Presidential Elections 22 September 2006

The Human Rights Environment

The Gambia had ensured the fundamental rights of its citizens through its Constitution which guaranteed democratic and political rights to freedom of speech, assembly and association. It had also adhered to a number of international conventions on human rights, including the International Covenant on Civil and Political Rights (ICCPR). Prior to the 2006 elections, a number of arrests and detentions during which persons were held longer than the 72 hours stipulated by law without being brought before a court and charged. This situation with respect to many categories

---

40 To which the author was adviser.

of persons including political opponents, journalists, lawyers, and others who were critical of government, illustrated the widespread concern. The case of a female Member of Parliament, Hon Dute A. Kamaso, who was detained in custody without trial for more than four months, heightened the concern about the government's commitment to human rights. Stakeholders expressed concern about freedom of speech, citing intimidation of journalists and the recent establishment of a National Media Commission and the repeal of the National Media Act. The powers of the National Media Commission were extensive in so far as it was a state-appointed committee with responsibility to license and register journalists and could require journalists to disclose their sources of information.

Structure of the Electoral Management Body

The Independent Electoral Commission (IEC) was a constitutional body composed of a Chairperson and four other members, appointed by the President for an initial period of seven years and may be reappointed once. Members of the Commission may be dismissed by the President for inability to perform their duties, or if circumstances arose whereby they would not be eligible for appointment to the position, or for misconduct subject to the procedure of the President appointing a tribunal of three judges of a superior court to inquiry into the matter and report on the facts. In the period 1996 to 2006, three Commission Chairpersons were removed from office and in July 2006, the Chairman and two Commissioners were dismissed by the President. Security of tenure of the IEC's members must have been an issue given the many dismissals over the last ten years. The Commission appointed its staff.

Voter Registration in Gambia

The Independent Electoral Commission (IEC) had responsibility for the compilation of the voters register. The requirement for registration was holding a National Identity Card issued by the Immigration Department, or a birth certificate, or a certification by five elders of their Gambian citizenship and age. After registration, the voter was issued with a voter's card with a polling station number on it. There was a period for public scrutiny in June and July 2006. The registration data was computerised. The register was 670,336 voters strong. Party agents were given copies of the registers. There were unverified reports that non-Gambians and under-age persons were included in the register.

The Campaign for the 2006 Gambia Presidential Elections

The Independent Electoral Commission (IEC) was responsible for issuing permits for campaign meetings by the candidates in coordination with the police. The IEC was responsible for ensuring security at rallies and airtime distribution to candidates during the campaign. Various methods were used to get the parties and candidates' message across to voters, including public rallies, posters, billboards, stickers, and T-shirts. The campaign language was temperate. Some posters were put on public buildings by the ruling party. A highly placed police officer was heard to express the view that there was nothing wrong with displaying posters anywhere as the police and army personnel were allowed to express their political preference. Stakeholders complained that the playing field was not level as the opposition felt intimidated because of the arrest of and detention without trial of political opponents and others critical of the government. The incumbent President during his campaign said that areas that did not vote for him would not be developed and that utterance was viewed as intimidation.

Unique Method of Voting

The Gambia had a unique method of voting using marbles, called ballot tokens which are deposited into the ballot drums of the voter's choice. There were three ballot drums for the 2006 elections, which were painted in the colours and party symbols and photos of each candidate, and the name of the party, were placed onto the drums. The drums were prepared by placing a layer of sand at the bottom of each drum to absorb the sound as token hit the bottom. Upon the verification of the voter's documents, his/her name was marked off the register, the index finger marked with indelible ink, and then he/she was given a voting marble. The voter took the voting marble to the voting compartment and placed the voting marble in the drum of his/her choice. The sound of the bell signified that he/she had voted. The unique voting method required special counting equipment which involved the use of sieves to sift the marbles from the sand in the ballot drums, and then trays holding 200 or 500 marbles, to count them. The ballot drums were opened in alphabetical order of the candidates' names and the number of ballot token for each candidate was counted. The trays were then shown to all the party agents and observers.

The Burmese Referendum of 10 May 2008.

The Electoral Environment

The Burmese Referendum of May 10 2008 was described as illegitimate. The atmosphere was not conducive to holding a ballot, coming in the wake of a terrible cyclone coupled with gross intimidation of the electorate by the ruling military regime, the State Peace and Development Council (SPDC). The military crackdown on monks and pro-democracy protestors in August and September of 2007 led to intense intimidation of political opponents of the military regime. There was denial of basic freedoms of expression, association and assembly. Further, there was large scale arbitrary arrest and detention. The environment in Burma in 2008 did not allow for the free expression of the will of the electorate. Indeed most Burmese had no access to a copy of the draft constitution which the referendum was seeking to approve. The draft instrument which was some 194 pages was printed in Burmese and English but not in the minority languages, and was available on sale in selected bookshops for about a month. The document was not subjected to national debate and discussion, and those who opposed it openly were jailed. Several prominent journalists were detained. The ban on gatherings of more than five people inhibited free discussion.

A Vote to Nowhere

Some stakeholders dubbed the referendum of May 10 in Burma the 'vote to nowhere'. They saw the draft constitution as nothing more than consolidation of the power of the military regime. Certain provisions of the draft constitution were directed against the opposition; and in particular the National League for Democracy (NLD). Chapter III Article 4 of the draft constitution barred anyone from becoming President of the Union whose parents, spouse or children and their spouse was a citizen of a foreign country. It was believed that the foregoing stipulation of the draft constitution was aimed at the opposition NLD whose leader, Aung San Suu Kyi, was the widower of a British citizen, and had two children who were British citizens. Other provisions were aimed at keeping large numbers of opposition supporters from contesting elections to the Parliament by excluding persons who had been punished for an offence that made him/her lose qualifications for election to Parliament.

A Flawed Referendum Vote

The lead up to and conduct of the referendum vote in Burma was marred by fraudulent tactics by the State Peace and Development Council (SPDC). Stakeholders reported a tenfold exaggeration of the number of eligible voters, lack of transparency in the counting procedure, allowing multiple votes in some cases and denial of votes to others. Intimidation of voters by threatening them with three years imprisonment or other serious punishment as razing villages or forced relocation, if they voted no. Many civil servants were compelled to vote in advance and in front of their superiors. There was intrusive presence of soldiers which intimidated some voters to vote yes. Voters name and ID number was noted down which caused voters to believe that the secrecy of the ballot was compromised. The media was completely controlled by the SPDC, which proclaimed a large turnout of voters and victory by a wide margin.

The Mongolia Parliamentary Election June 2008.

Electoral Environment

The electoral environment in which many of the pre-election processes were carried out was generally calm. The voters register was 1, 500,000 and most stakeholders seemed comfortable with the register. The voters had a wide choice between parties as 12 political parties, one coalition and 45 independent candidates, fielding a total of 356 candidates to contest the elections. There were 26 multi-member constituencies, each having between 20-30 candidates, depending on the number of seats in a particular constituency. Each candidate had to receive a license from the General Election Commission and registered before commencing their campaign which ended on midnight on the 27 June 2008. All the campaign advertisement material was then removed from public places. No campaigning was allowed on the day before election or on Election Day.

The Voting Process

Election observers and stakeholders gave the electoral managers high marks generally, although there were reports of vote buying. In particular many elderly voters reported that they were given vouchers to vote for a particular candidate. Stakeholders expressed satisfaction with various aspects of the polling arrangements, such as the location of polling stations, the absence of campaigning near to polling stations, there was no shortage of materials at polling stations, the opening of the poll procedures were followed, and polling agents and observers were allowed to see all aspects of polling. The overwhelming majority of voters voted without difficulty. The voting procedures were generally applied correctly, except in some cases the secrecy of the ballot was not observed, as family and friends viewed how each others voted. Generally, there were no unauthorised persons in polling stations.

Although 67% of Mongolians thought the process up to the poll was free and fair, there was post-election conflict because some opposition parties were unhappy with the results.

Nepal Constituent Assembly Elections 10 April 2008

The Electoral Environment

The general environment was one of a post-conflict atmosphere. Some of the pre-election clashes appeared to be a reflection or spill over of the violence from the years of conflict. Some 18 serious pre-election clashes were reported to have caused injuries to 82 people. However, despite serious sporadic violence, the elections were peaceful and well-managed. The campaign was lively and competitive. The old parties, the Nepali Congress (NC) and the Communist Party of Nepal (UML) were outdone in political campaigning by the Communist Party of Nepal (CPN(M)) Maoists who used intimidation against their opponents. The Maoists were at the receiving end of campaign violence also when some 15 of their activists were killed. The constituent assembly (CA) elections resulted in a more representative body than in the past. The inclusive nature of the CA consists of castes, ethnic, religious and regional representatives. Stakeholders and observers pronounced the elections to be credible despite the strong-arm tactics used by some of the parties, including the Maoists.

The Election Campaign

The constituent assembly election campaign in Nepal was fiercely competitive as to give way at times to irregularities and violence. There were many political parties campaigning, many of whom focussed on the first past the post seats. The Code of Conduct for parties and candidates adhered to and the Election Commission did not succeed in enforcing it. Many stakeholders expressed admiration for the Maoists' campaign, although some elements were objectionable in so far as it was directed at obstructing the campaign of other parties and threatening to return to war. The Maoists' campaign was credited with discipline, motivation and strategic planning. Their cadres were more energetic than those of other parties. They were well trained, managed and educated in the party's position, but their weakness was developing good working relations with other parties.

The Electoral Machinery

The election machinery was well managed by the Election Commission. Polling stations were well managed and the electoral officers were generally well-trained and performed their duties in a competent manner. The Code of Conduct was generally followed, although some officers expressed the view that it was too ambitious and put a flexible interpretation on it. All materials were delivered to the polling stations on time and with adequate security. The election officers were well trained including temporary staff. There were weaknesses in the identification of voters some names were not on the list and the procedures made it easy for illegal proxy voters to escape detection. Stakeholders were pleased with the technical management of the election.

Polling in the Constituent Assembly Elections

Polling started on time at 7a.m. and closed a 5p.m. Although the day was largely peaceful, there was trouble in isolated areas where three people were reported killed, including an independent candidate who was shot by unidentified gunmen. Voter turnout was good the first past the post (FPTP) recorded 61.7 per cent and the proportional (PR) 63.3 per cent. The difference between the FPTP and the PR could be explained as due to government officials, security personnel, and the Maoist Provisional Liberation Army members, were listed as 'temporary' voters and only allowed to vote in the PR race. The turnout was uneven. Many migrants to urban areas returned to the home village to vote often given free transportation by Maoists. Nepalese abroad were not able to vote. Since the cut-off date for registration was mid-November 2006, many young persons could not vote in the Constituent Assembly elections.

Disruption, Intimidation and Cheating

Despite the high marks given to Election Commission and many of the contestants in the election, there were some low points in the organization, particularly the campaign. Some singled out the Maoists' attempt to disrupt the campaign of other parties in selected areas, but there were many clashes that did not involve Maoists. The CPN(M) directed its disrupted activities consistently at the royalist parties. Reports suggested that the Nepali Congress (NC) and the Communist Party of Nepal (UML) also used tactics to intimidate their opponents. There were allegations from different sources that some NC and UML candidates imported hired thugs into their constituencies to support their campaigns. Short of open violence, all parties were said to employ devious tactics to boost their vote. Some used the proxy procedure to organize unauthorized proxy voting, particularly using migrants whose names were on the roll, but could not turn up to vote. The Maoists were reported to have invested substantial resources in visiting households in advance of the election to check up the number of persons who would be present to vote and to cross-check the number with the electoral roll. It was reported that some parties put up 'dummy candidates' who would have agents inside the polling stations to assist their real party.

Thailand's Parliamentary Election 23rd December 2007.

Electoral Environment

The electoral environment in Thailand leading up to the December 2007 elections was confused and could not be described as conducive to the holding of free and fair elections. In May 2006, the Constitutional Court annulled the results of elections held in April and the Elections Commission set new elections for October 2006. Before the elections could be held, the military carried out a coup d'etat on 19 September 2006. The King endorsed the coup leader, General Sonthi Boonyaratglin, as the head of an interim governing council. The ousted Prime Minister, Thaksin, and many of his supporters were targeted with legal action and their assets were frozen. In August 2007 a new constitution was approved and elections were set for 23rd December 2007.

The New Constitution of Thailand 2007

The new Constitution was a product of the post-coup administration and was to a large extent reforming the pre-coup structures of government. Many political analysts and democratic activists viewed the new Constitution as a backward step as far as democracy was concerned. It set term limits for prime ministers, and made it easier to impeach the Prime Minister. The electoral changes included changes to the electoral system and decreasing the size of the Parliament. The number of seats in Parliament was reduced to 480 from 500, and the 400 seats were based on the first past the post system and 80 would be elected on the proportional representation basis. The number of multi-member constituencies was 157, while four provinces had single-member constituencies. The multi-member constituencies had two or three members. For the proportional representation seats, the country was divided into eight zones each of which had between 7.6 and 7.9 million inhabitants and was represented by 10 members. The threshold for a party to receive a seat was 5% of the total vote. Independent candidature was not allowed.

Electoral Administration

There were five Election Commissioners one of whom served as Chairman. They were supported by a Secretary General who headed the Office of the Election Commission. That office had five departments and each of the country's 76 provinces had a replica of the central office. The mandate of the Commission (ECT) was couched in broad terms such as 'to control and arrange to hold elections' and to 'determine measures and controls of financial contributions to political parties and candidates'. It was further mandated to conduct investigation and inquiry for fact finding and to adjudicate and make decisions on problems or dispute. In inquiring into disputes, the ECT had power to requisition documents or take evidence from individuals or summons any person to give evidence, as well as powers to request the Courts and any public officials or local government organizations to take action. The ECT had power to disqualify candidates and dissolve political parties. It also had power to order new elections in any or all polling stations where there was credible evidence that elections was not conducted in a fair and honest manner, provided that such was taken within 30 days after the elections. The ECT could enlist the support of other state institutions to assist their work.

Vote Buying in Thailand

The December 2007 elections in Thailand witnessed 'vote buying' elevated to the nation-wide agenda during the campaign. The issue was challenged on three fronts, namely, the Elections Commission (ECT) put on high profile voter education programmes, there were government sponsored initiatives to tackle the problem, and the legislature passed stiffer measures to punish offenders. There was a limit on the expenditure of each candidate contesting constituency seats and each political party contesting the election on the proportional basis also had a limit on expenditure for each constituency contested and an additional amount of twenty percent of the total expenditure for an election on a proportional basis for each political party. The party treasurer had to disclosure accounts of expenditure when the election campaign was over. There were restrictions on distribution of cash, in-kind gifts and community projects and any promise of such benefits in the future. The transportation of voters on polling day as an incentive to cast a vote for a particular party was banned. The punishment for selling or buying votes was harsh—ranging from denial of voting in a future election to jail for five years or a fine of 100,000 baht. Despite some success in some provinces, stakeholders' reports suggested that the problem had not gone away and might have increased in certain forms such as in-kind gifts, cash handouts, and electronic transfer of funds, payment to attend rallies, sightseeing trips, birthday parties, supermarket coupons and telephone cards. There was evidence that longer-term lock-in arrangements whereby the transactions of vote-buying took place months before the election campaign began. There were reports that some vote buyers would pay money in advance to village heads and pay the remainder if the results showed that a certain target was achieved for the candidate concerned. Some vote buyers took advantage of the fact that election results were posted up at the stations by making a list of those who promised to vote for the party and compare it with the result sheet, if the two lists matched roughly voters would be paid by the canvasser.

Adjudication- 'Red Cards' and 'Yellow Cards'

The Elections Commission of Thailand (ECT) had exclusive jurisdiction to adjudicate cases of election violations within 30 days after the elections, after which its judgment on all cases were considered by the Supreme Court. The ECT had wide powers which could be exercised against candidates, parties or voters by way of imposition of fines, imprisonment, or banning of parties. In order to determine nature of the offence committed by a candidate offender, he/she was issued with a 'yellow card' or a 'red card'. The issuance of such card indicated that the result of the election in the constituency was disqualified and a re-election would be held. The 'red card' violator would not be able to contest the re-election and was banned from contesting a seat for a year, while the yellow card holder was allowed to contest the re-election. Where a political party executive was directly involved or implicated in an election violation, the party as a whole could be punished, but dissolution of a party had to be done by the Constitutional Court. The re-elections resulting from the issuance of yellow and red cards were generally conducted well.

Afghan Legislative Elections September 18 2005.

Electoral Environment

The legislative elections were held along with provincial elections. The electoral system was the single non-transferable vote (SNTV) in which each voter cast a single vote even though there were multiple members to serve their respective electoral district. Some stakeholders complained that the electoral system marginalized and limited the potential influence of political parties, and would lead to unrepresentative parliament of local leaders. The SNTV resulted in many candidates winning with small numbers of votes. The Political Parties Law was passed in 2005 and Election Law was passed in 2004. The Law provided that voters would vote for individual candidates rather than for parties in the parliamentary elections, but candidates were allowed to run under party banner. Candidates could also run as independents nominated or endorsed by political party, but political symbols could not appear on the ballot.

Voter Registration

The registration exercise for the 2005 elections in Afghanistan went well yielding some nine million out of an estimated 9.8 million eligible persons. However, aggrieved stakeholders claimed that there were blatant irregularities with more registered persons than estimated eligible persons, particularly in provinces along the Pakistan border where attacks were frequent. Further, there was over-registration in six Pashtun dominated provinces. Fifty-seven percent of the eligible population registered, although three provinces recorded more than 100 percent voter registration.

Legal Landscape

The legal landscape in Afghanistan in September 2005 was dominated by Islam which was central to the Constitution. The scene was also informed by the adherence of the State to the Universal Declaration of Human Rights which provide for freedom of thought, conscience and religion. The Constitution established a presidential system in which the president served as head of state or government, and a bicameral legislature. There was also a Supreme Court with High Courts and Appeals Court. There were no separate religious courts. The equality of women was guaranteed under the Constitution. Each of the 34 provinces had at least two female candidates to fill the seats guaranteed by 27 percent of the Assembly for women. The President appointed one-third of the members of the House of Elders, Meshrano Jirga, 50 percent of these members should be women. There was separation of powers, the executive, legislature and the judiciary which was independent. The President may be impeached by Loya Jirga. The President had veto power with respect to legislation, but the veto may be overruled by two-thirds vote of the Wolesi Jirga which also had power to approve or otherwise judges appointed by the President.

Human Rights

In Afghanistan, it was a crime to convert from Islam punishable by death. That provision exposed the contradiction in Afghanistan which is a party to the Universal Convention on Human Rights which guarantees freedom of thought, conscience and religion. Human rights advocates often draw attention to the pervasive intimidation and violence against girls and women. They pointed out that Afghan women and girls are faced with constant threat of abduction and rape, forced marriage, and fear of being traded for debts. Much of the rural population in Afghanistan were under the control of tribal chiefs and warlords who had supreme jurisdiction. Afghan women participate rarely in public life and human rights violations against woman ranged from threats to rape.

Indonesia Parliamentary Elections 5 Aril 2004

Election Environment

Election campaign was largely peaceful and took the form of outdoor rallies and motorcycle convoys, as well as television advertising. There was scant campaigning in the troubled province of Aceh due to fear of disruption. There were reports of political parties engaging in 'money politics', although the practice was against the law. Some sections of the public in Indonesia were ambivalent about 'money politics', as many media houses encouraged individuals to accept the money, goods or other offers, from anyone who offered it, but to vote for whomsoever they wished. The inducements were often small, such as bags of rice or sugar, or small amounts of money. The 'money politics' scenario was facilitated by the house-to-house canvassing by local officials and village heads who encouraged villagers to vote for a particular party. The voter registration was done by the Central Statistics Agency. In order to vote, a person had to produce a voter registration card and a personal invitation. Some voters had neither stipulated forms of ID and the Indonesian General Elections Commission (KPU) revised the technical guidelines to allow personal ID, but the new guidelines did not filter down to the general public in a timely manner. The lack of registration cards was felt more in the rural areas. The issue of distribution of voting materials, particularly ballot papers, was of concern to many stakeholders, but the measures taken to avoid shortages of late deliveries were by and large successful.

Polling Day in Indonesia 5 April 2004

Polling day was peaceful. It was treated as a community event and large sections of communities participated in preparing voting sites. There was no evidence of interference with voters or with the process, except for sporadic incidence of violence in Aceh. Election observers reported that polling stations were generally well laid out and sited in neutral locations. Stations were in general well equipped with election materials and supplies, some of which were supplied by international partners, such as Australia and Japan. There were clear signs that election officials were well trained. Stations were opened on time and the procedures were followed. Stakeholders such as security officers and political parties followed the applicable rules. Party agents were positioned in the stations where they could see the polling activities. The main irregularities reported on by stakeholders were failure to check the ink on the people's fingers before they were allowed to vote; there were isolated incidence of polling officers helping people to cast their ballot; elderly voters had difficulty folding the ballot in a manner that the polling station staff (KPPS) Head's signature was on the outside; and some voters had difficulty putting the ballot papers in the box.

The Counting of Votes in the April 2004 Elections

Many international election observers and local stakeholders gave the counting process good marks for openness and transparency. Everyone present at the count could see the validity of the votes and the count and that the votes were generally accurately recorded. Party agents were free to record the votes. The number of invalid ballots was relatively small, and indeed some of the invalid ballots were believed to come about accidentally when the nail went through two ballot papers instead of one ballot paper that was intended. Although some parties put out confusing messages to voters that they should only vote for party, nevertheless, most voters voted for parties and individual candidates. The counting process was slow, but the transparency offset the complaints that would otherwise have been levelled against the Indonesian General Elections Commission (KPU). The ballot boxes were stored over night in some rural areas where the count had not been finished, but observers reported that the boxes were adequately secured.

Haiti Legislative & Local Elections May 21 2000

Election Environment

The national registration of voters began January 24 2000 and ended on March 19 2000. A total of 3, 959, 571 voters were registered out of an estimated 4, 245, 384 eligible persons. The registration was carried out by the Provisional Electoral Council (CEP). The registration exercise was declared as being adequately completed by the Organisation of American States (OAS). The candidates' registration went off smoothly and 29,500 candidates for about 7,500 positions. Polling day was postponed some three times, but was finally set for May 21 2000.

Polling and the Aftermath

It was estimated that about 60 percent of voters went to the polls. Most voters were able to locate their station with ease, but voters had to wait in long queue before voting. Following the counting of votes, the relatively calm environment quickly deteriorated into violence in some localities. Armed groups burnt ballots boxes in the election offices in the Departments of the Centre and the North. Other areas of the country experienced disorganization in the final stages of the closing stages of electoral process. In the final preparatory stages for the elections, sporadic incidents of violence resulting in seven deaths of party activists and some candidates. The immediate post election disturbances triggered a state of disorganization and lack of transparency in the compilation of results and delays in posting up results in many of the communes. There were long delays in posting up results in some commune for several weeks. Opposition candidates were detained and subsequently released. In some communes, the election results were not posted up at all, while some high-ranking electoral officials left their posts and never returned to their duties. According to the Organization of American States (OAS) observer mission, several Senators and a few Deputies, who should have contested the run-off elections, were declared winners at the first round.

The Nature of the Irregularities Perpetrated

In one department, Northwest, Haiti, the independent candidate who came first, lost 1,000 votes and the second-place candidate gained 16,000 votes, thus changing the order in which the senatorial candidates won. The Provisional Electoral Council (CEP) decided to re-hold elections in three communes, but in two of them in Bahon and Dame-Marie, the reason was disputed as the tally sheets that were believed to be lost were subsequently found. The original results in those two communes showed that the opposition parties had won. The Organization of American States (OAS) observer report found that the legislative elections were adversely affected by irregularities. The posting up of results at communes and department was haphazard and lacked transparency. Both the Chamber of Deputies and the senate elections were riddled with irregularities and challenges and complaints were not treated in a systematic, transparent or professional manner. There was grave and systematic under counting of the percentage of votes received by senatorial candidates. The law required that a senatorial candidate should receive an absolute majority of the valid votes cast, and if not, the candidate should participate in a runoff election. The CEP issued a statement in which it appeared that the results were based on absolute majority based on a limited number of candidates (usually the first four candidates with the most votes) instead of the total number of valid votes. The upshot of that approach was that 17 senatorial seats were decided in the first round, of which 16 winners were from a particular party, but if the calculations of absolute majority were based on the total number of valid votes cast, 10 senatorial races would have had to go to a second round. Despite on and off acknowledgement by the CEP that the calculation of absolute majority was an error, attempts to correct the error met with difficulties. Some members of the Commission resigned and the Chairman resigned and left the country without correcting the error. The OAS observer mission found that the election was fundamentally flawed and suspended all its observation activity for the second round.

Iraq—Representative Elections 2005

Electoral environment

The Independent Electoral Commission of Iraq (IECI) consisted of a nine-member Board of Commissioners. There were seven voting members (including a Chief Electoral Officer) appointed by the Iraqi and two non-voting members were international experts appointed by the United Nations Secretary-General. The IECI was in charge of the December elections, assisted by 18 governorate electoral offices, a regional office for Kurdistan region, and local district electoral offices. The IECI was a transitional body whose mandate was to conduct the December elections. The IECI employed a lottery procedure to recruit polling staff of 220,000. Additional polling staff of 800 was recruited for the province of Anbar. The IECI was assisted by some 50 international experts.

The Legal Environment

The legal environment for the Council of Representative elections consisted of a new constitution and electoral law. There were provisions dealing with political rights and freedoms and improved representation of women. The voting and counting procedures met democratic standards, except that the party agents were not entitled to receive a copy of the statement of the poll. Access to the media was good during the campaign and was established by law. Out-of-country voting was permitted and special voting was scheduled for detainees, hospital patients, and security forces. A mechanism to deal with complaints was established and complaints could be made by e-mail or submitted at polling stations, although there was no time frame set to dispose of complaints.

Annex

Countries-elections tracked and mapped

Afghanistan, Albania, Antigua & Barbuda, Armenia, Bangladesh, Belarus, Belize, Bermuda, Bhutan, Bosnia and Herzegovina, Bulgaria, Burma, Canada, Cambodia, Cameroon, China, Croatia, Democratic Republic of Congo, Dominican Republic, East Timor, Egypt, Ethiopia, Fiji Islands, France, Gambia, Ghana, Gibraltar, Guatemala, Guyana, Haiti, India, Indonesia, Iraq, Ireland, Jamaica, Kazakhstan, Kenya, Kyrgyzstan, Liberia, Lesotho, Malawi, Madagascar, Malaysia, Maldives, Mali, Mauritius, Mexico, Moldova, Mongolia, Montenegro, Mozambique, Namibia, Nepal, Nicaragua, Nigeria, Northern Ireland, Pakistan, Palestine, Panama, Papua New, Paraguay, Peru, Philippines, Russia, Rwanda, Saint Kitts & Nevis, Seychelles, Sierra Leone, South Africa, Solomon Islands, Spain, Sri Lanka, Swaziland, Switzerland, Taiwan, Tajikistan, Tanzania, Thailand, Togo, Trinidad & Tobago, Turkey, Uganda, Ukraine, United Kingdom, USA, Uzbekistan, Venezuela, Zambia, Zanzibar (Tanzania), and Zimbabwe.